The political economy of New Labour

Labouring under false pretences?

Colin Hay

Manchester University Press
Manchester and New York

distributed exclusively in the USA by St. Martin's Press

Copyright © Colin Hay 1999

The right of Colin Hay to be identified as the author of this work has been asserted
by him in accordance with the Copyright, Designs and Patents Act 1988.

Published by Manchester University Press
Oxford Road, Manchester M13 9NR, UK
and Room 400, 175 Fifth Avenue, New York, NY 10010, USA
http://www.man.ac.uk/mup

Distributed exclusively in the USA by
St. Martin's Press, Inc., 175 Fifth Avenue, New York,
NY 10010, USA

Distributed exclusively in Canada by
UBC Press, University of British Columbia, 6344 Memorial Road,
Vancouver, BC, Canada V6T 1Z2

British Library Cataloguing-in-Publication Data
A catalogue record for this book is available from the British Library

Library of Congress Cataloging-in-Publication Data applied for

ISBN   0 7190 5481 8   *hardback*
        0 7190 5482 6   *paperback*

First published 1999

06 05 04 03 02 01 00 99   10 9 8 7 6 5 4 3 2 1

Typeset by Ralph Footring, Derby
Printed in Great Britain by Bell & Bain Ltd, Glasgow

To my parents, who have laboured hard,
but never under false pretences

The political economy of New Labour

MANCHESTER
UNIVERSITY PRESS

Contents

List of figures and tables	*page*	viii
Preface and acknowledgements		x
List of abbreviations		xiii

1   Contextualising Novelty: the legacy of Thatcherism,
the prospect of globalisation   MODERNISATION? EXCEPTONTY?   1

2   Labour's Thatcherite Revisionism: the Policy Review
process and the 'politics of catch-up'   THATCHERISM   42

3   On New Labour's Ups – and (Anthony) Downs   76

4   That Was Then, This Is Now: the politics of
conspicuous convergence   CONVERGENCE   105

5   Studiously Courting Capital: the economic politics
of accommodation   145

6   Labouring Under False Pretences? Dedication,
industrial capacity and indigenous investment   181

Bibliography   212

Index   237

Figures and tables

Figures

3.1 Hotelling's spatial model of bipartisan (electoral)
competition   *page* 86
3.2 Bipartisan competition with elastic demand   88
3.3 A normal distribution of preferences:
bipartisan convergence   90
3.4 A bimodal distribution of preferences: bipartisan divergence   91

Tables

1.1 Endogenous, comparative and contextual novelty   *page* 13
1.2 Class dealignment, 1964–97   25
1.3 Structure and agency in the modernisation of the
Labour Party   33
2.1 Assessing the Thatcher legacy: strategy, ideology
and policy   49–52
2.2 Britain: social democracy or market liberalism?   55
4.1 Bipartisan convergence in Britain, 1992–7: trade union
reform   109
4.2 Bipartisan convergence in Britain, 1992–7: employment
law   112
4.3 Bipartisan convergence in Britain, 1992–7: education
policy   115
4.4 Bipartisan convergence in Britain, 1992–7: training policy   116
4.5 Bipartisan convergence in Britain, 1992–7: pension
provision   118
4.6 Bipartisan convergence in Britain, 1992–7: family policy   118
4.7 Bipartisan convergence in Britain, 1992–7: National
Health Service reform   119
4.8 Bipartisan convergence in Britain, 1992–7:
welfare/workfare   119

4.9 Consolidating welfare retrenchment: Labour's changing
attitude to welfare reform 122
4.10 Bipartisan convergence in Britain, 1992–7: economic
policy 124
4.11 Bipartisan convergence in Britain, 1992–7: industrial
policy 125
4.12 Bipartisan convergence in Britain, 1992–7: privatisation
and the public sector 128
4.13 Bipartisan convergence in Britain, 1992–7: media
regulation 129
4.14 Bipartisan convergence in Britain, 1992–7: constitutional
reform 131
6.1 Standardised levels (rank on Maddison's scale) of savings,
investment and growth 187
6.2 Asset allocation of UK pension funds in 1979 and 1989 198
6.3 Overseas holdings of UK pension funds, 1993 198

Preface and acknowledgements

This book, as is so often the case, has taken rather longer to write than I had originally anticipated. During the intervening time the target of its attentions has shifted dramatically, a process (or series of processes) that has become the principal focus of the present volume. Stimulated initially by a certain frustration with the path down which Labour seemed to be travelling in the mid to late 1980s, the book is as much a normative intervention as a theoretical and analytical contribution. Many (perhaps the majority) of its readers will no doubt disagree with my assessment of the 'modernisation' process and of the room for alternatives both in opposition and now in government. Nonetheless, I do hope to raise a number of key theoretical and analytical issues that cannot so simply be dispensed with. Indeed, it is my central contention that they must be addressed if we are to adjudicate claims as to the obsolescence or indeed the continued viability and vibrancy of social democracy in contemporary Europe in a context of globalisation. In this respect, I can only hope that I have not been labouring under false pretences.

Given the rather lengthy gestation of my thoughts on this subject, I have incurred an unusually extensive array of debts, both personal and intellectual. A very large number of colleagues and friends have commented at various stages upon draft chapters and papers whose contents have found their way in some form into this text. Still others have badgered me into clarifying, amplifying and developing my position in a strange variety of locations – from seminar rooms and lecture theatres to buses, trains and pubs. Amongst those who spring immediately to mind are (alphabetically): Eric Bleich, Mark Blyth, Jim Buller, Andreas Busch, Lorna Chicksand, Howie Chodos, David Coates, Fiona Devine, David Dolowitz, Josef Esser, Steven Fielding, Paul Furlong, Andrew Gamble, Peter Hall, Jonathan Hopkin, Chris Howell, Bob Jessop, Jim Johnston, George Katsifiacis, Ira Katznelson,

Michael Kenny, Peter Kerr, Colin Leys, Tom Ling, Stuart McAnulla, Rianne Mahon, David Marsh, Andy Martin, Mick Moran, Mark Motte, Sue Penna, Paul Pierson, Frances Fox Piven, Peter Preston, Trevor Purvis, David Richards, Eric Shaw, Paul Thompson, Brian Waddell, Richard Weiner and Daniel Wincott. I must also thank the Center for European Studies and the Department of Political Science at the Massachusetts Institute of Technology for putting me up (or putting up with me) whilst most of this book was written and my colleagues and friends in the Department of Political Science and International Studies at the University of Birmingham for putting up with my periodic trips to the US. Nicola Viinikka and Pippa Kenyon at Manchester University Press have provided precisely the right blend of infectious enthusiasm, encouragement and common sense.

I would also like to acknowledge a variety of yet more significant debts. A series of exchanges, both in the journals and in the seminar room, has been crucial to the development of the argument here presented. I must thank Martin Smith and Mark Wickham-Jones in particular for being exemplary and exacting interlocutors and for never taking personally our theoretical, analytical and normative disagreements.

This brings me to my two most important debts of all. The first is to Matthew Watson. Over the past two years we have worked, at times fairly tirelessly, on the political economy of New Labour – about which, I fear, I have learned rather more from him than he has from me. Many of the ideas presented in this book could not have been formulated without his almost constant input. I can only reiterate that without our discussions and, in particular, his encyclopaedic knowledge of contemporary economics, this book could simply not have been written. I would also like to thank him for permission to draw on draft sections of a co-authored article (on which, thankfully, we had a very clear division of labour) in the final chapter. My most considerable debt, however, is, as always, to Elspeth Stewart, who has, once again, heard rather more about New Labour than anyone could have cared to. She has been a constant source of inspiration and an equally constant reminder that there are many more important things than writing! I can only apologise for so frequently giving the impression that there weren't!

Finally, and more formally, I would like to express my thanks to the editors and publishers of the following journals for permission to reprint, in some cases in heavily revised form, arguments first presented in their pages. Parts of chapter 2 first appeared in *Political Studies* (Volume 42, Number 5). Chapter 4 is based largely on an article that first appeared in *New Political Science* (Volume 20, Number 1). Parts of chapter 5 first appeared in *Politics and Society* (Volume 25, Number 2). Parts of chapter 6 first appeared in *New Political Economy* (Volume 3, Number 3).

September 1998
Cambridge, MA

Abbreviations

CBI	Confederation of British Industry
DHA	district health authority
DTI	Department of Trade and Industry
ETI	economically targeted investment
GDP	gross domestic product
HMSO	Her Majesty's Stationery Office
IMF	International Monetary Fund
MDAs	metropolitan development agencies
NCB	National Coal Board
NEC	National Executive Committee
NHS	National Health Service
NIB	national investment bank
NUM	National Union of Mineworkers
PLP	Parliamentary Labour Party
PSBR	public sector borrowing requirement
RDAs	regional development agencies
RIBs	regional investment banks
RTAs	regional training agencies
SRI	socially responsible investment

1 Contextualising Novelty: the legacy of Thatcherism, the prospect of globalisation

Every generation since the industrial revolution has believed that it is living through a period of unprecedented economic change. (Tomlinson 1997: 11)

A new stage in the development of the world economic and political system has commenced, a new kind of world order, which is characterised both by unprecedented unity and unprecedented fragmentation. Understanding this new world order will require new modes of analysis and new theories, and a readiness to tear down intellectual barriers and bring together many approaches, methods and disciplines which for too long have been apart. What is required is a new political economy which combines the breadth of vision of the classical political economy of the nineteenth century with the analytical advances of twentieth-century social science. (Gamble *et al.* 1996: 5)

We have been elected as New Labour, we will govern as New Labour. (Tony Blair, speech to Labour Party workers, Royal Festival Hall, London, 2 May 1997)

If Tomlinson is right and every generation since the industrial revolution has, indeed, believed itself to be living through a period of unprecedented economic change, then there would nonetheless appear something qualitatively distinct about the near constant invocation of novelty in the analysis, interpretation, rhetoric and practice of contemporary British politics and political economy. No self-respecting critical analyst or commentator can possibly but shiver at the proliferation of entities, processes, institutions, theories, disciplines and now parties to which the ubiquitous prefix 'new' has been appended in recent years. We inhabit, variously, a 'new world order', a 'new world disorder' or 'new times'. Our politics exhibits all the characteristics of a new consensus fashioned around the ideas of the new right and

1

reflected in a spirit of 'new realism' espoused, embodied and internalised most vigorously by New Labour. Should we require yet further evidence of the ubiquity of novelty, we need look no further than the world of political discourse. Here we discover, once again, New Labour leading us tirelessly and inexorably down the road to New Britain, armed with its post-neo-classical endogenous growth theory, to find a new place within a new Europe aided and abetted by a renewed special relationship with Blair's fair-weather cousins across the pond, the New Democrats. Given the perhaps understandable nausea which such a proliferation of markers of innovation might, and invariably does, engender, a dispassionate assessment of claims of an epochal shift in the contours of contemporary capitalism, the domestic political economy and New Labour's place within this new constellation of constraints and opportunities is particularly difficult. It is, nonetheless, long overdue.

Yet, lest this convey the wrong impression, the present volume does not provide (nor indeed could it provide) a neutral and dispassionate assessment of the 'modernisation' of the British Labour Party in recent years. My aim in this volume, and in this introductory chapter in particular, is to raise and to render as explicit as possible the theoretical and analytical issues which would have to be resolved were such an assessment to be attempted. These, as we shall see, principally concern questions of change – its temporality, nature, pace, duration and consequences, and the means by which it might be identified, adjudicated, analysed and interpreted (on such themes see also Hay 1999a, 1999b). Though rarely acknowledged explicitly, and even less frequently addressed explicitly, claims as to the continuous/incremental or discontinuous/punctuated nature of complex institutional change, the relative significance of economic, political and ideological factors, and the more or less contingent or determined nature of political and economic dynamics are routinely and intuitively appealed to in the analysis of the modernisation process (on these themes more generally see Hay 1998a; Marsh 1996; Marsh *et al.* 1999). My aim in this chapter is to place the analysis, interpretation and assessment of Labour's transformation in recent years and its prospects, which are advanced in later chapters, in the context of such theoretical concerns. The argument proceeds in three stages. In the following section, I consider the conception of novelty itself before moving on in the next section to consider the various contexts within which Labour's modernisation has been situated and against whose backcloth it might be assessed and adjudicated. In the final section I seek to draw out of this discussion a series of theoretical and methodological issues crucial to the analysis of subsequent chapters yet at best dealt with implicitly, intuitively or tangentially in the existing literature. These are: the relationship between structure and agency, context and conduct appealed to in accounts of Labour's modernisation; the relationship between the material and the discursive or ideational in driving political and economic dynamics; the relative significance of political, economic and cultural factors, and domestic and international processes and practices in shaping the trajectory and nature of Labour's modernisation in an era of much-vaunted globalisation.

Conceptualising novelty

Old Labour, New Labour

The term 'new', as Butler and Kavanagh observe in their commentary on the 1997 general election campaign (1997: 64), occurred some thirty-seven times in Blair's speech to the 1994 Labour Party conference and a further 104 times in the *Road to the Manifesto* document (Labour Party 1996a). Indeed, since the public launch of 'New Labour' – and with it the promise to build a 'New Britain' – at the 1994 conference, one might be forgiven for thinking that Labour had claimed exclusive rights to its use. In 'rebranding' itself, 'New Labour', with all the associated advertising blitz, Blair has effectively claimed that the party's modernisation is over. In so doing, he has also served to complete this modernisation by distancing himself and the party symbolically and rhetorically from its past. Yet New Labour's relation to this past is by no means uncomplicated. For, in emphasising the rupture that the 'Blair revolution' represents, the party has juxtaposed its present to a variety of rather different historical 'others' (Mandelson and Liddle 1996). Two are perhaps of particular significance.

First, New Labour has sought to distance itself from the spectre of 'Old Labour' in government (the period 1976–9 in particular). The British economy's precipitous spiral into economic recession following the first oil-price shock in 1973 under the Wilson and then Callaghan governments, its embarrassing 'bailout' by the International Monetary Fund (IMF) once all normal channels of credit had been exhausted, the effectively enforced abandonment of a Keynesian full-employment strategy and, above all, the footage of picket lines, rotting rubbish and unburied corpses during the Winter of Discontent (1978/9) have cast a long pall over Labour's previous period in government.[1] The confidence that this spectre has finally been laid to rest is reflected in the assertiveness with which Labour proclaims its novelty.

Second, in declaring itself 'new', Labour is also seeking to distance itself from associations with aspects of its more immediate period in opposition (as symbolised by the unapologetic leftism of the period 1979–83 and by the events of the miners' strike of 1984–5). Where it previously stood to suffer from its perceived associations with this period of 'unbridled leftism' and 'socialist extremism', it can now, it appears, only benefit from emphasising (indeed, grossly exaggerating) the paranoid protectionism, unguarded opportunism and suicidal disregard for public opinion held to characterise this period. Accordingly, the party no longer feels obliged to apologise for this temporary aberration, as reflected in the suggestion by Hughes and Wintour (not untypical of party sympathisers) that, in 1983, 'even 28 per cent of the vote, the party's lowest since 1918, seemed more than the party deserved' (1990: 6). Mandelson and Liddle's opprobrium is no less pronounced, reflected in their comment that in the period after 1979 Labour's enduring commitment to social justice had been 'completely distorted by indulgent policies framed to appeal to sectarian activists and minority pressure groups' (1996: 36). Thus, in an at best partial and simplistic, at worst wilful and cynical (and quite clearly *convenient*) historical revisionism, Labour chose to depict (and construct) the immediate aftermath of the 1979 election as a hasty, temporary and profoundly undemocratic and unrepresentative victory for an arcane and anachronistic leftism (for rather different interpretations see Elliott 1993: 126–34; Panitch and Leys 1997: 134–214; Shaw 1994: 1–29; Wickham-Jones 1996: 189–208; for an analysis of New Labour's reinvention of its past see Hassan and Shaw 1996).

If these are New Labour's most obvious 'others', then it is important that we should not lose sight altogether of at least one further 'other': the modernisation process itself. This may be a more contentious point, but the argument is a simple one. In proclaiming itself 'renewed' and 'rejuvenated' after a protracted period of transformation, the party has effectively wrapped up (at least symbolically) the modernisation process. In so doing, it conjures a simple periodised narrative of its recent development: of a past to be transcended, of a process of transcendence and, eventually, of an end-state (a state of

'New Labour'), now happily achieved. This suggests a certain ambivalence regarding Blair's role, in particular, in the modernisation process: should the modernising project be imputed to Blair (à la Mandelson and Liddle's *The Blair Revolution*)? Or should Blair be seen as the recipient of a <u>modernisation project conceived and largely</u> executed under the leadership of <u>Kinnock</u> (and, latterly, Smith) and now simply bequeathed to him? This ambivalence may tell us much about New Labour's symbolic politics (on which see Bale 1996). For Blair does not wish to be associated directly with a party undergoing modernisation (and hence a party in need of modernisation), when he can be associated instead with a party which is already modernised. At the same time, there are obvious advantages to being seen, and/or constructed, as the immediate agent of the party's modernisation – and hence as the immediate recipient of the approval such modernisation might engender.[2] Moreover, that Labour now seems to want to distance itself from the modernisation process tells us something about the party's attitude towards this often conflictual and, at some points, largely directionless process of transformation. New Labour simply does not wish to recall the means by which – in the party's latest version of its recent history – (sections of) the leadership, the National Executive Committee (NEC), the Parliamentary Labour Party (PLP), the trade unions and constituency members alike were dragged, often kicking and screaming, into the latter decades of the twentieth century. With the benefit of distance and hindsight, modernisation is now cast as a necessary, long-overdue, but rather unsavoury and perhaps unduly protracted interlude that has now been safely negotiated. Its success, the very condition of New Labour's electoral triumph, was symbolically secured in the rewriting of Clause IV of the party's 1918 constitution (on which see especially Bale 1996; Kenny and Smith 1997a).

New Labour's invocation of novelty, however, should not be seen to imply a strictly chronological, far less linear, conception of historical time. For, in its somewhat stylised reconstruction of its own history (more accurately, perhaps, the *pre*-history of New Labour) in terms of binary oppositions, the Labour Party has sought to reclaim as much as it has rejected. Thus, whilst going to considerable trouble to distance itself from the 'old labourist' politics of the Wilson/Callaghan government, Foot and even, where convenient, Kinnock, it exhibits a certain selective nostalgia for the politics of renewal and modernisation associated in particular with Attlee and the Wilson of 1964 (if not, perhaps, his later reincarnation). In the last case, it is the rhetoric and symbolism of opposition rather than the (all too predictable) compromise, disappointment and betrayal of office that draws New Labour towards an at least partial rehabilitation of Wilson.[3] What impresses the party today is, presumably, the combination of 'technocratic modernism' and the (rhetorical) juxtaposition of a moribund Conservatism on the one hand with Labour's visionary dynamism on the other (Mandelson and Liddle 1996: 49). As Noel Thompson notes:

> There is a considerable electoral virtue in a concept open to disparate interpretations and satisfying a variety of political tastes. Harold Wilson's 'big idea' of a New Britain forged in the 'white heat of technological revolution' proved effective in these respects ... it was not only sufficiently nebulous to be embraced by the technocratic Right and the pro-planning, public-ownership-supporting Left, but also, in capturing something of the spirit of the 1960s, it served to rally a significant swathe of the aspirant middle and working classes to the cause of Labour. (1996: 37)

Ironically, the inspiration for Wilson's 'big idea' was drawn primarily from the reinvigoration of the Democrats under Kennedy, some thirty years before Blair would seek to draw similar inspiration from Clinton's New Democrats (Panitch and Leys 1997: 16). One can perhaps only hope that the analogy with the first Wilson administration does not prove portentous for New Labour. For the disparity between that promised and that delivered (arguably Labour's most obvious Achilles' heel) was greater for the Wilson government of 1964–70 than perhaps any post-war Labour administration – previous or subsequent.[4] Its rhetorical radicalism ran aground to expose both a distinct lack of conviction and the institutional inertia imposed by the (narrowly conceived) sectoral interest of its 'social partners' on both sides of the capital–labour relation (see Crossman 1985; Elliott 1993: 74–81; Howell 1980: 251–67; Panitch 1976; Ponting 1990: chapter 3; for a more sympathetic reappraisal see Coopey *et al.* 1993). Almost three decades later, things may be somewhat different. Arguably New Labour has got its betrayals in earlier (indeed, prior to its election), promising little substantively whilst continuing to espouse a rather vague sense of renewal and rejuvenation now projected from the 'new model party' on to Britain itself (the view, for instance, of Marquesee 1997; Panitch and Leys 1997: chapter 11; and P. Smith 1997: 175–81). Whether this will prove sufficient to satisfy the palpable sense of expectation and anticipation which accompanied Labour's landslide (the party's extended exercise in expectation suppression in the eighteen months before polling day not withstanding) is another matter.

Labour's desire to associate itself with the 'spirit of 1945' and Attlee's 'New Jerusalemism' has been, perhaps understandably, altogether less qualified and more vocal. In Blair's speech to the Fabian Society commemorating the fiftieth anniversary of the 1945 election victory, the comparison is very clearly drawn:

> Then, as now, we faced enormous changes in the global economy and in society. Then, as now, Labour spoke for the national interest and offered hope for the future; the Tories spoke for sectional interest and represented the past. Then, as now, Britain needed rebuilding and the voters turned to Labour to take on that task; because, then as now, the people knew that market dogma and crude individualism could not solve the nation's problems ... I have no hesitation whatsoever in describing the 1945 Labour government as the greatest peacetime government this century. (Blair 1995: 1–2)

At the same time, however, Blair is anxious to distance himself from the substantive concerns of the Attlee administration, arguing that just as it was a 'government for its time', New Labour must become a government for new times. The similarities with Attlee's cautious radicalism, then, are reflected less in any attempt to emulate the latter's programmatic vision of a New Jerusalem (or, indeed, its radicalism) than in the desire to 'set out how the enduring values of 1945 can be applied to the very different world today'.[5] In this way, New Labour can present itself as the rightful heir (and, in certain respects, the *first* rightful heir) to the spirit of Attlee whilst, at the same time, drawing an unequivocal distinction between 1945 and the contemporary 'global' context within which such a spirit might be reinstantiated. In one sense, then, Labour here conjures a cyclical conception of political time – of long periods of stasis and incremental evolution punctuated only infrequently by the modernising spirit of renewal and rejuvenation which animated Attlee and (if to a lesser extent) Wilson as it now animates Blair. Blair's New Labour is, in this revisionist auto-biographical history, the reincarnation of Attlee's New Jerusalemism.

Interestingly, as the recent historiographic reappraisal of the initial post-war experience has demonstrated, what the Attlee and Wilson governments shared (and what distinguishes them from other post-war administrations) was an explicit and interventionist productivism – a prioritisation of the (perceived) interests of industrial over financial capital. This found itself reflected in the associated desire (ultimately unsuccessful) to restore a competitive edge to, and to modernise, British industry through consistent supply-side intervention. In both cases, however, such modernising ambitions were thwarted by a combination of narrowly conceived sectoral interest on the part of capital and labour and a rather more deeply entrenched economic orthodoxy than the public rhetoric would suggest (Tiratsoo and Tomlinson 1993; Tomlinson 1993).[6] Given New Labour's fairly comprehensive retreat, in recent years, from the industrial modernisation strategy of the period 1983–90 (see chapters 4 and 5), it is thus doubly ironic to find it reinvoking the spirit of Attlee at precisely the moment at which contemporary revisionist historiographers have come to emphasise the latter's own variant of 'supply-side socialism'. It is, frankly, rather difficult to imagine New Labour succeeding where its more professedly reformist progenitors failed (in its avowed attempts to restore an industrial growth dynamic to the British economy).

Old times, new times
In projecting itself as New Labour, the party has not merely sought to distance itself from certain aspects of its past (and those who would seek to reconstruct the party in their image) whilst selectively appropriating others. It has also invoked, as it has relied upon, certain conceptions of the external environment upon which its 'new' politics must be projected. Thus, arguably, as crucial to the party's modernisation as its understanding of its own history and tradition as a party (and, perhaps, its disavowal of its history and traditions as a movement) has been its conception of the contemporary global political economy. More particularly, in appealing to the distinction 'Old Labour – New Labour', the party has frequently invoked (whether implicitly or explicitly) a similar distinction between 'old times' and 'new times'. Where, for instance, the Keynesianism, (quasi) corporatism, collectivism, egalitarianism, expansive welfarism and, indeed, socialism of Attlee or Wilson were appropriate to the post-war period, the fiscal conservatism, individualism, social (or even neo-) liberalism, moralism and, in Blair's terms, 'social-ism' of New Labour are appropriate to new times.[7]

This is a crucial point, central to much of the argument of proceeding chapters. For it suggests that claims as to the qualitative novelty of the social, political and, above all, economic context in which New

Labour finds itself have been central to the modernisation process – and must, accordingly, be central to any assessment of the trajectory, extent and appropriateness of Labour's transformation. Remarkably, however, both in the literature on New Labour and in Labour's own accounts of its modernisation, precious little detail is provided as to the precise nature of this epochal shift and the constraints (or indeed opportunities) it might be seen to impose (or present). Clearly, the reliance upon a distinction of the type 'old times – new times' logically entails, as it implies, an epochal shift in the contours of the advanced industrial societies occurring at some point between the zenith of Keynesian social democracy (presumably in the late 1950s or early 1960s) and Labour's consignment to the electoral margins in the 1980s. Closer scrutiny of this period might suggest that the rise of the new right (in Britain, of Thatcherism) be seen as marking precisely such a rupture (and perhaps even an irreversible break) with the past (on which see Hay 1996b: 147–55). Yet what is also clear is that New Labour and commentators sympathetic to the modernisation process reject this attribution of responsibility for 'new times' to the new right. Accordingly, rather than depict the passing of Keynesian social democracy as a political (and hence contingent) response to the widely identified crisis of the 1970s, exponents and proponents of modernisation alike have tended to rely instead upon a rather more deterministic logic of economic necessity. Indeed, rather than see Thatcherism as *initiating* a break with the past, it is seen as a *response* to the distinctive economic (and presumably the attendant political) pressures of new times. Martin Smith is by no means unrepresentative of the literature when he suggests that 'many of the factors which led to the Policy Review were external to Thatcherism and to some extent *also explain the changes that have occurred in the Conservative Party*' (1992a: 14, emphasis added; see also Kenny and Smith 1997b; Mandelson and Liddle 1996: 12–14). This is certainly not an unequivocal passage (and is perhaps all the more representative of the literature for that), yet it does appear to imply an overriding economic and/or social logic narrowing the realm of the politically possible and operating in large part 'above' (independently and beyond the control of) political actors. This impression would seem to be confirmed by Michael Kenny and Martin Smith's more recent comment that 'a line has to be drawn between the policies of earlier eras and those appropriate to today's conditions' (1997b: 226). That this is indeed the case might appear intuitively appealing, obvious even. However, as in so much of the existing literature, it is precisely such a sense of intuition – rather than any more substantive analysis – on which we are asked to rely. Kenny and Smith are, then, in good company in failing to tell us why such a line need be drawn in the first place, precisely where it should be drawn, what it delineates and what are the processes which have taken us from 'there' to 'here'. Much of what follows is an attempt to adjudicate and assess, in the light of the evidence available, such intuitively appealing if frequently undefended and often implicit claims as to the nature and distinctiveness of the times we inhabit.

Without wishing to prejudge the issue, it is important to note at this stage the long and distinct pedigree of the concept of 'new times' in debates on the need for, nature and extent of the modernisation required if Labour were to overturn the ascendancy of the new right established in the 1980s. The term was first coined in this context in the pages of *Marxism Today*, a journal with which Blair was himself quite closely associated (see Terry 1997: 39–58). What is interesting here is the extent to which, in the face of consistent criticism, those previously most committed to the notion of a qualitative shift in the contours of contemporary capitalism (necessitating a new accommoda-tion with the changed realities of a new epoch) have qualified significantly such claims in recent years – in no small part in the light of Labour's modernising zeal. Thus Stuart Hall, intellectual guru of *Marxism Today* and the neo-Gramscian revival in Britain more gener-ally, suggests in a recent interview:

> I feel a peculiar responsibility for the Blair phenomenon. Blair was quite close to *Marxism Today* at one stage as a reader. We launched the modernisation programme which Blair took up. We mean different things by it but we are implicated in some of the shifts because we've always argued that Labour could not just go back to its old stamping ground and reaffirm the past. In a funny way, then, we're responsible for launching some of these new ideas which have then been appropri-ated cosmetically and installed in a different kind of project. (Terry 1997: 55)

Though Hall is by no means committed to the idea that Labour could simply revamp the Keynesian social democracy of the post-war years, he does nonetheless regard Labour's modernisation as resting on a fundamental misconception and, in particular, a conflation of the necessities of new times with the contingencies of neo-liberalism (see also Hall 1995). Invigorated perhaps by the suggestion of a new epoch,

Labour, he argues, has mistaken the politics of welfare retrenchment, labour-market deregulation and fiscal austerity for the only game in town in a post-Keynesian, post-corporatist and post-social democratic context. For Labour, this is an exceedingly dangerous, however well intentioned, move – its consequence, to restrict the limits of the possible, the feasible and the desirable to that imaginable within the ascendant neo-liberal world view. Given the rapid and embarrassed retreat of authors like Hall from the 'new times' thesis and what he now sees as its unfortunate implications (principally the tendency to confuse and even conflate the contingencies of the new right for the exigencies of globalisation), the onus is surely on those who would defend such a claim to provide some justification for the assertion that the limits of Labour's radicalism exhaust (if not exceed) the limits of contemporary radicalism in the context of global(ising) capitalism.

It is both telling and ironic that Hall, former doyen of the 'new times' thesis, should be one of the first to retract publicly the legitimation it might otherwise be seen to confer upon Labour's modernising trajectory and to beat the retreat to precisely the 'outmoded' ideas that so many of Labour's sympathisers have been so swift to reject. Hall, of course, was not the only proponent of the 'new times' thesis, though he has certainly been the most vocal in distancing himself from it. Ironic though it may seem, New Labour can claim amongst its most influential advisors a number of 'new timers' who have moved on to greater things since the demise of *Marxism Today*. Chief amongst these has been Geoff Mulgan, who moved from *Marxism Today* and the Communist Party to found Demos (an independent think-tank of the non-aligned centre-left) and, more recently, to head the 'special projects' team in the Prime Minister's office. Needless to say, he has been less anxious publicly to recant his faith in the mantras of new times.

The nature of novelty: reconceptualising and recontextualising New Labour

As the above discussion suggests, New Labour's self-conception of its trajectory from the languor of seemingly permanent opposition to the prospect of 'natural government' has been couched in terms of two principal narratives: the first a story of the conversion and wholesale transformation of a political party whose structure, fraternal allegiances and ideology had become anachronistic; the second a story of the globalisation and resulting transformation of the external social and economic environment in which that party was forced to compete for power. Yet these are by no means the only stories which can be told about Labour's modernisation, nor the only contexts with respect to which the party's proclaimed novelty might be assessed. Indeed, in what follows I will seek to identify five rather different contexts with respect to which claims about Labour's modernisation and trans-formation may be adjudicated. Before doing so, however, it is perhaps useful to reflect conceptually upon the nature of novelty itself.

There is, of course, nothing particularly remarkable about novelty. If we follow Marx's oft-cited aphorism and view history as in a constant state of being made by actors, if not in circumstances of their own choosing, then, ontologically, the very nature of being itself is that of the production of novelty. In this most trivial sense, Labour may not need to prove very much to demonstrate its novelty – save, perhaps, that it exists. What is clear, however, is that, in claiming novelty, New Labour is invoking a much more fundamental and abrupt conception of change. This immediately complicates the picture, raising questions of political temporality and, more specifically, the difficult issue of the degree of change sufficient to warrant the identification of a 'new' stage in the development of a system, institution or organisation.

Claims of novelty are, of course, essentially relative, as novelty can only be claimed (and indeed evaluated) with respect, say, to a particu-lar tradition, ideology, environment, institution or history. A number of such contexts are relevant, as we have already seen, to claims about Labour's modernisation, not least those made by the party about itself. Here, however, it is important that we differentiate between three rather different senses of novelty. These might be termed: *endogenous novelty*, *comparative novelty* and *contextual novelty* (see table 1.1). Though claims about each are frequently related, it is important that we keep these senses at least analytically distinct.

The first sense, that of *endogenous novelty*, relates to claims made about an institution or party with respect to its own immediate history or tradition. Where it is argued, for instance, that New Labour's ideology, appeal to the electorate, party ethos and/or internal structure are novel and serve to set it apart from 'Old Labour', this is a claim to endogenous novelty. Such claims invoke (at least implicitly) a period-isation of the party's development and, in their simplest terms, a distinction between 'Old Labour' and 'New Labour'. Yet claims to

Table 1.1 Endogenous, comparative and contextual novelty

	What is novel?	With respect to what is this novelty assessed?	Does this imply a changed external environment?	Does this imply a change in party image, structure or appeal?
I. Endogenous novelty	Party image, electoral appeal, strategy and/or structure	Party's ethos, tradition, style and history	Not necessarily	Yes
IIa. Comparative electoral/ideological novelty (domestically)	Party image, electoral appeal, strategy and/or structure	The current electoral strategy/appeal of other domestic parties	Not necessarily	Yes – relative to competitor parties
IIb. Comparative electoral/ideological novelty (internationally)	Party image, electoral appeal, strategy and/or structure	The current electoral appeal/strategy of other labour/social democratic parties	Often, but not necessarily	Yes – relative to other labour/social democratic parties
III. Contextual novelty	External environment; the degree of fit between this context and party policy/appeal	Degree of political latitude; contours of external context; fit between policy and context	Yes	Generally, but not necessarily

endogenous novelty need imply no assessment (favourable or otherwise) of the appropriateness of such party traits and characteristics,
merely that they have changed in such a way as to differentiate the
party now from its past.

Notions of *comparative novelty* rely upon an altogether different
kind of judgement. Here the party's conduct is assessed not in terms of
its own historical traditions, but with respect to the contemporary
conduct of other parties. For authors wishing to make such a claim,
New Labour's novelty might be seen to reside in the distinctive and
contemporary nature of its appeal to the electorate, say, when compared either with that of other competitor parties, or with parties in
different political systems which traditionally share a common lineage
or ethos (in this case, other social democratic or labour parties). Again,
such a comparison need not necessarily imply the appropriateness or
desirability of the novelty in question. Critics of New Labour, for
instance, might plausibly argue that the party's comparative ideological novelty amongst (former) social democratic parties in western
Europe has served to act as a model for the further dissemination of
neo-liberalism (see for instance Mommen 1999).[8] Clearly, this need
not imply that such novelty is either warranted by the contours of the
external environment or desirable. For such authors it is rarely either.
Furthermore, this type of comparison need not imply any terribly
dramatic process of modernisation on the part of the party in question –
merely that in comparative terms its ideology, ethos and/or appeal to
the electorate are qualitatively distinctive and somewhat more contemporary than those of the parties with which it is contrasted.

Finally, we might posit a conception of *contextual novelty*, implying
some fit between party form, ideology and function on the one hand and a
changed (and hence novel) external environment on the other. The much-
vaunted correspondence of New Labour and new times provides a good
example of precisely such a claim. It should be noted, however, that to
point to a qualitative shift in the external environment is not necessarily
to imply the need for wholesale party modernisation to (re-)establish a
favourable fit between party conduct and external context, just as such a
modernisation is in itself no guarantee of (re-)establishing such a fit.
Nonetheless, to identify contextual novelty in this way is, generally, to
imply the appropriateness of policy to a qualitatively novel social,
political and economic context posing qualitatively novel challenges.

If it is important to differentiate at least analytically between
endogenous, comparative and contextual claims to novelty, it is equally

important to disentangle the various endogenous and exogenous contexts with respect to which claims about Labour's modernisation have
been, and might be, made. Though by no means an exhaustive list, five
potential contexts arise fairly naturally out of the above discussion,
providing a useful way of departmentalising the existing literature on
Labour's transformation in recent years. These various contexts and
the literatures to which they have given rise can be arranged, as
follows, in terms of the degree to which they privilege either endogenous or exogenous factors. They are: (i) the party's internal history
and traditions; (ii) the development of the British state and economy in
the post-war period; (iii) demographic and other socio-economic
trends; (iv) the development of European social democracy in the post-
war period; and (v) the development of the international or global
political economy. We consider each in turn.

The development of the Labour Party
The first, and perhaps most obvious, context with respect to which
Labour's modernisation might be assessed is that of the party's traditions, history and ideology. As we have seen, claims to the comparative
novelty and distinctiveness of New Labour arising from the party itself
are most frequently couched in terms of a narrative of the modernisation of the party. Here 'Old Labour' is counter-posed to 'New Labour',
as a clear break with the structure, ideology and practice of the party
throughout the post-war period is posited. At the same time, however,
a certain ambivalence regarding party philosophy or ethos often ac-
companies such claims. Blair's (1995) speech to the Fabian Society
commemorating the fiftieth anniversary of Attlee's electoral triumph is
a case in point. For whilst anxious to distance himself from the spirit
of paternalism, universalism and collectivism of an earlier time, Blair
was nonetheless keen to highlight the 'enduring values of 1945':
values which, of course, remained largely unspecified in the speech
itself. A very similar sentiment is captured in a rare comment by Blair
on the notion of 'modernisation' itself:

> The process of what is called 'modernisation' is in reality ... *the
> application of enduring lasting principles for a new generation –*
> creating not just a modern party and organisation but a programme for
> a modern society, economy and constitution. It is not destroying the
> Left's essential ideology: on the contrary, it is retrieving it from an
> intellectual and political muddle. (Blair 1996: 221–2; emphasis added,

from the Charities Aid Foundation's tenth Arnold Goodman Charity
Lecture, London, 8 July 1993)

Given the centrality of such endogenous claims to novelty to the
party's understanding of its own identity, it is not surprising that much
of the secondary literature on Labour's modernisation has also tended
to concentrate on the internal dynamics of Labour's transformation
(see for instance Heffernan and Marquesee 1992; Hughes and Wintour
1990; Jones 1996; Kenny and Smith 1997a; Marquesee 1997; Shaw
1994; Smith and Spear 1992; Taylor 1997).[9] This literature has charted
and chronicled, often in meticulous detail, the complex contours of
Labour's trajectory since the late 1970s, providing both a wealth of
empirical evidence and considerable insight – evidence and insight on
which the present study draws heavily.

Despite its often highly descriptive nature, such debate has, nonetheless, been characterised by considerable dispute and controversy. In
particular, authors have disagreed over the precise nature of New
Labour's break with the past, the timing of its modernisation, the more
or less cumulative, incremental or punctuated nature of the process, the
relative significance of the Policy Review period and of the leadership
of Kinnock, Smith and Blair. Eric Shaw, for instance, in perhaps the
most comprehensive study to date of the transformation of the party
since 1979, identifies a clear trajectory from the 'revisionism' that had
characterised the Labour Party in opposition and government throughout the post-war period to the 'post-revisionism' of the 1980s and
1990s:

> Whilst the revisionist model affirmed the capacity of the state to steer
> the market, and hence adjust private economic interests to the needs of
> society at large and thereby secure the basic social democratic goals of
> higher growth, full employment and an expanding welfare state, post-
> revisionism ... took a much more sanguine view of what could be
> achieved. (Shaw 1994: 105)

As he goes on to explain, for post-revisionists,

> it was only the private sector that could create the conditions for full
> employment, growth and therefore the wherewithal to finance improved
> public services ... post-revisionism regarded the central Croslandite
> proposition, that democratic government had the ability to prevail over
> the power of business, as false. (105–6)

Others, however, have reached an almost antithetical conclusion, emphasising instead New Labour's return to the spirit (if not quite the substance) of Croslandite revisionism following a temporary victory for the left during the early 1980s (see for instance Jones 1996; Smith 1992a: 24–7, 1994: 709).[10] Thus, as Smith concludes his own study of the Policy Review process, 'the Labour Party has ... to some extent returned to the revisionism of the 1950s and 1960s and to the social democratic traditions that had been important throughout its history' (1992a: 28; though see Kenny and Smith 1997a: 125, 1997b: 223–4). The rewriting of Clause IV of the party's 1918 constitution under Blair's leadership often features prominently in more recent accounts (prompting a series of comparisons between Gaitskell and Blair).[11] Tudor Jones, for instance, is altogether less equivocal than Smith:

> Viewed against its historical background, Tony Blair's successful bid in 1995 to rewrite Clause IV of the Labour Party Constitution may with justification be regarded as the culmination of a revisionist project within the party – concerned both with demoting public ownership and endorsing the market economy – that was initiated in the 1950s. (1996: 149)

In fact, the potential for some reconciliation between these seemingly antithetical positions does exist. Gregory Elliott's comment on the internal debate within the Labour Party in the 1950s and 1960s is here suggestive: 'Whereas the revisionists sought to endow Labour with the theory of its contemporary practice, their critics strove to (re-) dedicate it to the practice of its traditional "theory"' (1993: 67). In this passage, revisionism is taken to imply little more than a certain quietism with respect to capitalism's iniquities, a pragmatic as distinct from ideological ethos and a perhaps rather opportunistic attempt to rationalise theoretically that already considered practically necessary. On such an understanding, Old Labour in the 1950s and New Labour in the 1990s do indeed share a certain revisionism. Yet any closer scrutiny of the party's 'theory of its contemporary practice', then and now, can only serve to emphasise the rather different substance of Labour's contemporary revisionism. Suffice it to note at this stage that even the description of Labour's trajectory since the early 1980s, once set in a historical context, is highly contested.

The question of revisionism, however, does not exhaust the disputed contemporary history of the Labour Party. For, whilst popular accounts (and, frequently, those offered by the party about itself) often credit Blair with the party's transformation (for instance, Mandelson and Liddle 1996), the secondary literature is rather more divided in its assessment and interpretation of the origins and timing of Labour's modernisation. Thus, perhaps rather surprisingly given the historical and comparative focus of their collection, Brian Brivati and Tim Bale's introduction to *New Labour in Power* speaks of 'Tony Blair's project to reform the Labour Party' without any reference to Smith or Kinnock (1997: 2). Nick Ellison's emphasis, later in the very same collection, is somewhat different, pointing to the significance of the reforms initiated by Kinnock and continued, if at a rather more leisurely pace, under Smith. 'Blair's successful "transformation" of the party', he argues, 'would have been unthinkable without the prior initiatives taken by Kinnock and Smith' (1997: 53). Similar sentiments have, of course, been expressed by Blair himself, who has been quick to acknowledge publicly his debt to his immediate predecessors (even before his election as party leader):

> With Neil Kinnock's election as leader we began a long march of renewal. That project was taken forward by John Smith. We owe it to them both ... to finish the journey from protest to power. (Blair 1996: 3; from his leadership election statement, 1994)[12]

It is Shaw (1994), however, who perhaps goes furthest in emphasising the significance in establishing Labour's trajectory of internal and subsequently programmatic reform of Kinnock's period as party leader. Others ostensibly sympathetic to such a view tend to trace the origins of the process of modernisation to the Policy Review – initiated as a response to the party's third consecutive electoral debacle in 1987 (Crewe 1993: 23–4; Jenkins 1987: 252–3; see also Hughes and Wintour 1990; Smith 1992b: 9–12). Yet Shaw, in a comprehensive, compelling and ultimately convincing account, places the emphasis instead on the period 1983–7. In so doing, he stresses the organisational and institutional difficulties confronting modernisers (like Kinnock) in 1983.[13] In pointing both to Labour's 'multiple crises' and to its institutional inertia at this time, Shaw serves to establish precisely the extent of the internal transformation of the party required before anything so bold, strategic, centralised or co-ordinated as the Policy Review could even be contemplated, yet alone successfully negotiated (1994: 29–52). In so doing, he provides an important corrective to much of the existing literature (though for similar assessments of the timing, pace and duration of Labour's modernisation see Eatwell 1992: 334–5; Hay and Watson 1999; Leys 1997; Panitch and Leys 1997; Wickham-Jones 1995a: 698–9, 1996).

The above paragraphs have only begun to touch upon the bewildering variety of often seemingly incommensurate perspectives on New Labour that have been couched simply in terms of the internal dynamics of the party and its history. Nonetheless, it should be noted that many of the apparent divergences (and associated disagreements) between such authors derive less from fundamental differences of interpretation so much as from rather different starting points. Clearly, for instance, were one to periodise Labour's transformation in recent years in terms of the development of policy, one might end up with a rather different mapping of the modernisation process over time than if one were to periodise the same process with respect to the structure and governance of the party (in terms, say, of the degree of centralisation of power, the influence of the trade unions, and so forth). Whereas the former might result in an account emphasising the significance of the immediate run-up to the 1987 general election, the Policy Review process itself and the extended 1997 general election campaign, the latter might by contrast point to the immediate aftermath of electoral defeat in 1983 and, perhaps, the period 1994–6. Despite superficial appearances to the contrary, then, the two might in fact provide complementary narratives.

This may seem like an overly conciliatory gesture. My aim, as proceeding chapters will make clear, is not to suggest that all perspectives on New Labour can so easily be reconciled – far from it. Yet it is surely important to emphasise that if we are to be clear about what divides us, it is crucial that we are able to render as explicit as possible the premises upon which we build. What is also clear is that if we are to adjudicate claims as to the relevance and appropriateness of Labour's modernisation, whatever its origins and timing, we can do so only by locating this process within the broader social, political and economic context, both domestically and internationally. It is to these exogenous contexts that we now turn.

The development of the British state and economy in the post-war period

Unsurprisingly, the most frequently considered external context for Labour's modernisation has been the immediate political and economic setting. Yet given the obvious importance of locating Labour's transformation and its political and economic implications in terms of the development of the state and economy in the post-war period, there have been remarkably few systematic analyses of New Labour in terms of the legacy of the Thatcher and Major years (though for more cursory assessments see the debate[14] between Martin Smith, Mark Wickham-Jones and myself in the pages of *Political Studies*).

Interestingly, those more sympathetic to the trajectory of Labour's transformation and, often, more persuaded by arguments about its necessity have tended not to concern themselves with a consideration of the legacy of Thatcherism – or, at least, only dismissively and in response to criticism (see for instance Smith 1994; though cf. Kenny and Smith 1997a: 221–2). Sceptics, by contrast, have tended to lavish much more attention on the extent to which Labour's changing policy commitments (at least since the Policy Review) have represented a capitulation or accommodation to aspects of the Thatcherite legacy (see for instance Elliott 1993; Hay 1994, 1997a; Leys 1990, 1997; Panitch and Leys 1997). In the end, as we shall see in the following chapter, much hinges on the interpretation of Thatcherism itself. For if the legacy of the Thatcher/Major years is seen either as relatively inconsequential (or at least far less significant than often argued – see for instance Kerr and Marsh 1999; Marsh and Rhodes 1992a, 1992b; McAnulla 1999), or as largely epiphenomenal (and hence more appropriately attributed to globalisation or the transition to post-Fordism – see for instance Hughes and Wintour 1990; Mandelson and Liddle 1996; Smith 1992a), then a direct assessment of New Labour's policy programme in the light of Thatcherism might indeed seem unnecessary. Clearly, however, for authors emphasising the comparative radicalism of the Thatcher and Major years (for instance Kavanagh 1997) or even the incremental yet cumulative nature of the break with the past which they marked (Hay 1996b; cf. Kerr *et al.* 1997), there can be no more urgent task than to assess the degree of convergence between the parties in recent years. Given, as will by now be clear, my sympathies for this latter view, it is precisely this task which I set myself in proceeding chapters.

The legacy of almost two decades of Conservative government and the nature of New Labour's accommodation to that legacy (in whichever sense of the term) raise a further and perhaps equally contested issue – that of consensus. 'Consensus' is perhaps the most disputed term in the academic vernacular of post-war British political history. In so far as a conventional narrative of the period exists amongst political scientists, it posits a punctuated history – of moments of significant transformation giving way to slower periods of incremental change. The Attlee and Thatcher governments emerge, within this clearly stylised history, as agents of transformation in the context of war and the crisis of the 1970s, respectively, to challenge the orthodoxies of the time. Between these flurries of political innovation, a much longer period of relative tranquillity and bipartisan consensus can be identified, lasting largely unchallenged from the early 1950s until the mid-1970s. Yet this in itself is a highly contested account (proponents of the consensus thesis include Addison 1975; Kavanagh 1987, 1992; Kavanagh and Morris 1994; Lowe 1990; Seldon 1994; for the sceptical view see Kerr 1999; Kerr and Marsh 1996; Marlow 1996; Pimlott 1988, 1989; for a review of the literature see Hay 1996b: 42–65).

The rather entrenched and protracted nature of the debate (which, one might be forgiven for thinking, has made little progress in the last decade despite its proliferation) owes much to the inherent ambiguity of the concept itself. At the risk of stating the obvious, consensus is a relative concept. Accordingly, whether one sees consensus or not depends largely on evaluative judgements (inherently subjective decisions, for instance, as to the precise degree of bipartisan accord that would warrant the label consensus) and the specific comparative context and time frame chosen (for a more detailed exposition see Hay 1996b: 47–8). Proponents of the post-war consensus thesis may, on occasion, seem to be invoking some conception of absolute consensus – this is certainly how their claims are most frequently read by their critics. Yet this is rarely (if ever) the case. More frequently, they are merely suggesting, for instance, that the period following the initial post-war reconstruction was characterised by a rather greater degree of agreement between the parties as to the legitimate scope and scale of government than that it immediately proceeded. Clearly, a catalogue of instances of bipartisan or intra-governmental discord in no way constitutes a refutation of such a thesis (despite the proliferation of rhetorical pronouncements to the contrary). Yet this is, of course, not necessarily to imply that the notion of a post-war consensus is of much utility either. Arguably, its inherent ambiguity and the conceptual confusion evidenced in the debate reviewed above render the term at best something of a hostage to fortune. Nonetheless, in strictly comparative terms, the evidence for a degree of bipartisan convergence unusual in Britain by historical standards and characteristic of the post-war period does seem quite compelling.[15]

The notion of a 'return to consensus' in recent years is, if anything, more contentious still (though it has, as yet, to give rise to anything like the volume of literature as the post-war consensus). Thus, whilst a number of authors have come to identify a certain convergence between the parties in recent years – a convergence initiated by Labour and reflected in a 'post-Thatcher' yet basically Thatcherite consensus (Hay 1994, 1997a, 1998b; Kavanagh 1997; Kavanagh and Morris 1994; see also Elliott 1993; Panitch and Leys 1997; Russell 1996) – others continue to emphasise the perceived ideological and programmatic gulf between the parties (Brivati 1997; Kenny and Smith 1997a; McAnulla 1999; Smith 1994).

Though the subject of even less systematic attention, the trajectory of the British economy during the post-war period and, in particular, the question of relative economic decline provide an important domestic context with respect to which Labour's modernisation might usefully be situated (on the question of decline see in particular Coates 1994; Cox *et al.* 1997; Eichengreen 1996; Gamble 1994; Kitson and Michie 1996; Newton and Porter 1988). The question of relative economic decline has proved a perennial theme of British political discourse since the mid-1960s. Moreover, Labour's attitude towards and diagnosis of the condition of the British economy provide a rather useful way of periodising its political economy over the post-war period. Indeed, it is instructive to recall that the notion of modernisation itself is by no means a recent addition to Labour's lexicon. The need for a comprehensive industrial modernisation lay at the heart of Labour's appeal to the electorate most famously in 1964, but also in 1945 and indeed throughout the 1970s (Coopey *et al.* 1993; Newton and Porter 1988; Tiratsoo and Tomlinson 1993; Tomlinson 1994). It is, in fact, not a little ironic that at the seeming high point of the party's self-modernisation, the 1997 general election, it should so comprehensively have abandoned any systematic programme for industrial modernisation and 'supply-side socialism' (Watson and Hay 1998). These are themes to which we return in subsequent chapters. Suffice it to note for now that Labour's political economy, in particular its diagnosis of the British affliction and of the measures likely to restore a high-growth dynamic, must lie at the heart of any assessment of the party's transformation and of its prospects for government (on which compare Commission on Public Policy and British Business 1997; Hutton 1996; Layard 1997).

Socio-economic and demographic trends

A rather different context with respect to which Labour's modernisation might be evaluated is provided by the political sociology and psephology of contemporary Britain. Following consecutive election defeats in 1979, 1983, 1987 and 1992 it was not surprising that the attention of psephologists in particular would be drawn to the long-term socio-economic factors which might account for Labour's seeming consignment to the electoral wilderness. Mirroring similarly pessimistic conclusions in the early 1960s (see, most famously, Abrams *et al.* 1960), a number of commentators and analysts began to ask themselves whether Labour would ever win another election, positing quite seriously the notion of Britain as a 'one-party state' (Heath *et al.* 1994; King 1993; Margetts and Smyth 1994; Nairn 1994). Needless to say, their diagnoses of the nature of Labour's predicament seem to have endured rather longer than the problem itself – a result, it might be argued, of the latter stages of Labour's modernisation (and in particular the impact of the techniques of psephology on that process).[16] That diagnosis – of incremental yet cumulative changes in the social structure increasingly militating against a Labour victory – has, arguably, contributed to the transformation of the party's electoral strategy. Thus, in recent years Labour has increasingly sought to project itself as a 'catch-all', as distinct from a primarily 'class-based', party (Norris 1997; Sanders 1998; see also Denver 1997, 1998; Harrop 1997).

Though the strategic implications may in the end be very similar, the specific diagnoses offered by psephologists and political sociologists to account for Labour's electoral marginalisation in the 1980s have varied considerably. The most prevalent view suggests that parallel processes of class and partisan dealignment have served effectively to render anachronistic any appeal to the electorate based on class or, indeed, traditional party identification (Crewe 1986, 1992; Franklin 1985; Särlvik and Crewe 1983). Such an analysis, which has become something of an article of faith amongst contemporary British psephologists, had clear strategic implications for a traditionally class-based party such as Labour. These were simple: 'labourism' could be maintained only at the cost of electability; and the party would have to loosen its ties (institutional and ideological) with the labour movement and seek to reproject itself as a modern 'catch-all' party. Similar conclusions have been drawn by some comparative political economists in seeking to account for the seeming crisis of social democratic corporatism in western Europe (see for instance Kitschelt 1994; and the various contributions to Piven 1991).

The class dealignment thesis, however, has not gone uncontested. Political sociologists, such as Anthony Heath, Roger Jowell and John Curtice, have argued that whilst an absolute decline in class voting may be observed (in the sense that a smaller percentage of the electorate tends to vote today for its 'natural' class party), this in fact masks a 'trendless fluctuation' when cast in terms of relative class voting (Heath *et al.* 1985, 1987, 1991, 1994).[17] Despite the emergence of a genuine third party (albeit one disproportionately penalised by Britain's first-past-the-post electoral system) and the absolute (and continuing) decline in the size of the working class, Labour remained in the 1980s a class-based party, albeit a less successful one. In fact, they argue, class dealignment, if genuine, might very well have advantaged Labour. For were there no relationship between class and voting whatsoever: (i) the size of the working class would become an irrelevance in assessing Labour's electoral prospects; and (ii) there would be no potential conflict in seeking to reconcile an appeal to an expanding middle class and its traditional working-class electoral base alike (1994: 282). Though the analysis was rather different, the immediate strategic implications were very similar: if Labour re-mained a party primarily of the working class it was likely to find itself consigned to the opposition benches in ever smaller numbers.[18]

Recent developments, however, appear to have changed the picture somewhat. As David Sanders, for instance, notes, 'the pattern of voting in the 1997 general election put paid to any lingering doubts that class-based voting played anything like the role in the late 1990s that it had in previous decades' (1998: 220). As he goes on to explain, 'the class–vote relationship – whether measured in "absolute" or "relative" terms – progressively weakened from the 1960s to the 1990s ... the process may even be accelerating as Britain approaches the millen-nium' (see table 1.2).

This latter comment is particularly significant, for it suggests a potential explanation for this observation – that Labour's modernisa-tion has been accompanied by a change in electoral strategy as the party has sought to project itself as a 'catch-all' party. If this is indeed the case (and the influence of the class dealignment thesis upon Labour's own assessment of electoral strategy should not be under-emphasised), then it is hardly surprising to observe an accelerating secular decline in class voting (both absolute and relative) in the

Table 1.2 Class dealignment, 1964–97

	Index of absolute class voting [a]	Index of relative class voting [b]
1964	76	6.4
1966	78	6.4
1970	64	4.5
1974 (Feb.)	64	5.7
1974 (Oct.)	59	4.8
1979	52	3.7
1983	45	3.9
1987	44	3.5
1992	47	3.3
1997	29	1.9

[a](Non-manual Conservative vote – non-manual Labour vote) + (manual Labour vote – manual Conservative vote) (%).
[b](Non-manual Conservative vote/non-manual Labour vote) / (manual Labour vote/ manual Conservative vote).
Source: Sanders (1998: 220, table 8.1).

1990s. In what sense it can be taken as a confirmation of the class dealignment thesis (as a scientific hypothesis) is another matter altogether.[19]

A further socio-economic factor which has received precious little attention in the discussion of the limits of the possible for a New Labour government is projected demographic change (though see for instance M. Campbell 1998). Despite this persistent oversight, the 'demographic time bomb' (as it has increasingly come to be known) of an ageing population may place considerable strains upon the welfare state into the millennium. As Geoffrey Garrett perceptively observes:

> There is no doubt that government budgets throughout the industrial democracies will be put under increasing stress in the coming decades. But globalisation is not the source of these pressures. Rather, the root causes of the looming welfare state crisis are, in the context of stable working-age populations, significant increases in steady state rates of unemployment and, more importantly, the growing ranks of the aged populations entitled to state pensions and health benefits. (1998: 150)

The advanced industrial economies are, of course, rather differently exposed to such demographic challenges – the projected impact of fertility rates and growth in life expectancy varying markedly. Thus, whilst Italy (with falling fertility rates, high life expectancy and relatively comprehensive public pensions provision) is projected to suffer an increase in government spending on health and pensions of some 10 per cent of gross domestic product (GDP) by 2030, the figure for the UK (with higher and more stable fertility rates, a slower rate of growth of life expectancy and less generous public pensions provision) is only 2 per cent (Organisation for Economic Cooperation and Development 1996; Walker and Maltby 1997). Such demographic pressures have precipitated a sense of a public pensions crisis in many European economies, resulting in radical reforms in Sweden (in re-sponse to a perceived taxpayers' revolt), proposals for significant public pensions reform in Italy, and an ongoing and comprehensive review of public pensions provision in the UK (M. Campbell 1998; International Social Security Association 1995; Scherman 1995; Walker 1996). In all these countries, the general thrust of policy reform is to replace defined benefit regimes with defined contribution regimes (Stephens 1997; Walker and Maltby 1997). Whatever one's assessment of such developments, it seems clear that a combination of demo-graphic and other socio-economic trends has transformed, or at least threaten to transform, the context within which labour and social democratic parties compete for office and may subsequently govern.

British social democracy in comparative context

The above discussion serves to introduce an important, though fre-quently neglected, comparative dimension into the analysis. In this respect it is not exactly representative of the existing literature. For, with few exceptions, commentators and analysts of Labour's mod-ernisation have failed to draw much insight from the burgeoning comparative literature on the crisis and continued viability of European social democracy and the contemporary prospects of the antipodean labour parties (though see Albo 1997; see also *en passim* Bell and Shaw 1994; Padgett and Paterson 1991; Paterson and Thomas 1986; Piven 1991; Sassoon 1996, 1997).

This diverse and disparate literature is not easily summarised and much of its detail will have to await elaboration in later chapters. Nonetheless, a handful of key themes can be identified, which place recent developments in the Labour Party in a much broader context.

They provide a rather different light to that cast by more parochial contextualisations.

First, a consideration of contemporary British social, political and economic processes and institutions can only serve to highlight the specificity of British capitalism. The comparative political economy of the advanced industrial economies, for instance, has identified a variety of relatively distinct national 'models of capitalist accumulation' (see for instance Albert 1993; Berger and Dore 1996; Brenner 1998; Coates 1999; Gerschenkron 1962; Hart 1992; Pollin 1995; Shonfield 1965; Zysman 1983; for a review of this literature with respect to the specificity of British capitalism see Watson and Hay 1998). Within such a schema, Anglo-US capitalism, in contrast to the German, Japanese or Scandinavian variants, is characterised by a 'capital market-based' (as distinct from 'bank-based') financial system and by a correspondingly arms-length relationship between finance and industry and a limited role for government (Pollin 1995, 1997; see also Orrù 1993). This is reflected, in turn, in some of British capitalism's distinctive pathologies: pervasive short-termism, 'fluid' as opposed to 'dedicated' capital, high target rates of return on venture capital, the constant threat of hostile take-overs, a lack of committed and long-term investment and correspondingly low levels of manufacturing investment, capacity and growth (Gourevitch 1996; Porter 1996; Woolcock 1996). This diagnosis of Britain's economic affliction clearly provides a useful perspective from which to base an analysis and evaluation of New Labour's economic and industrial strategy (for similar diagnoses see Bond and Jenkinson 1996; Cowling and Sudgen 1990; Hutton 1996; Michie and Smith 1996; Watson and Hay 1998). It also suggests that the pathologies of Britain's institutionally distinctive capitalism may well require equally distinctive solutions (cf. Hutton 1996).

Despite an emphasis upon the institutional specificity of distinct national capitalisms, the comparative political economy of contemporary Europe, North America and the antipodes also serves to highlight certain pervasive transnational (perhaps even global) tendencies. Principal amongst these has been the widely identified crisis of social democracy – and of the Keynesian welfare state more generally – originating in the mid-1970s and the associated (and, some would argue, global) rise of neo-liberalism (for a range of rather different interpretations of which see Blyth 1998a; Esping-Andersen 1996; Garrett 1998; Huber and Stephens 1998; Kitschelt 1994;

Kitschelt *et al.* 1999; Pierson 1996; Scharpf 1991). Such observations would suggest that, whatever the distinctiveness of the British case, Labour's modernisation cannot adequately be understood without seeing it as part of a much broader process with international, as much as domestic, conditions of existence. The extent of convergence, the limits of national political autonomy and the precise nature of the processes involved are all highly contested (for very different inter-pretations compare Berger and Dore 1996; Garrett 1998; Hay 1997b; Hay and Watson 1998; Hirst and Thompson 1996; and Notermans 1997; with Cerny 1990; Kurzer 1993; Moene and Wallerstein 1995; Moses 1994; Scharpf 1991; Wickham-Jones 1995b). Nonetheless, it would appear that the fate of social democracy and/or labourism in Britain may well be bound up with that of social democracy and/or labourism within the advanced capitalist economies more generally. The nature of the options available to New Labour in government and, indeed, the very prospects for the welfare state and the future of British social democracy cannot, then, be gauged without a detailed consideration of the processes (both domestic and international) which are held to have undermined Keynesianism, corporatism and social democracy – in short, all democratic alternatives to neo-liberalism – throughout the advanced capitalist economies.

The development of the international or global political economy
This brings us, eventually, to the development of the international or global political economy – of which, perhaps unremarkably, rather more has been made in accounts of New Labour's modernisation. In part, as we shall see, this may well be because party modernisers have themselves frequently invoked arguments about the changing contours of the global political economy in pointing to the (perceived) necessity of the modernisation project on which they embarked in the 1980s (for a commentary see Hay and Watson 1998).

Two related, though nonetheless distinct, bodies of literature are here of particular significance: the first detailing a qualitative shift in the contours of contemporary capitalism, taking us from the Fordist stage of capitalist development (more precisely, the Fordist regime of accumulation and the attendant mode of regulation) that had character-ised the post-war period, via the crisis of the 1970s, to an emergent post-Fordism; the second positing a rather more inchoate and incre-mental process of globalisation that has, nevertheless, served to transform fundamentally the landscape of contemporary capitalism.

Regulation theory, the first body of literature considered here, might be seen as the very antithesis of the comparative political economy of authors like Gerschenkron, Albert and Zysman considered in the previous section. Whereas this latter perspective tends to point to the institutional distinctiveness and inertia of specific capitalisms (which are held to exhibit distinctive national traits over extended periods of historical time), the former by contrast tends to downplay the significance of national variations, emphasising instead stages of capitalist development (as reflected in institutional similarities between nations during phases of sustained economic growth). Thus, whereas the former places its emphasis upon national variation across time, the latter places its emphasis upon historical variations in the form of capitalist accumulation which transcend national specificities. If, for comparative political economists such as Albert, what was important about British institutions in the 1960s was that they were British, for regulation theorists what was important about them was that they were Fordist. In this latter schema, what is important about British institutions today is that they are either post-Fordist (Hall and Jacques 1989) or in the process of becoming post-Fordist (Amin 1994; Jessop 1993, 1994).

Such a view has clear implications for an assessment of the economic and political latitude of the New Labour government. If the institutional architecture of contemporary capitalism has indeed undergone a qualitative transformation and the world we inhabit is essentially and irredeemably post-Fordist, then Labour in government has no choice but to adapt to this new constellation of constraint and opportunity (for critiques of this implied 'logic of inevitability' see Hay 1998c; Taylor-Gooby 1996). If, as a number of authors have recently suggested, the political economy of post-Fordism calls forth a new form of the capitalist state – whether a 'Schumpeterian workfare state' (Jessop 1993, 1994, 1995) or a 'competition state' (Cerny 1990, 1997) – then Labour must also accommodate itself to this *political* reality. Whether, and to what extent, such an account is seen to imply an economistic and deterministic logic of inevitability is a matter of some contention – and clearly of considerable significance. Much hinges on the degree of institutional latitude that post-Fordism is seen to 'allow'. If the political economy of the current stage of capitalist development is held to be synonymous with neo-liberalism, then the logic of the argument is that New Labour has no choice but to capitulate to the latter's inexorable embrace. If, on the other hand, post-Fordism (as in Jessop's formulation) can sustain a variety of different regimes (neo-liberal, corporatist and social democratic) then all that this implies is that Labour needs to revise its social democracy in tune with such post-Fordist tendencies.[20]

Whatever its weaknesses, the undoubted benefits of the post-Fordist or regulationist perspective (at least in the somewhat crude form in which it has tended to be imported into debates on the political economy of contemporary Britain) are its clarity and precision. Fordism was then; post-Fordism is now; we must adapt. The same, unfortunately, cannot be said of the voluminous literature on globalisation, which, though equally portentous in its conclusions, is decidely less clear about the mechanisms, processes and actors involved. In recent years the notion of globalisation itself has become something of an 'essentially contested concept' (Connolly 1993; Gallie 1956), deployed in a frightening diversity of senses by a frightening diversity of politicians, analysts, commentators, academics, media and management gurus. Nonetheless, and despite the well documented vacuousness of many of its central propositions, a certain orthodoxy can be identified (for critiques of which see Hay and Marsh 1999a; Hirst and Thompson 1996). This posits an increasingly 'borderless world' (Ohmae 1990) in which labour and ('footloose' multinational) capital flow freely – down gradients of unemployment and social protection, and taxation and labour cost, respectively. The result is a much more fully integrated global economy in which the Darwinian excesses of international competition drive out 'punitive' taxation regimes, 'overregulated' labour markets, social protection, all but residual welfare regimes and Keynesian economics. This, in turn, serves to establish a pervasive logic of international economic and political convergence – a convergence on neo-liberal terms. At a stroke, it would seem, the liberalisation of capital flows, the deregulation of financial markets and the growth of instantaneous communications technology have eliminated all alternatives to neo-liberalism within the contours of the new global political economy (Barnet and Cavanagh 1994; Levitt 1983; Ohmae 1990, 1996; Reich 1992; Sachs and Warner 1995).

This is hardly a comforting picture for social democrats, suggesting, as it does, that the indulgent 'luxuries' of the post-war period (principally, full employment, redistribution, a comprehensive and universal welfare state and corporatism) can simply no longer be afforded. Whilst reluctant perhaps to accept all the ramifications of this 'business school' globalisation thesis, (former) social democrats across western Europe have tended to deploy disarmingly similar arguments about the 'harsh economic realities' of globalisation in preparing their supporters for their comparative moderation in government (for a comparative analysis see the various contributions to Glyn 1998). Whether (and to what extent) such claims, in the end, reflect a sharp narrowing of the realms of political and economic possibility or, indeed, merely a convenient excuse for policy revisions made for altogether different reasons, the significance of globalisation and claims made about globalisation to the political economy of New Labour can scarcely be overstated. A critical analysis and interrogation both of the literature on this subject and of New Labour's own understanding of the constraints it imposes are, then, a central and necessary aim of the present volume.

Contextualising novelty: analytical and theoretical considerations

In the preceding sections, I have sought to identify some of the principal substantive issues which any balanced assessment and evaluation of Labour's transformation and its prospects for government must consider, together with the bodies of literature appropriate to such a project. In this concluding section, I move from the comparatively concrete realm of such substantive considerations to the more abstract realm of the analytical and theoretical issues raised by such concerns. My argument here, echoing that of an earlier, collaborative study of the whole post-war period (Marsh *et al.* 1999), is that the principal positions in the debate on Labour's modernisation, like those on the periodisation of political development in post-war Britain, rest on generally unstated assumptions about a core set of basic analytical questions. Rendering these explicit at the outset, it is argued, may serve to clarify the nature of the debate and the precise character of the specific positions adopted by its principal protagonists (for a further elaboration of this rationale see Hay and Marsh 1999b; Marsh 1999).

In making this argument, I identify four central issues, each of which serves to highlight different aspects of the question of causality: (i) the relationship between structure and agency, context and conduct; (ii) the relationship between the ideational and the material, between the ideas held about the world and that world itself; (iii) the relative significance of political, economic and cultural factors; and (iv) the relative significance of domestic and international factors.

Structure and agency, context and conduct

The debate on the modernisation of the Labour Party provides yet further evidence of a social scientific truism: when engaged in abstract reflections of a theoretical kind, social scientists are keen to extol the virtues of a complex or dialectical view of the relationship between structure and agency; yet, when it comes to more substantive concerns, the allure of structuralist and intentionalist positions is often too great.[21] It is perhaps all too easy, then, to call for a more complex view of the relationship between structure and agency than that exhibited in much of the existing literature.

Nonetheless, some appeal surely needs to be made to contextualise political conduct on the one hand and to consider the mechanisms by which political context is constantly shaped and reshaped on the other.[22] For it is only by so doing that we can resist the tendency, characteristic of intentionalist accounts, to view Labour as so radically unconstrained by its environment that pragmatic and contextual (as distinct from normative and ethical) considerations simply did not enter into the equation when charting a course for the party's modernisation. Similarly, it is only by so doing that we can resist the tendency, characteristic of structuralist positions, to imply such a rigidly delimited realm of political autonomy that the trajectory of the party's modernisation might almost be derived from a consideration of the environment in which it took place independently of the actors involved.

Nonetheless, as table 1.3 demonstrates, those positions within the existing debate which have placed their emphasis either upon structure/context or upon agency/conduct have tended to do so without exclusively privileging one over the other. Thus, for example, those analyses which have sought to account for Labour's trajectory in recent years in terms of a strategic struggle for the party's soul (as reflected in the shifting balance of power within the party) have generally felt the need to introduce a range of contextual and structural factors – the balance of power itself at any given moment in time, the strategic resources at the disposal of particular actors, the constitution and institutionalised practices of the party and so forth. Similarly, accounts privileging the harsh economic realities of a newly globalised political economy have nonetheless had to invoke some conception of agency – if only as the immediate mechanism by which the party's commitments might be brought in line with a new external environment. It might seem tempting at this stage to suggest some middle ground, or even a potential rapprochement, between these contending structural and more

Table 1.3 Structure and agency in the modernisation of the Labour Party

Explanations emphasising context/ structure	Explanations emphasising conduct/ action/agency
(1) *Economic*. The transformation of the global economic context rendered 'Old Labour' policies anachronistic – Keynesianism, social democracy and an inclusive welfare state are no longer sustainable in an era of globalisation. The aspirations of the past had to be sacrificed on the altar of economic competitiveness – 'harsh economic realities' necessitated the modernisation of the party.	(1) Tony Blair's 'charismatic' leadership of the party and his commitment to a vision of a 'new' party have transformed 'Old Labour' into 'New Labour'.
(2) *Political*. The grim reality of almost two decades in the electoral wilderness and the marginalisation of Labour from its core constituencies under Thatcher and Major necessitated a move to the new centre ground – 'harsh political realities' necessitated the modernisation of the party and a move onto the terrain previously inhabited exclusively by the Conservatives.	(2) The changing balance of power within the party allowed for an overturning of the traditional relationship between Labour and the trade unions. This created a space for new (modernising) groups within the party committed to a revised labour agenda. In a struggle for the party's soul, these groups ultimately triumphed, resulting in an incremental yet cumulative process of modernisation of which Blair is merely the culmination.
(3) *Social*. A weakening of the relationship between class and voting behaviour and a shrinking of the working class had weakened Labour's traditional electoral base. 'Harsh social realities' called forth a transformation of the party and a courting of the new aspirational middle classes.	(3) After years in the electoral wilderness, a group of political analysts and marketing and advertising agents were given the latitude to transform the party's policy commitments, bringing them more into line with those ideas the electorate had consistently voted for since 1979 – giving the electorate what it wanted rather than seeking to make a case for what Labour believed in.

agency-centred accounts. Yet we should be extremely wary of any suggestion that essentially interpretative disputes over the assessment of Labour's modernisation (or of anything else for that matter) can simply be adjudicated by importing abstract considerations of structure and agency. Neither Giddens' structuration theory (1984) nor the strategic-relational approach (Jessop 1990, 1997) can resolve such essentially evaluative and empirical matters. As table 1.3 also indicates, those more structural accounts have consistently emphasised the qualitative novelty of the context in which New Labour finds itself, while those more agency-focused explanations tend to imply no such qualitative shift in the external context. Such a dispute cannot be resolved by theoretical fiat. In the end, choices have to be made. The best that can be asked for is that, having made such choices, analysts seek to defend and develop them in terms of a consistent and explicit view of the relationship between the actors involved and the context they inhabit.

Rhetoric and reality: the ideational and the material
Equally significant, though the subject of far less theoretical scrutiny, is the question of the relationship between the ideas we formulate about our environment and that environment itself (though on the relationship between ideas and institutions see Berman 1998: chapter 1; Blyth 1997a, 1998b; J. L. Campbell 1998; Hay and Wincott 1998; McNamara 1998: chapter 1). The significance of the realm of ideas (the ideational) can easily be traced from the question of structure and agency itself. For, if we accept that actors inhabit an environment external to themselves and within which they act, it is not a particularly large step to suggest that their conduct is influenced by the ideas they formulate about that external environment. What is more, as we know from (often painful) experience, no one-to-one correspondence can be assumed to pertain between the ideas we formulate about our surroundings (immediate or more distant) and those surroundings themselves. If we want to understand how actors behave, then it is essential that we give due consideration to their understandings of the context in which they are situated. This is no less so if we are seeking to understand and account for the actions and conduct of the Labour leadership in the modernisation of the party, in the formulation and reformulation of policy and, indeed, in government. An example from the discussion thus far may serve to make the point.

Recall the class dealignment thesis (Franklin 1985; Särlvik and Crewe 1983). During the 1980s, a number of prominent psephologists claimed to identify a secular trend in the relationship between social class and voting behaviour – it appeared that a smaller (and an ever diminishing) percentage of the electorate were voting for their natural class party (for the working class, Labour; for the middle class, the Conservatives). Critics protested that this conception of absolute class voting merely redescribed, rather than explained, Labour's predicament. Any shrink in the size of the vote for a party like Labour – whether the consequence of extraneous political factors[23] or of socioeconomic change – would result in an absolute drop in class voting. All that could be concluded, then, from such a measure was that Labour was not doing very well. What was required, to adjudicate the claimed weakening of the relationship between class and voting behaviour, was a measure of relative class dealignment. Moreover, such a measure showed no such secular trend (Heath *et al*. 1985).

The influence of the class dealignment thesis, however, did not wane in response to such criticism – far from it. This presents us, as already noted, with a certain difficulty in assessing its validity in the light of more recent evidence. For, during the 1990s, it would appear as though the absolute rate of class dealignment accelerated and, indeed, that a decline in relative class voting can now be observed. We are presented with a stark choice between two rather different explanations in accounting for this. The first is simple, intuitive, entirely conventional and gives no consideration to ideational factors. It is that proponents of the class dealignment thesis were right all along and have merely been vindicated by events subsequent to their initial hypothesis (Sanders 1998). The second, an ideas-based explanation, would point to the influence of the class dealignment thesis (and, more directly perhaps, the influence of some of its proponents) on Labour's strategic thinking. Labour, in the late 1980s, became convinced of the validity of the class dealignment thesis (whatever the relative class voting figures might have suggested). As a rational and, until then, a class-based party, it sought to modify its appeal to the electorate, reprojecting itself as a catch-all party, studiously courting the median voter. Any subsequent evidence of class dealignment (whether absolute or relative) might then be taken less as evidence of the validity of the thesis than of its influence. Quite simply, if Labour behaved as if the thesis were true, the predictions of the thesis would be confirmed. Moreover, this would be the case whether or not working-class voters would be inclined to respond to a more genuinely class-based appeal.

On the basis of the existing evidence, it is perhaps impossible to adjudicate finally between these two contending and mutually incompatible explanations – with very different implications for electoral strategy and the prospects for class-based electoral appeals. Nevertheless, whilst it remains plausible that the recent increase in both absolute and relative class dealignment may be a consequence rather than a cause of Labour's modernisation, it would seem dangerously presumptuous to conclude that socio-economic change has consigned class-based electoral politics to psephological history.

Similar arguments, as we shall see, may be made about the impact of globalisation – and ideas about globalisation – on New Labour's perceptions of the limits of political and economic feasibility (see Rose 1996: 354; Watson 1999a, 1999b). What both these examples serve to highlight is that, convenient though it may be to do so, we ignore the realm of political ideas at our peril. Most social scientists now seem happy to concede that we do indeed make history, though not in circumstances of our own choosing. Perhaps it is now also time to concede that, very often, we make our history in the image of the theories we construct about it or, indeed, in the image of the theories others construct about it.

The political, the economic and the cultural
As will by now be clear, I do not subscribe to the view that political analysis should restrict itself exclusively to a consideration of 'political' variables (often very narrowly conceived political variables at that), leaving other disciplines to fight over the remaining variance. Yet neither do I subscribe to the (perhaps increasingly prevalent) view that the 'best' theory is that which incorporates every variable and every interaction to produce a saturated model in which no variance is left unaccounted for. Parsimony, given the choice, is no bad thing.[24] Moreover, and more importantly, analytical and causal clarity are, or at least should be, fundamental imperatives of political analysis. Thus, although I do wish to argue for the significance of political, economic and cultural factors and, above all, the complex nature of the interaction between them, it is important to caution against the 'additive' conceptions of theoretical sophistication with which such arguments are so frequently associated. The political, the economic and the cultural are not independent arenas. Nor, worse still, are they 'dimensions'. Accordingly, we should be careful to avoid the implicit theoretical one-upmanship of the claim that politicism is one-dimensional,

political–economic explanations are two-dimensional, and that only an integration of the political, the economic and the cultural can provide the 'complete' picture – a three-dimensional view (of a three-dimensional world).[25]

That having been said, it is equally important to caution against the dangers of politicism and economism and to suggest that they may be countered by a consideration of the political conditions of economic dynamics and the economic conditions of political dynamics.[26] Politicism, in the literature on the renaissance of the Labour Party, tends to be associated with the rather blithe optimism which comes with intentionalism and a benign neglect of the external (above all economic) environment. Politicist accounts thus tend to emphasise the inherent contingency of the modernisation process (not necessarily a bad thing), often as a means to celebrate the considerable foresight, conviction and strategic nous of the modernisers (a normative judgement on which I will, for now, remain silent). Given that Labour in government will ultimately be judged in no small measure on the economic consequences of its policies, politicist accounts can provide only a very partial and limited basis from which to assess and evaluate Labour's prospects for government and hence the trajectory of its modernisation.

Economism is no less problematic. At its worst, it tends to view the political as either altogether irrelevant or as epiphenomenal of immutable and inexorable economic processes (such as globalisation). Not only does this frequently imply that there is simply no alternative to the policies that have been pursued (a dangerous and seldom defended assertion), but it also fails to acknowledge the political 'authoring' of processes such as globalisation. For, as a growing number of authors have demonstrated, in so far as globalisation exists, its origins can be traced to a series of highly political (and hence contingent) decisions to deregulate the financial markets and to liberalise capital flows (Evans 1997; Helleiner 1994, 1995, 1996; Watson 1999c; Weiss 1997). Once this is acknowledged, the logic of inevitability which it is so frequently seen to imply appears somewhat less imposing (Akyüz and Cornford 1995; Eichengreen *et al.* 1995; Haq *et al.* 1996; Watson 1999c).

If we are serious, then, about resisting tendencies to both structuralism and intentionalism, it is important that we also resist the narrow privileging of the economic and the political with which they have become so intimately connected.

The domestic, the international and the global
Finally, we return to the complex question of the relationship between the domestic, the international and the global. It is tempting, as in the above discussion of the relationship between the political, the economic and the cultural, to argue that we need to consider each moment and each moment in its articulation with every other moment. In one sense, though glib, this is true. However, as in the previous discussion, it will not suffice. For, ultimately, the relative significance of the domestic, the international and indeed the global (in whatever meaningful sense it can be said to exist in an analytically independent sense from the international) is an evaluative and empirical matter. If we are interested in Labour's economic and industrial policy, the international may be of rather greater significance than if our principal concern is with the prospects for a democratically elected second chamber to replace the House of Lords. No meta-theoretical invocation to balance the domestic and the international can then be posited.

Yet, if we are to reach a balanced assessment of New Labour's modernisation, it seems plausible to suggest that we can begin to do so only by locating the nature of the party's predicament in the early 1980s and its subsequent trajectory in some kind of international and comparative context.[27] It is only by so doing, for instance, that we could claim to dismiss the suggestion that international factors were of any relevance. In assessing the transformation of the Labour Party, then, an invocation to consider the domestic, the international and the relationship between the two now follows fairly directly from the discussion of preceding sections. If we are to move beyond the dangerous duplicity of structuralism–economism and intentionalism–politicism, then we can do so only by acknowledging – and reflecting both theoretically and empirically – the domestic conditions of existence of international political and economic dynamics and the international conditions of existence of domestic political and economic dynamics (see also Hay and Marsh 1999c). Though the ostensible concern of this volume is with the latter, a focus on the former constitutes an equally significant part of the argument which follows.

Notes

1 The continued popular resonance of such images is evidenced in the fact that at every election since 1979, images from the Winter of Discontent

(generally of rubbish rotting in the streets) have been used by the Tory tabloids. The 1997 general election was exceptional only in the rarity of such symbolic denunciations, with merely one example. That image, of rotting rubbish, was reproduced in the *Daily Mail* on 11 February 1997 under the headline 'Jobs for life? Look what happened when politicians made this promise.' On the symbolic significance of the Winter of Discontent in announcing the passing of the post-war social compromise see Hay (1996a).

2 Even if that construction is largely done by one's closest political allies, such as Mandelson.

3 On the gulf between the rhetoric of Wilson's 'white heat of technological revolution' and the rather more pedestrian reality of conciliation, compromise and concession see Howell (1980: chapter 9).

4 This view is perhaps most famously and eloquently expressed by Richard Crossman: 'This Government has failed more abysmally than any Government since 1931' (1985: 432).

5 This quotation is taken from the revised and abbreviated version of the speech reproduced as 'The Radical Coalition' in Blair (1996: 4).

6 There is now a voluminous literature on both the Attlee and Wilson governments' ultimately abortive attempts at institutional and industrial modernisation. In addition to that cited above, see, on the Attlee government, Johnmann (1991); Mercer (1991); Pollard (1992); and Tomlinson (1994). For a brief review see Hay (1996b: 34–5). On Wilson see Grant (1982); Lee (1996a); Longstreth (1979); Shanks (1977); Young and Lowe (1974); and Zysman (1983: 212–20).

7 As Paul Smith notes, 'never before, perhaps, has a single hyphen been made to represent so great a disconnection' (1997: 177).

8 Similar claims might also be made about both the Australian and New Zealand Labour Parties. For an admirable analysis of the latter see for instance Larner (1997).

9 Whatever the merits of such studies (which, as we shall see, may be considerable), their focus on internal dynamics has often been achieved at the expense of any extended discussion of the external context in which this has occurred, whether domestic and political or international and economic.

10 Without, again, wishing to prejudge the issue at this stage, Mandelson and Liddle's comments on Crosland would appear to bear out Shaw's identification of New Labour as post-revisionist. In *The Future of Socialism*, Crosland, they note, 'took the continuation of economic growth for granted, concentrating instead on issues of social equality'. This optimism, they conclude, was 'sadly misplaced' (1996: 10; see also 26). For an entertaining précis of Crosland's revisionism (as expounded in *The Future of Socialism*) see Elliott 1993: 7–9. As he suggests, 'The most compelling attempt in the annals of British social democracy to theorise

revisionism came from the pen of Anthony Crosland, the aspiring Bernstein of his generation, whose *The Future of Socialism* spelt out the rationale for the abrogation of an anachronistic liability' – namely Clause IV (8). See also Crosland (1956).

11 On which, see in particular Brivati (1996); Kenny and Smith (1997a).

12 Blair gives voice to a very similar sentiment in his speech accepting the party leadership (see Blair 1996: 29).

13 Reflected most clearly in Foot's failure, despite his best intentions, to secure a more Keynesian programme to present to the electorate for the election of that year (Shaw 1994: 12–13; see also Shaw 1988).

14 Hay (1994); Smith (1994); Wickham-Jones (1995a); see also Crouch (1997); Elliott (1993: 123–67); Hay (1996b: 158–77); Kavanagh (1997).

15 There may be reasons, however, for questioning the standard depiction of this consensus. As I have elsewhere argued, 'consensus there may well have been. Yet this consensus was not particularly Keynesian, not particularly interventionist and not particularly social democratic' (1996b: 63).

16 The ability of psephologists to change the very subject matter of their 'scientific' enquiries by formulating influential propositions about it, of course, renders psephology at best a rather unusual 'science' – and should, perhaps, make us rather wary of some of its most boldly stated conclusions. We return to this theme below and in chapter 3.

17 By relative class voting, Heath *et al.* refer to 'the relative strength of parties in different social classes'. As they explain, this 'measures the relationship between class and party after controlling for any across-the-board movements between the parties' (1994: 282).

18 The decline in the size of the working class, however, cannot in itself account for the scale of Labour's electoral decline in the 1980s. As Heath *et al.* note, 'if we recalculate the popular vote each party obtained in the 1992 election, using the *share* of the vote each party obtained from each social group in that election, but using the *size* each group had been in 1964, the Labour party would have attracted 5 points more and the Conservatives 4 points fewer in the 1992 election than they actually did' – a swing of some 6 per cent (1994: 284, original emphasis).

19 Once again, we witness ostensibly scientific claims made about an external reality being deployed in the very shaping and transformation of that reality. The conclusion (which one might naturally draw from the seeming confirmation of the class dealignment thesis) that only 'catch-all' parties can win elections in contemporary Britain may be entirely inappropriate if the decline in class voting is in fact a *consequence* of the demise of class-based electoral appeals. The class dealignment thesis (whether, at the time, accurate or not) may well have contributed significantly to both a relegation of class-based electoral politics and a studious courting of the median voter. Either way, it would seem as though the age of the catch-all party has indeed arrived and is here to stay.

20 It is, at this point, perhaps important to note that these already rather complex and difficult issues are only further clouded by authors who seem to take as their definition of social democracy 'that which Labour does'. We return to this definitional question in later chapters.

21 A similar point is made by Michael Kenny and Martin Smith in a recent review of the literature on New Labour under Blair's leadership (1997a: 225–6). Indeed, in making such an argument, they at least implicitly accuse me of precisely such an inconsistency – a charge against which I defend myself in chapter 2. For my own abstract and theoretical reflections on the question of structure and agency see Hay (1995).

22 To make such an appeal is not, of course, to imply that all existing accounts are guilty of one or other oversight. Indeed, it would probably be fairer to suggest that all existing accounts posit some relationship (however skewed, however inconsistent) between conduct (say, that of the party leadership) and context (say, that of the global political economy). It is, however, to emphasise the benefits of reflecting explicitly on the specific relationship between conduct and context posited and to caution against the consequences of the structuralist and intentionalist positions to which many authors seem drawn on occasion.

23 Such as the combination of political ineptitude and the appearance of a new party on the scene (in the form of the Social Democrats).

24 The question, of course, then becomes that of what is sacrificed on the altar of parsimony.

25 For a similar critique of the theoretical one-upmanship implied in Lukes' (1974) 'three-dimensional' view of power see Hay (1997c).

26 This should not be taken as a tacit invitation to 'culturalism'. My silence on the subject only reflects the absence, to date, of perspectives on New Labour which might be regarded as 'culturalist'.

27 It need hardly be pointed out that such a contextualisation is a necessary, though by no means sufficient, condition of balance.

2 Labour's Thatcherite Revisionism: the Policy Review process and the 'politics of catch-up'

> [Labour's] new programme accepts the basic parameters of the Thatcher Settlement, in much the same way that the Conservative government of the fifties accepted the parameters of the Attlee Settlement. It does not seek to extend the public sector or reverse privatisation to any significant degree. It does not propose to raise the overall level of taxation, but promises to adjust its incidence in a mildly more egalitarian direction. It does not substantially depart from the laws that now regulate industrial action, while rendering them a little more favourable to trade unions. It does not abandon the British nuclear deterrent. All these changes of the Thatcher years are uncontested. (Anderson 1992: 346)

So wrote Perry Anderson in 1992. Though perhaps somewhat less contentious now than then, it is the argument of this chapter that the basic substance of his judgement – Labour's acceptance of, and accommodation to, what he terms a 'Thatcher Settlement' – might have been made at any point from 1990 (if not before) to the present. In this sense, however tempting it may be to update, revise and extend Anderson's list of supporting evidence in the light of more recent developments, this is a temptation that I will resist for now (though see chapter 4). My aim in this chapter is to establish that by the completion of the Policy Review – and, perhaps, some time before that – Labour had ceased effectively to be a social democratic party, committed as it had by then become to a pervasive neo-liberal economic orthodoxy and to a basic acceptance of the legacy of the Thatcher years. In making this argument I suggest, in contrast to much of the existing literature on this period, that the Policy Review itself evidenced a 'Thatcherite revisionism' that reflected in turn the perceived exigencies for Labour of 'the politics of catch-up'.

Much hinges, as we shall see, on what such claims are taken to imply. The nature of the Thatcherite legacy is much contested, the notion of social democracy itself no less so and the concept of 'Thatcherite revisionism' is potentially ambiguous. It is thus imperative at the outset that we seek to establish some conceptual clarity. Before turning, then, to an analysis and assessment of the Policy Review process, we consider the nature of the legacy bequeathed by the Thatcher governments and the concepts of Thatcherite revisionism and social democracy, respectively.

Contextual preliminaries: the Thatcherite legacy

The literature on Thatcherism is vast and various. Moreover, however important an assessment of the legacy of the Thatcher (and Major) governments to an evaluation of the modernisation of the Labour Party, a comprehensive review would prove of limited utility at this point. Suffice it to note that political scientists who have focused on Thatcherism have tended, with rare exceptions, to resolve themselves into one of two camps.[1] In one grouping, a number of authors (often writing initially in the immediate aftermath of the Conservatives' victory in 1979 and in some cases even prior to that) sought to identify and detail the radical nature of the break with the post-war period which they saw 'Thatcherism' as marking (see for instance Hall 1979; Hall *et al.* 1978; Hall and Jacques 1983; Jacques 1979; Jenkins 1987; Moon 1993, 1994; Savage *et al.* 1994; Stephenson 1980). In the other grouping, a rather more homogeneous range of authors (writing subsequently and often in direct response to the earlier literature) sought to question and revise what they viewed as the overblown and exaggerated claims of those who had initially coined the term (see for instance Dolowitz *et al.* 1996; Jessop *et al.* 1988; Kerr and Marsh 1999; Marsh and Rhodes 1992a, 1992b, 1995; Riddell 1983).

The result, as I have argued at greater length elsewhere (Hay 1998d), has been the perhaps rather unhelpful and polarising dualism that has tended to characterise the debate on the impact of Thatcherism in Britain. The literature is fundamentally divided over the question of the extent, scale, reversibility and (if less explicitly) the temporality of the Thatcherite 'revolution'. Authors in the latter camp tend to draw on an implicitly incremental, gradualist and evolutionary institutionalism, stressing continuity rather than discontinuity, incremental evolution rather than punctuating crisis and revolution, inertia rather than dynamism. In so doing, they emphasise the rather unexceptional character of successive Thatcher administrations in the face of what they see as exaggerated claims to the contrary made by Thatcherite apologists (strategic or unwitting). Those across the barricades, by contrast, emphasise what they see as the specificity, singularity and exceptional character of the Thatcher governments, arguing that the election of Margaret Thatcher in 1979 marked a path-shaping moment of largely irreversible institutional and ideational transformation (and, in some accounts, even 'revolution'). Unsurprisingly, this polarity of views has generated a series of often confrontational exchanges and, arguably, rather more heat than light. Two exchanges in particular catch the eye: that between Jeremy Moon on the one hand and David Marsh and Rod Rhodes on the other in the pages of *Politics*;[2] and the rather milder debate between Stuart Hall and the self-styled 'gang of four', largely in the pages of *New Left Review* (see Hall 1979; Hall and Jessop 1985; Jessop *et al.* 1984, 1985, 1987, 1990; Leys 1990; for a review see Hay 1996b: 140–7).[3]

Driven, perhaps, by the passion of the exchange itself, in both cases the protagonists quite simply talk past one another, failing to appreciate that rather different objects of analysis are being appealed to. Thus, although Moon, Marsh and Rhodes, the 'gang of four' and Hall all refer to Thatcherism, arguably they mean rather different things by it. Herein lies the difficulty.

For Hall, as indeed for Moon, Thatcherism is understood, defined and hence periodised in terms of its distinctiveness. For Hall, in particular, that distinctiveness resides in its invocation of new-right ideology (a flexible and often contradictory articulation of neo-liberalism and neo-conservatism). For Jessop and his co-authors, as for Marsh and Rhodes, Thatcherism is understood in more classically institutional (even statist and economistic) terms. It is periodised, accordingly, in terms of its political and economic effects. In each case, the relationship between ideas and institutions (between paradigms and policy) is left untheorised and unspecified.

Once this is acknowledged, the possibility of some reconciliation and rapprochement between these contending and seemingly incommensurate views emerges. The basis for such a synthesis is the observation that what might be termed 'paradigm shifts' in the ideas influencing policy-making tend to take some considerable time to be reflected in substantive institutional and policy change (on paradigm shifts see Kuhn 1962; also P. A. Hall 1993). Accordingly, institutional effects and outcomes will tend to follow ideational change, often with a significant time lag. It should then come as no surprise that those who concern themselves principally with the realm of ideas tend to emphasise the radicalism, exceptionalism and relatively rapid nature of the Thatcherite 'break' with the past,[4] whilst those focusing on the consequences of policy (and institutional outcomes and effects more generally) should emphasise comparative continuity, incrementalism and either enduring inertia or, at best, cumulative radicalisation.[5]

A dualism in the interpretation of Thatcherism's radicalism thus reflects a dualism in the understanding of the relationship between ideas and institutions. The transcendence of this latter dualism thus offers the potential to reconcile previously divergent and polarised strands in the literature on Thatcherism. Such a view might posit a more abrupt period of ideational change or paradigm shift (as captured by authors like Stuart Hall) followed by a much more drawn out process of incremental yet directional and cumulative institutional transformation (as detailed, for instance, by Marsh and Rhodes). To reiterate, even if a new paradigm (that, say, of Thatcherism) becomes ascendant relatively swiftly within the corridors of Westminster and Whitehall, it may take an extremely long time before its consequences are reflected to any significant extent in the institutional architecture of the state itself. The institutions of the state did not look remarkably different six months or even five years after Thatcher entered Downing Street, despite her obvious commitment to a radically different conception of the political 'good' to that of her predecessor.

At this point, two potential objections might be raised. First, the notion of a paradigm shift (from that, say, of Keynesian social democracy to Thatcherite neo-liberalism occurring almost instantaneously in the late 1970s) is simply too neat. Second, little or no consideration is given to the difficult and often contradictory process of implementation – it being assumed, all too easily, that a neo-liberal or neo-conservative institutional blueprint might be translated directly and unproblematically (if incrementally) into a corresponding institutional architecture. These are important points. Indeed, it is crucial to establish that the perspective developed above in highly schematic terms need imply neither assumption.

The notion of a paradigm shift is merely a convenient theoretical shorthand for what is, in fact, likely to prove a rather complex and contested process of ideational struggle (in Gramsci's terms a 'war of position') by which significant changes in the ideas informing policy are assimilated within the corridors of power (and may later become institutionalised). It should not then be seen to imply an instantaneous 'Gestalt switch' in which an entire body of cognitive assumptions, norms and conventions is overturned and replaced by another.[6] More-over, to suggest that Thatcherism should be seen as a paradigm need not imply that it should also be seen as a clear and unambiguous 'blueprint' for institutional change. Riddell's (1983, 1991) conception of a 'Thatcherite instinct' comes rather closer to the sense I wish to convey (Hay 1996b: 135). Far from a well articulated, tightly honed and comprehensive reform programme, the Thatcher governments came to power with, at best, a loosely articulated sense of the evils and excesses of the post-war period and a vision (however vague) of the political 'good' and of the 'vigorous virtues'. This would serve to guide their efforts to formulate a more substantive agenda in power. It is in this sense, and this sense alone, that I refer to Thatcherism as a paradigm and to the election of the first Thatcher government, in the context of a widely perceived state and economic crisis, as marking a 'paradigm shift'.

Once clarified in this way, the objection that such a formulation posits too simple and direct a correspondence between an institutional blueprint and institutional effects is easily dealt with. For, clearly, the implementation process is likely to throw up a series of unintended consequences which may not only alter significantly the path of institutional change over time, but also the incumbent party's assess-ment of the politically feasible and desirable. To posit directional and cumulative change is not, then, to imply the existence of a tightly scripted narrative of institutional design written in advance and instan-tiated over time nor any simple process by which aspirations might be translated into outcomes.

The significance of Thatcherite radicalism

As a preliminary to an assessment of New Labour's modernisation, it may seem somewhat perverse to have devoted so much attention to the nature of the break with the past that the election of the first Thatcher government marked in 1979. As we shall see, however, this is a crucial question for two rather different reasons. First, our assessment of the comparative radicalism of the Thatcher years will influence consider-ably our evaluation of the extent and irreversibility of the Thatcherite legacy. A second and a more subtle point needs also to be noted, however. The emphasis placed in the above discussion on the role of ideas and in particular paradigm shifts in altering the trajectory (if not necessarily the pace) of institutional change is suggestive of what is required to challenge such a legacy. More specifically, it indicates that a 'battle for hearts and minds' and an attempt to supplant the dominant paradigm by an alternative conception of the political good may be the very condition of post-Thatcherism.

The legacy of Thatcherism is scarcely less contested than the nature of the break with the past which the election of Thatcher is seen to represent. Unsurprisingly, positions on both questions are closely related. Those who have sought to downplay the exceptional character of the Thatcher governments have tended to view the Thatcherite legacy as more ephemeral and transient. Those, on the other hand, anxious to emphasise the qualitative novelty of Thatcherism as a state and/or hegemonic project have generally pointed to what they see as a fundamental transformation in the character of the relationship between the state and the economy, civil society and the public sphere, since the early 1980s. A certain amount of ambiguity nonetheless persists, particularly in the former view. Thus, whilst in their earlier work on the implementation of Thatcherite policies Marsh and Rhodes (1992a, 1992b) were quick to point to a substantial 'implementation gap' (a disparity between stated ambitions and actual policy outcomes), going so far as to suggest that the Thatcherite revolution is 'all rhetoric and no reality', in response to criticism their position seems to have shifted somewhat (1995). Indeed, in more recent work, Marsh and a variety of co-authors have pointed to the Thatcher (and Major) governments' progressive radicalisation over time and to the cumulative consequences of almost two decades in government (Dolowitz *et al.* 1996; Kerr and Marsh 1999; Kerr *et al.* 1997; see also Jessop *et al.* 1988; McAnulla 1999). Though still perhaps resistant to the suggestion that the previous two decades might be seen as exceptional, unprecedented even, by post-war British standards in terms of the extent of such cumulative change, this latter reading would indeed imply a considerable and (given the incremental character of institutional change) largely insurmountable Thatcherite legacy. Clearly such a position stands in some tension with the earlier emphasis upon the exaggerated nature of claims made about the Thatcher years.

To some extent, however, even these seemingly different interpretations can be reconciled. First, it should be noted that it was in a study of the first two terms of the Thatcher government that Marsh and Rhodes came to identify an 'implementation gap'. It is certainly not impossible, then, that the notion of a progressive radicalisation over time, particularly one most evident after 1987, might be reconciled with an emphasis on the less than revolutionary nature of policy implementation up until that point. Second, to identify an implement-ation gap and hence a disparity between stated policy objectives and policy outcomes need not imply continuity. Indeed, if there is a 'strategic gap' (a disparity between strategic and stated policy ob-jectives – Hay 1996b: 152–3) or if policy-making occurs in an unpredictable environment (and is hence characterised by unintended consequences) one would expect to see evidence of an implementation gap independent of the degree of radicalism of the government. This in turn suggests the need to consider not only stated policy objectives (and the extent to which they are realised) in any assessment of the Thatcherite legacy, but also strategic motivations for policy and unintended consequences. Precisely such an assessment of the Thatcher governments from 1979 to 1990 is presented in table 2.1, which also includes an indication of the extent to which Labour's policy stance following the Policy Review represented an acceptance of, or depart-ure from, the Thatcher legacy.

Though table 2.1 is by no means comprehensive, it does suggest that, at least in the policy areas considered, the disparity between stated aims and ambitions on the one hand and policy outcomes on the other was rather wider than that between strategic objectives and the policy record. It also suggests that in each of these policy arenas the Thatcher governments, by 1990, had made considerable strides in altering the character and extent of the state's responsibilities and its degree of intervention. The nature of the Thatcherite legacy, then, would appear considerable.[7]

Conceptual preliminaries: Thatcherite revisionism and social democracy

Having considered the extent of the inheritance bequeathed to any incoming Labour administration after 1990, it is important that we devote some attention to the concepts with which we might describe Labour's relation to this legacy.

'Thatcherite revisionism'

The notion of 'Thatcherite revisionism' deployed here is, as noted above, potentially ambiguous and hence in need of some clarification

Table 2.1 Assessing the Thatcher legacy: strategy, ideology and policy

---

Privatisation and denationalisation

Ideological justifications	Reassert market mechanisms; introduce the discipline of the market to promote competitiveness, efficiency and modernisation; reduce the public sector borrowing requirement (PSBR) and hence decrease taxation whilst increasing incentives; roll back the frontiers of an overextended state.
Strategic motivations	Retrenchment of public sector trade unions; transform material interests of employees and consumers alike; transfer responsibility from the state; secure windfall revenues allowing tax cuts to the wealthy and reductions in the PSBR; create a share- and property-owning, Tory-voting democracy.
Policy record (1979–90)	Slow start with sale of assets and stakes in private companies; from 1984 privatisation and denationalisations to include Jaguar, British Telecom, British Airways, British Aerospace, British Gas, British Airports Authority, British Steel, Rover Group, regional electricity and electricity-generating companies, water and sewerage companies.
Assessment and reversibility	The crux of Thatcherite economic policy – providing a series of one-off windfall payments to the Exchequer; destroyed the power of former public sector trade unions; displaced responsibility to the private sector; and disseminated share ownership. Almost completely irreversible in the medium term (revenue gained has been squandered).
Labour's policy stance after the Policy Review	Acceptance of the reality, if not the principle, of privatisation and of a radical shift in the balance between the public and private sectors; commitment to return essential services (such as the privatised utilities) to the public sector and to full compensation of shareholders (providing the 'fair market price').

Table continues over

Table 2.1 continued

Trade union reform

Ideological justifications	Regeneration of market mechanisms; end interference from trade unions capable of 'holding the country to ransom'; restore democracy to industrial governance by replacing corporatist structures; modernise the economy; retrench the responsibilities of the overloaded state and cut demands placed upon it.
Strategic motivations	Secure revenge for defeat of the Heath government at the hands of the miners; weaken the trade unions before embarking upon a policy of labour-market deregulation likely to result in a deterioration of pay and conditions and a rise in structural unemployment; link Labour with the militant extremists of the 'loony left'.
Policy record (1979–90)	Restriction of picketing and strike activity; tight constraints placed upon the closed shop; union assets rendered liable to sequestration; systematic preparation for a show-down with the National Mineworkers' Union (planned since the 1978 Ridley report) resulting in a year-long confrontation and ignominious defeat for the miners.
Assessment and reversibility	Dramatic decrease in trade union influence and membership; delegitimation of the trade union movement; dismantling of corporatist structures; destruction of power of public sector unions. Completely irreversible in the medium-term.
Labour's policy stance after the Policy Review	Selective repeal of Thatcherite trade union reform while accepting its central tenets; secondary picketing legal only where a second employer is actively involved in frustrating a legitimate industrial dispute; sympathy action legal only where a shared direct interest is demonstrated; emphasis on economic partnership; commitment to European Social Chapter.

Table 2.1 continued

Local government reform

Ideological justifications	Increase the accountability and responsibility of local government to the electorate; decrease the political autonomy of 'loony left' local authorities to charge high rates at the behest of electors paying no rates; extend the free market by selling off local assets and contracting-out of services.
Strategic motivations	Roll back the frontiers of the welfare state by increasing local responsibility for welfare provision yet imposing centralised fiscal controls; displace responsibility for welfare services where possible whilst increasing top-down control; impose universal charge/rate capping on all authorities.
Policy record (1979–90)	Initial pledge to abolish rates thwarted by the Treasury; rate support grant dramatically cut from 61 per cent (1979) to 47 per cent (1987); abolition of Greater London Council and the six (Labour-controlled) metropolitan councils; rate-capping introduced and extended to all authorities; poll tax fiasco; council tax introduced in 1993.
Assessment and reversibility	Contracting-out of local services has undermined public sector trade unions; responsibility displaced from central state to the local for service delivery increasingly constrained from the centre; poll tax seriously undermined legitimacy of the Thatcher government. An irreversible restructuring but at the cost of delegitimation.
Labour's policy stance after the Policy Review	Commitment to the repeal of the poll tax (also a Conservative pledge by the 1992 election); acceptance of the principle of universal capping; no commitment to the restoration of funding to pre-1979 levels; commitment to repeal Section 28 of the Local Government Act (1988).

Table continues over

Table 2.1 continued

Social welfare reform

Ideological justifications	Sever relationship of dependency created between the 'nanny state' and 'welfare scroungers'; reassert traditional values of family support, care and a patriarchal domestic division of labour; cut public spending to create incentives through decreased taxation; introduce discipline and efficiency of the market.
Strategic motivations	Further erode the power of the public sector trade unions; encourage the population to take out private health cover; generate an internal market within the National Health Service; divest the state of responsibility for welfare where possible; subsidise private welfare, creating a new Thatcherite constituency.
Policy record (1979–90)	Internal markets introduced throughout the welfare state (most notably in the National Health Service); creation of hospital trusts, fund-holding general practitioners and an immense health care bureaucracy; care in the community (by unpaid women in the family) to replace state welfare; selling-off of council housing.
Assessment and reversibility	Commodification of welfare; stimulus to the private sector; displacement of responsibility to the local level; deterioration in the quality of care; transformation of the material interests of large sections of the population. Again, largely irreversible due to the costs of reorganisation despite the nostalgia for the 'old' welfare state.
Labour's policy stance after the Policy Review	Selective modifications to the policy legacy of the Thatcher years cast within the basic framework of the new welfare settlement; commitment to the restoration of earnings-linked pensions; review of National Health Service bureaucracy and restoration of hospital trusts to district health authorities; acceptance of principle of the internal market; refusal to challenge the subordination of welfare reform to economic priorities.

Source: adapted and developed from Hay (1996b: 154–5).

at the outset. To appeal to the concept of revisionism itself in this context is, of course, to invoke the Labour Party's long tradition of revisionist social democracy – of a peaceful, incremental and, above all, democratic 'road to socialism' paved with egalitarian, redistributivist and collectivist intentions (see, especially, Crosland 1956; Haseler 1969). To identify Labour's 'Thatcherite revisionism' might then be seen to imply a number of rather different claims about the party today:

1 that the party retained its long-established tradition of revisionism (of a peaceful and democratic transition to socialism) but replaced its social democratic conception of the path to socialism with one which was essentially Thatcherite;

2 that the party rejected (as either unfeasible or undesirable) the very notion of a road from capitalism to socialism (democratic or otherwise), preferring instead to make revisions to the Thatcherite legacy in tune with a 'social-ism' compatible (and perhaps even synonymous) with liberal democracy;

3 that the party came to accept what it saw (however reluctantly) as the largely irreversible legacy of the Thatcher years and sought to reconcile and modify its social democratic aspirations and sensitivities in the light of this insurmountable inheritance;

4 that the party came to accept somewhat more enthusiastically the considerable extent of the Thatcherite legacy, which it preferred to attribute to a new stage in the development of capitalism necessitating a new revisionism for new times – in so doing it engaged in an enthusiastic process of downsizing its anticipations in tune with a 'Thatcherite settlement' whose basic parameters it came to accept;

5 that the party underwent an ideological conversion (on the road to socialism) from social democracy to Thatcherism, becoming in turn a Thatcherite party committed to the democratic road to neo-liberalism.

Given the considerable disparity between some of these senses of the term, it is important that we eliminate the potential for misinterpretation at this point. Of the alternatives listed, the first and last are perhaps the most implausible. Whatever else has happened to the party since the early 1980s, not even the most zealous of modernisers have been anything other than reluctant and partial converts to Thatcherite ideology. Moreover (Blair's comments on 'social-ism' not

withstanding), to my knowledge, Thatcherism has yet to be presented
as a means to socialist ends. This leaves three potential and by no
means incompatible candidates. If Thatcherite revisionism is understood in any of these senses, then the claim that during the 1980s the
Labour Party came to exhibit a Thatcherite revisionism is, I would
contend, plausible. That having been said, however, the definition
which comes closest to that I will defend in the pages which follow is
the fourth – that the party came to accept the considerable extent of the
Thatcherite legacy, which it preferred to attribute to a new stage in the
development of capitalism, necessitating a new revisionism for new
times.[8]

Social democracy

> [I]t is otiose to commend or condemn Labour for abandoning some-
> thing – socialism – it never espoused; and for embracing, in its stead,
> something – social democracy – it had already jettisoned. (Elliott
> 1993: xiii)

The notion of social democracy presents an altogether different and
more difficult conceptual challenge. For not only is the term frequently
deployed in the existing literature in a great diversity of ways, but it is
also virtually never defined – it being assumed, falsely, that protagonists in the debate and readers alike share a common and largely
intuitive sense of its essence. Things become all the more complicated
if we consider the historical, theoretical and comparative uses of the
term.

To take the last first, comparative political economists of post-war
and contemporary western Europe frequently use the concept of social
democracy as a means of differentiating the political–economic regimes of a number of northern European (archetypally Scandinavian)
economies from other political–economic regimes such as 'market
liberalism' (see for instance Garrett 1998; Huber and Stephens 1998;
Pontusson 1992; Rothstein 1996). This, on the face of it, may seem
unproblematic. Yet in so doing, such authors consistently present
Britain as an example of market liberalism, not of social democracy
(nor even of political–economic 'incoherence'). This remains the case
after the 1997 election and, given the (empirical) criteria by which
such assessments are made (Garrett 1998: 59–69), it is difficult to
imagine that Britain is likely, any time soon, to join the ranks of the
social democracies (see table 2.2).[9]

Table 2.2 Britain: social democracy or market liberalism?

	Trade union membership, 1990 (%)	Number of unions, 1990	Government spending, 1980–90 (% GDP)	Highest effective rate of marginal corporation tax, 1980–90
Britain	38	76	44.3	41.5
Social democratic regimes (Austria, Denmark, Finland, Norway, Sweden – average)	65.8	24.2	52.1	48.5
Incoherent regimes (Belgium, Germany, Italy, the Netherlands – average)	35.8	17.8	51.4	43.3
Market liberal regimes excluding Britain (Canada, France, the USA, Japan – average)	28	87.3	40.9	40.5

Clearly, it should come as no great surprise that Garrett (1998) should find in 1990 empirical indicators of Britain's market liberalism as distinct from its social democracy. The point, however, is that such indicators are hardly likely to converge rapidly (if at all) on the characteristics of social democratic regimes under a Labour administration. Indeed, it seems likely that they will in fact continue to diverge. This suggestion might seem to render problematic any description of New Labour as a social democratic party.

Source: calculated from Garrett (1998).

What this suggests, at minimum, is that British social democracy, as and when it can be said to (have) exist(ed), is somewhat distinctive in comparative terms (Howell 1980; Panitch 1976). Nonetheless, it may still be appropriate to speak of a British tradition of social democracy if we are, at the same time, clear to differentiate it from the concept of social democracy more familiar from the comparative political economy of post-war western Europe.

Yet our problems are only beginning. For quite simply, how do we differentiate, on the one hand, between modifications to and developments of a political philosophy, tradition and practice which represent appropriate and necessary responses to a changing external environment and those, on the other, which represent a departure from and betrayal of that tradition? This takes us to the crux of the matter. Three potential strategies naturally present themselves – the first two of which resolve (or fail to resolve) the dilemma by displacement. The first strategy is to specify a number of social democratic parties and to argue that social democracy is, like Herbert Morrison's view of socialism, simply 'what social democratic parties do'.[10] This strategy, though frequently deployed, is seldom defended explicitly (for a rare exception see Kitschelt 1994: 1). According to such a view, social democracy will persist almost indefinitely – indeed, by definition – regardless of the context in which it is expressed. Though clearly neat, such a conception fails to resolve our dilemma in any satisfactory way. Equally evasive is to define social democracy historically in terms of the practice of nominally (or self-proclaimed) social democratic parties at some point in their heyday (say in the mid-1960s). According to such a view, social democracy (often prefixed with the label 'Keynesian') is largely a thing of the past – a conception which, however elegant, gives us little purchase on contemporary developments in the parties which continue to bear its name or proclaim its faith. Finally, we might seek to extrapolate from the history of social democracy as both an ethical tradition (or imperative) and a political practice a series of (potentially) trans-historical premises and values. Such fundamental normative and ethical principles of social democracy might be adapted to a variety of different contexts and environments (more or less conducive to their realisation). According to this view, the extent (if any) of New Labour's social democracy might be judged in terms of evidence (or otherwise) of its enduring commitment to this core set of ethical tenets. It is only this last strategy which offers us the possibility of any comparative historical analysis of social democracy.

Despite the rather stark nature of the choice between these three definitional strategies, there is a certain tendency in much of the literature sympathetic to Labour's modernisation to conflate this last definitional strategy with the first considered above. This has resulted in the search (one can only surmise an arduous one) for a set of basic social democratic values which does not serve to differentiate Old from New Labour. Mark Wickham-Jones, for instance, chooses his definition of social democracy carefully as 'a commitment to reformist measures' (1995a: 700). Reformism is, of course, no less vague a concept than revisionism and Wickham-Jones gives us little more to work with, going on to suggest, rather unhelpfully, that 'there remained policies in the party's 1989 programme which were social democratic in their orientation (and which gave concern to capitalists)' (1995a: 700). Presumably, then, social democracy implies nothing more than a certain gradualism with respect to the reform of capitalist institutions (a definition so vague and all-encompassing that it scarcely eliminates Thatcherism itself) and the equally nebulous notion that the extent of a party's social democracy might be gauged by the degree to which its policies provoke consternation on the part of capitalists (a definition which hardly differentiates well between Labour and Conservative governments in the post-war period).

For present purposes, a rather more exacting definition is proposed (see also Blyth 1999). Social democracy in the following chapters will be taken to imply: (i) a commitment to *redistribution* – to the principle that the distribution of social advantage within any capitalist society at any time can never be equitable and must be addressed through a constant imperative to redistribute (see also Shaw 1994: 6); (ii) a commitment to *democratic economic governance* – to the principle that the market, left to its own devices, can only generate outcomes which are inefficient, inequitable and unacceptable and that, accordingly, the state must take responsibility for market outcomes and for the degree of intervention required to ameliorate their excesses (cf. Przeworski 1985: 207–11); and (iii) a commitment to *social protectionism* – to the principle that it is the primary responsibility of the state to ensure that its citizens are provided for in terms of health, education and welfare in its broadest sense and across the life span (see also Shaw 1994: 6). By such a definition, the Labour Party throughout the post-war period was social democratic in its stated aspirations and ideology, though far less frequently social democratic in practice. In the late 1970s, in government, it came to subordinate its, by that stage somewhat beleaguered, social democratic aspirations to the perceived (and, to some extent, externally imposed) imperatives of economic prudence (Burk and Cairncross 1992; Hay 1999c). In opposition in the 1980s it first reclaimed and subsequently repudiated (if gradually) its social democratic aspirations and ideology, as these were again subordinated to economic exigencies.

These, then, are the claims that I seek to defend in this chapter: that by the completion of the Policy Review process the Labour Party had essentially committed itself, should it gain election, to a form of 'Thatcherite revisionism'; and that, by this time, it had effectively repudiated and abandoned its at best rather sketchy tradition of social democratic advocacy and, less frequently, social democratic practice.

Modernisation or accommodation?

Few commentators and analysts would deny that between the mid-1980s and the completion of the Policy Review process in 1989–90, the Labour Party underwent a profound transformation of both internal structure and policy. More contentious, however, has been the assessment of the nature, extent and timing of such change. During this period, did the party accommodate itself to the terms of an emerging Thatcherite settlement and political consensus, or did it merely update its policies in the face of a transformation in the very structures of the global political economy? Moreover, given that Labour underwent such a process of radical, perhaps unprecedented, reform, when did this originate and to what might it be attributed? I review (more fully in the next section) perhaps the most prominent attempt to deal with these issues – the 'modernisation' thesis (Hughes and Wintour 1990; Seyd 1993; Seyd and Whiteley 1992; Shaw 1993; Smith 1992a, 1992b). This account suggests that Thatcherism has merely provided the immediate opportunity for Labour to begin a long overdue modernisation, as an extended period in opposition forced the party to come to terms with the extent to which the external environment had changed since last it was in power. The resulting Policy Review, it is argued, led to the emergence of a 'reinvigorated Labour Party which appears ... to have overcome its apparently fundamental divisions' (Smith 1992b: 3).

It is the argument of what is to follow that such an account runs the risk both of conflating the appearance of electability in 1990 (an appearance that would all too rapidly fade) with reinvigoration and of celebrating the party's accommodation to a Thatcherite settlement. That settlement was always likely to prove damaging to Britain's long-term economic performance. Indeed, its smouldering contradictions, though present from its inception, were to become all the more visible in September 1992.[11]

In place of the modernisation thesis, I propose an alternative analysis. This accepts that between 1983 and 1990 the party underwent a profound transformation of structure and policy.[12] However, it suggests that in so doing, the party came to accept and, to a significant extent, to embrace the terms of a *post-Thatcher*, yet nonetheless *Thatcherite*, settlement. The basic contours of this settlement are charted in table 2.1. The Policy Review thus marks the symbolic return to consensus politics in Britain (see also Crouch 1997; Kavanagh 1997). The structures and perceived responsibilities of the state around which this consensus has been forged are, needless to say, fundamentally different from those that characterised the post-war consensus (see also Crewe 1993: 23–6).[13]

This alternative account suggests that changes in the patterns of global economic production, distribution, ownership and competition in recent years, however considerable, do not of themselves necessitate the defensive and reactionary 'politics of catch-up' to which Labour would seem to have restricted itself. Indeed, the Thatcherite state project and the neo-liberal accumulation strategy upon which it was premised exacerbated the persistent structural weaknesses of the British economy (on which see Eichengreen 1996; Hutton 1996; Kitson and Michie 1996; Watson and Hay 1998; on Thatcherism's economic pathologies see Buxton *et al.* 1998; Michie 1992). It is thus somewhat ironic that Labour should begin to draw electoral benefits from its 'Thatcherite revisionism' at precisely the moment at which the subject of that revisionism should begin to reveal its contradictions in a most visible form – as, from autumn 1992, the Conservatives lost their reputation for economic competence (Sanders 1996). It is the argument of this and subsequent chapters that such contradictions (likely to prove the most enduring feature of the Thatcherite legacy) now lie at the heart of Britain's current political and economic impasse. At the time of writing, that impasse is largely camouflaged by the stage in the economic cycle. However, any longer-term view can hardly fail to recognise that current and previous economic cycles trace a secular and, somewhat alarmingly, an accelerating spiral of decline (Watson 1997).[14] Further doses of neo-liberal medicine, spoonfuls of sugar notwithstanding, would seem to offer little in the way of a solution and arguably something of a catalyst.

In what is effectively a preview of later chapters, it is my argument that the current impasse (however well camouflaged for now) can be resolved only by a rejection of Thatcherite neo-liberalism – and its (blind) faith in the market's own self-restorative mechanisms.[15] Comforting though such a philosophy of benign neglect has proved, as a means to promote productive investment, capacity expansion and indigenous growth it is worse than useless. It is certainly no substitute for a more developmental and dirigiste role for the state. The case for such supply-side interventionism, however, could not make itself.[16] It required, as it still requires, Labour's rejection of the politics of *preference-accommodation* ('the politics of catch-up') and its adoption of a *preference-shaping* strategy based on the politics of advocacy (on which see Dunleavy and Ward 1991; see also Epstein 1980; Krieger 1991: 48; Lindblom 1977: 135–7; Petty and Cacioppo 1986; Shaw 1994: 60–1, 216–17). It is perhaps only then – with an incumbent Labour government committed to a truly post-Thatcherite developmental state and armed with a strategy to address the persistent structural weaknesses of the British economy – that we might speak of a truly reinvigorated and genuinely social democratic Labour Party.

Devising and revising revisionism: the 'modernisation' thesis

Though varying somewhat from author to author, the outline of a distinctive 'modernisation' thesis can be traced within the recent literature on the Labour Party (in addition to the literature cited above see also Butler and Kavanagh 1992: 43–66). Its central tenets can be summarised in four related hypotheses:

1 that by questioning the assumptions of the Keynesian orthodoxy of the post-war period, Thatcherism has transformed the terms of contemporary political debate in Britain;
2 that in so doing it has in fact facilitated the necessary accommodation of the Labour Party to a qualitatively novel global economic environment characterised by the heightened (if not quite perfect) mobility of goods, labour and, especially, capital;
3 that, as a consequence, Labour's Policy Review and resulting 'renewal' should be seen, somewhat ironically, as the product of the

party's years in the electoral wilderness during the 1980s and the requirement to face up to the future that this imposed;

4 that the Review should not therefore be seen as a concession to Thatcherism, but rather as an overdue modernisation which had, for too long, been thwarted by the cloying influence of the trade unions and the inertial impulses of left extremists.

A couple of points might usefully be made about the structure of such a thesis. First, it is important to consider what is implicit here. The argument underlying the 'modernisation' thesis is that, by 1987, the sensitivities, sensibilities and policies of Labour's past had been rendered anachronistic (and hence in need of 'modernisation') as a consequence of changes in the external (above all, global economic) environment. Accordingly, the thesis stated that for Labour to become electable once more, it had to adapt itself and its policies to the new constellation of economic opportunities, challenges and constraints (with the emphasis, of course, being on the latter).[17] What is particularly interesting and significant about this is the implicit theory of the voter on which it relies. Adaptation and accommodation to 'the harsh economic realities' of the new global political economy are here seen as a condition of *electability*. This implies a rather sophisticated electorate, apparently well versed in (one must assume neo-classical) economics. For here, as in so many of the arguments advanced to account for and/or to justify Labour's modernisation, (perceived) electoral expediency and (perceived) economic necessity are simply and conveniently conflated. It is assumed that only those (economic and social) policies that represent 'good economic sense' in an era of globalisation will be rewarded at the polls. Good economic sense is good psephology. This, it might be protested, is an extremely implausible assumption. Rather more plausible are the suggestions that voters do indeed have relatively well developed conceptions of what is economically feasible; that such conceptions are shaped, to a considerable extent, politically;[18] and that these conceptions may, as a consequence, bear very little relationship to any dispassionate assessment of what constitutes 'good economic sense'. The consequence for the modernisation thesis of exchanging these assumptions is devastating.

We can take the argument a stage further, however. For what we know is that in the context of a widely perceived economic crisis, the Conservatives were elected in 1979 arguing that the Keynesian economic orthodoxy of the incumbent Labour government had become little more than an historical anachronism. Keynesianism, they suggested, was simply no longer possible and had been superseded by neo-liberalism. Though the election of the first Thatcher government was hardly the mass mobilisation of public support of some popular depictions, the new right was nonetheless extremely successful in shaping popular perceptions of what was and, above all, what was no longer economically possible (Marshall *et al.* 1988).[19] If much of the electorate had indeed become convinced of the (unfortunate) necessity of neo-liberalism in the context of globalisation – as the evidence would suggest – and Labour did indeed seek to revise its economic convictions in the light of existing electoral preferences, then it is not difficult to see how 'modernisation' might have produced Thatcherite revisionism.

The second point to make about the structure of the modernisation thesis is that it is reminiscent of the 'new times' thesis initially popularised within the pages of *Marxism Today* and discussed briefly in the previous chapter (Hall and Jacques 1989). Both accounts seek to promote (or, in the case of the modernisation thesis, enthusiastically acclaim) the long overdue 'modernisation' of the Labour Party or the left more generally, based on a realisation of the qualitative transformation in the contours of contemporary capitalism. The 'new times' thesis relies on the simplistic counter-posing of Fordism ('old times') and post-Fordism ('new times'), suggesting that the left must accommodate itself to the new constellation of opportunities and constraints (again, the latter tends to be emphasised) which constitutes the post-Fordist present. Interestingly, what the very same authors in the pages of the very same journal previously ascribed to Thatcherism (a term they coined), they here came to attribute to post-Fordism (compare Hall and Jacques 1983 with 1989; for critiques along precisely such lines see Hay 1993; Rustin 1989). In so doing, they replaced the contingency of a strategic political dynamic for the air of inevitability summoned by an inexorable and irreversible economic dynamic (the transition from one stage of capitalist accumulation to the next).

The more recent and influential modernisation thesis is less explicit about the nature of the contemporary global economic context (periodic allusions to post-Fordism notwithstanding). Nonetheless, there are interesting parallels. Arguably both theses are incapable of making the distinction between:

1 inexorable global economic dynamics over which individual nation states may exercise only a minimal influence and which serve to

establish the strategic context within which specific state and economic projects (such as Thatcherism) are conceived and instantiated;

2 the specific economic and political strategies of an incumbent government or successive governments (the Thatcher administration, for instance) and their consequences for the broader political–economic environment.

Much follows from this inability to differentiate between aspects of the relevant political–economic context which, from the vantage point of an incoming administration, are immune to political intervention (and hence, effectively, immutable) and those which are not. In particular, contingent political strategies (even those, such as Thatcherite neo-liberalism, deeply deleterious to sustained economic growth) may be mistaken for simple economic necessities. It is not, then, surprising to find, in both accounts, neo-liberal economic mantras (principally, wage competitiveness, flexibility and labour-market deregulation) identified as 'conditions of British competitiveness' within the new global economy.[20] The economic orthodoxies of Thatcherite neo-liberalism and the bases of structural competitiveness are thus simply conflated, the specificity of Thatcherism thereby reduced to the particular ideological inflexion it has given to such 'necessities'.

The dangers of this failure to separate out global economic tendencies, on the one hand, and national political responses to such tendencies, on the other, can be seen if we consider Martin Smith's important and influential attempts to assess the political and ideological legacy of Thatcherism. He is by no means unrepresentative of the modernisation theorists when he suggests that:

> by arguing that the state did not have responsibility for employment, or the economy, and that nationalised industries should be returned to the private sector, Thatcherism changed the terms of political debate. (Smith 1992b: 7; from rather different perspectives see also Anderson 1992: 328; Letwin 1992: 309)

This is an interesting and perceptive point and, as we have seen, one that might lead us to question the extent to which economic preferences can be taken as indicators of 'good economics'. Given Smith's broader thesis that the Policy Review should not be seen as a form of Thatcherite revisionism, it might also be seen as a rather surprising observation. Indeed, the only way of reconciling these two central claims is to suggest that the 'rolling back of the frontiers of the state' and the neo-liberal strategy upon which this was premised were in fact necessitated by global economic dynamics over which individual nation states had minimal control. The argument was, and remains, empirically suspect, theoretically flawed and politically dangerous. It is based upon an inherently reductionist consideration of the political, in which 'functional' state projects can effectively be read off from global economic dynamics. Such an approach fails to reflect or consider the multitude of *potential* strategies for growth that can be sustained within a given set of global (and, one might add, domestic) economic constraints.[21] Moreover, it provides an implicit apology for Thatcherite economics since it assumes that the neo-liberal strategy of abstention from intervention would most successfully address Britain's need for structural competitiveness.[22]

What Smith's observation does suggest, however, is that it is primarily through the discourse of the new right that the need for economic modernisation (or at least heightened competitiveness)[23] has come to be understood in British political debate (though cf. Buxton 1998; Hutton 1996). This influence largely derives from the success of the organic intellectuals and think-tanks of the new right in Britain and the USA in colonising the debate on the nature of the state and economic crisis of the 1970s. This gave neo-liberal economics a stranglehold (which it has yet to relinquish) over the import of new economic insights into the political arena. This stranglehold is re-flected not only in the 'modernisation' of the Labour Party, but also in the revising and attendant downsizing of (Continental) European social democracy and antipodean labourism more generally (for a range of different interpretations of which see Blyth 1999; Gillespie and Paterson 1993; Glyn 1998; Huber and Stephens 1998; Notermans 1997).

What the above analysis surely serves to demonstrate is the need to distinguish clearly between:

1 the range of economic strategies compatible with, and the degree of accommodation necessitated by, any transformation and develop-ment of the global political economy;
2 the particular ideological and political inflexion given to such developments in dominant political discourses such as those of the new right.

If changes in the global economy have indeed necessitated a rethinking of the orthodoxies of the post-war period (of the possibility of 'Keynesianism in one country' for instance),[24] then it becomes imperative that this does not lead us to overlook the failures of Thatcherism and Reaganomics to yield sustained and sustainable economic growth. It is surely somewhat ironic that the culmination of the Labour Party's conversion to the economic nostrums of the new right should have coincided with Britain's deepest and most protracted recession since the 1930s – coming at just the time when the latter's harmful consequences were becoming most apparent (see for instance, Jessop 1992: 35–6; Jessop *et al.* 1990: 89–92; Rubery 1989: 172–5). These observations demonstrate the need, in the early 1990s as today, for a detailed reconnaissance by the left of the structures, processes and dynamics of the global political economy; the institutional specificity of the British economy (in particular its distinctive relationship between industrial and financial capital); and of how some complementarity between the two might be achieved on the basis of a novel accumulation strategy promoting a more developmental role for the state. Such a rethinking is today, as then, the condition of a reinvigorated Labour Party capable of identifying the contemporary crisis of the British state and of resolving the contradictions of the post-Thatcher settlement.

Such a genuine strategy of renewal must acknowledge:

1 the passing of the Keynesian era;
2 the limitations and failings of an abstentionist neo-liberal accumulation strategy;
3 the persistent structural weaknesses of the British economy;
4 the strategic opportunities as much as the constraints that international economic restructuring and greater regional economic integration present.

Labour's reinvigoration as a realistic alternative to Thatcherism – as opposed to the pursuit of 'Thatcherism by other means' (or 'new labourism by Thatcherite means') – can then be secured only by the construction of a new accumulation strategy. Such a strategy cannot represent a return to the past, either to the compromised Keynesian orthodoxies of the 1960s or to their protectionist revision in Labour's Alternative Economic Strategy of the 1970s and early 1980s (on which see Aaronovitch 1981; for an admirable commentary see Wickham-Jones

1996). With Labour in power, the likelihood of such a paradigm shift in the party's economic thinking (thinking which it now has to do aloud) has become all the more remote as it has become all the more difficult and, arguably, all the more necessary.

After 'modernisation': from preference-accommodation to preference-shaping

A central claim of the modernisation thesis is that the Policy Review represented 'an attempt to widen the appeal of the party and to win back some of the working class who voted Conservative in the 1980s' (Smith 1992a: 15; Seyd 1993; Sanders 1993). This is undoubtedly the case. However, advocates of, and commentators sympathetic to, Labour's 'modernisation' have tended not to consider the full range of alternative strategies available to the party in reconstituting its appeal to the electorate. In suggesting that the Policy Review was shaped profoundly by the need to win back lost voters, the implicit assumption was made that the only way in which this could be achieved was through a strategy of accommodation to the new-found preferences of the electorate – preferences, it should be noted, which saw the Conservatives re-elected in 1983 and 1987 with sizeable majorities. This psephologically inspired 'politics of catch-up' consigned Labour to a reactive and defensive, preference-accommodating approach – to what Colin Leys terms 'market-research socialism' (1990: 119; see also Shaw 1994: 216–7).

The dangers of such a strategy are threefold. First, in the wake of a crusading government intent on transforming not only the structures of the state but also the 'hearts and minds' of the British electorate,[25] there is a considerable risk of an unwitting accommodation to a Thatcherite agenda internalised within the sensitivities and sensibilities of the electorate. Indeed, by seeking to gauge such preferences as a means of repackaging and representing them as its own, Labour merely served further to establish them as the new 'common sense' in a way that the Conservatives could never have done on their own. It seems plausible to argue, as above, that such perceptions of the parameters of political and economic possibility had been circum-scribed significantly by the new right's narration of the crisis of the 1970s. They were, moreover, at considerable odds with any attempt to restore an indigenous growth dynamic to the British economy. If this is indeed the case, then it would seem that Labour in fact conspired in reinforcing the very attitudinal changes which would now seem to preclude all but the most orthodox and restrictive of macro-economic stances.

Second, as Labour would find to its cost in 1992 (and, arguably, had already done so in 1987), preference-accommodation – especially for a traditionally 'programmatic' party (Epstein 1980; Shaw 1994: 60) – was not likely to reap rapid electoral rewards. The risk is that in the initial attempt to poach the core constituencies of one's opponent, the perceived distance between the parties becomes so narrow that, as in 1992, the electorate adopts the view that it is simply 'better to vote for the devil it knows than the devil it doesn't' (see Sanders 1993: 213).[26]

Finally, if the above two propositions are indeed accurate, it is likely that by the time an opposition achieves power by the pursuit of such a preference-accommodating strategy, it will have done so only because the policy implementation of the outgoing government has proved so damaging as to undermine the electorate's faith in its competence. The clear danger is that the incoming party will secure for itself political office at precisely the moment at which the contradic-tions of the policy paradigm to which it, too, subscribes first become apparent to the electorate. The political fallout arising from any difficulty in establishing economic competence under such conditions may serve to ensure that any period in power is in fact short-lived. Whether this will prove the case for New Labour or not is largely an empirical matter. It is likely to depend on two key factors: (i) the ability of the Conservative Party in opposition to regroup and to define for itself a new political and economic programme; and (ii) Labour's ability to make swift decisions and to establish a hierarchy amongst its current wish list of rather contradictory priorities as, and when, the inevitable recession occurs (on the need to establish a clear sense of priorities see Panitch and Leys 1997: 253; Thompson 1996).

The basis for Labour's renewed appeal to the electorate has not, then, been an attempt to formulate an altogether novel conception of, and response to, the British impasse. Rather, it has sought to appeal to the pre-formulated sensitivities of the electorate, viewed as a fixed constraint to which policy appeals must be oriented. This tendency to 'reify' the attitudinal preferences of the electorate arguably prevented Labour in opposition from learning the lessons of Thatcherism's success, whilst making the party at least somewhat complicit in the latter's dubious achievements. As John Kingdom observes:

It seemed that socialism could live only by not being socialist; it was
not only Thatcherites at the graveside as the earth was shovelled over
the coffin of social democracy. (1992: 5–6; see also Crewe 1992: 23;
Leys 1990: 127)

Thatcherism's success, we should recall, was premised on the
ability of the new right to present the moment of the late 1970s as one
of crisis. In so doing, it proved itself capable of changing if not the
hearts and minds of the electorate then certainly the predominant
perceptions of the political context, recruiting subjects to its vision of
the 'necessary' response to the crisis of an 'overextended' stated 'held
to ransom' by the labour movement (Hay 1996a). However incomplete
and however far from hegemonic its project remained, its initial
success surely lay in this ability to mould perceptions of the nature of
the crisis of the 1970s and of the 'painful' remedies required.

There is much that Labour might have learned from this. The
similarities between the late 1970s and the early 1990s were considerable. Indeed, both contexts might be seen as providing rare
opportunities for the successful pursuit of *preference-shaping* (as
opposed to preference-accommodating) strategies. To avail itself of
such an opportunity, however, Labour would have had to distance
itself from the dominant political and economic orthodoxies of the
time, just as the new right did in the 1970s. What applied to
Thatcherism[27] then might as easily have been applied to Labour in
1992. Both contexts might be characterised in terms of profound and
protracted state failure and economic recession. Moreover, in 1992, as
in 1979, the symptoms of such state and economic dislocation were
widely perceived and experienced, providing a considerable opportunity for the mobilisation of a populist political and economic project
organised around the identification of the nature of the crisis and a
vision of an alternative.

Though the more recent 'crisis' might have been defined in a
number of different ways, all capable of finding resonance with a
variety of personal experiences of state and economic failure, some of
the core economic contradictions of the Thatcherite project can be
summarised as follows:

1 By pursuing both financial deregulation and a monetarist counter-
   inflationary strategy, Thatcherite neo-liberalism served to compound
   conditions discouraging investment in the 'real' economy, thereby

exacerbating a persistent structural weakness of the British economy. This has resulted in a situation in which Britain invests more of its available resources overseas than does any of its competitors (Pollin 1995; Watson and Hay 1998).

2 The 'rolling back of the frontiers' of the social democratic state has persistently been pursued for political advantage to the detriment of economic responsibility. This is evidenced in: (i) the short-term asset-stripping of the public sector for the sake of a 'share- and property-owning democracy' and cosmetic reductions in the public sector borrowing requirement at the expense of long-term improvements in competitiveness and industrial performance; and (ii) the revenue-maximising strategy of transferring public monopolies to the private sector rather than promoting competition by dissolving them. There is little evidence to substantiate Conservative claims that off-loading firms to the private sector has directly improved their performance and competitiveness (Bishop and Kay 1988; Foreman-Peck and Manning 1988; Haq and Temple 1998: 481–8; Parker 1995; Vickers and Yarrow 1995; Yarrow 1986, 1989).

3 The economic strategy of successive Conservative governments during the 1980s and 1990s was directed to securing tax cuts rather than to the channelling of tax incentives and public expenditure towards industrial investment, research and development, training, innovation and (re-)skilling. The result – consumer booms (most notably the 'Lawson boom' of the late 1980s) and import penetration – has undermined the prospects of sustained and sustainable economic growth without a significant expansion in industrial capacity (Michie and Smith 1996).

4 The policy of selective disengagement (if not perhaps outright abstention) from economic intervention resulted in the effective disintegration of both private and public sector training initiatives under the Thatcher governments. This led to a situation in which Britain's training system was, in the judgement of David Ashton *et al.*, 'just about the worst of our international competitors' in an economic context placing an ever greater premium upon reskilling and skill diversification (1989: 137; see also Chapman 1998; Finegold and Soskice 1988). As Bob Jessop and Rob Stones observed, 'at a time when high-grade flexibility depends upon polyvalent skills, the government sponsors flexibility through hire-and-fire industrial relations legislation and adopts a low-cost, low-skill training policy. This has reinforced the low-skill,

low-wage, low-productivity character of British industry' (1992: 187). Since the early 1980s, it would appear as though Britain has been forced to compete on the basis of a strategy of 'social dumping in one country' (Hay 1996b: 163–4).

5 The persistent failure of Conservative governments to develop a coherent industrial *strategy* – as distinct from a neo-liberal-engendered neo-Darwinism in which only the fittest have survived – has led to situation in which, as Jessop observes, 'Britain is fast losing [if it has not already lost] the last vestiges of an independent and coherent manufacturing base which could serve as the basis for an effective national economic strategy' (1992: 37; see also Cowling and Sugden 1990; Glyn 1989; Rowthorn 1989).

6 The systematic stripping of the strategic capacities of the state for intervention on the supply side[28] has compromised its (always meagre) ability to address the persistent pathologies of the British economy and, hence, to promote an investment-led manufacturing renaissance (Ashton *et al.* 1989; Jessop 1992; Jessop *et al.* 1990; Michie and Smith 1996; Watson and Hay 1998).

This list is certainly not exhaustive, but it does begin to illustrate the profound nature of the impasse that is the direct economic legacy of Thatcherism. Its social legacy is no less pronounced and no less inauspicious (see for instance Hills 1996; Oppenheim 1993; Walker and Walker 1987; Webb *et al.* 1996). Once this is considered, it becomes clear that there were – and are – alternatives to the Thatcherite revisionism to which the Labour Party had by 1990 restricted itself. Moreover, the construction of such alternatives was, by that point, a necessary (though not in itself sufficient) condition of Britain's emergence from persistent economic decline and social dislocation.

Conclusion

As I have sought to make clear in the preceding pages, the case for an alternative to Labour's chosen 'politics of catch-up' was in the early 1990s, as it remains today, a compelling one. The deep and palpable dissatisfaction with the policies and personnel of the Major government, which intensified considerably following Britain's ejection from European Exchange Rate Mechanism in September 1992 (Sanders 1996), only demonstrates the potential that existed for Labour in opposition to reap the electoral benefits of preference-shaping. If the crisis of the 1970s was, in the popular fiction of the new right, a crisis of overload and ungovernability, then altogether more plausible was the view that the crisis of the 1990s was, and is, a crisis of *under-load* – of an under-extended, retrenched and debilitated state stripped of the capacity for strategic economic intervention. The adoption, then, of a preference-shaping and, ultimately, a state-shaping strategy might have provided Labour with the basis from which to build a populist political project capable of transcending neo-liberalism and of providing the modernising role that the free play of the market has consistently failed to deliver. Whether that option still remains is a crucial question but one which must be left for subsequent chapters.

What is certain, however, is that such an alternative could not and cannot be constructed out of a nostalgia for a past to which there can be no return. On this much New Labour is surely right. The Keynesian welfare state is gone. The post-war settlement cannot be resurrected. An alternative vision is required. Yet, like all realistic visions, it must be grounded in a tightly focused analysis of the current conjuncture. This presents a considerable challenge to those who would like to present themselves as the 'organic intellectuals' of a resurgent and renewed left. The contradictions of the Thatcherite inheritance are all too apparent. Yet without an alternative vision, we remain ensnared within this 'catastrophic equilibrium' in which the 'old is dying and the new cannot be born' (Gramsci 1971: 176).

Notes

1 There is much wilderness between these two camps and the tents in each are rather liberally spaced – neither group could easily shelter under the same fly sheet.
2 The titles alone give something of a clue to the character of the debate. Moon's 'Evaluating Thatcherism' (1994) was followed by Marsh and Rhodes' 'Over the Moon or Sick as a Parrot' (1995) with the final salvo delivered by Moon in 'Evaluating Thatcher: Did the Cow Jump Over?' (1995). The exchange might, I suppose, be seen as further evidence that 'he who laughs last, laughs longest'.
3 To suggest that debates of this kind have generated rather more heat than light is not to downplay the significance and prescience of many of the observations made in the course of the exchange. It is, however, to suggest that the very genre of debate (of charge, rebuttal and counter-charge) –

with its rhetorical preference for polarity – does not lend itself easily to the kind of careful theoretical and empirical elaboration by which such observations might best be developed.

4 As well as the work of Stuart Hall cited above, see also Wolfe (1991); O'Shea (1984); Letwin (1992).

5 See the work of Jessop *et al.*, Marsh and Rhodes, and Dolowitz *et al.*, cited above. On the Thatcher governments' cumulative radicalisation see in particular Kerr and Marsh (1999); Kerr *et al.* (1997).

6 The term 'Gestalt switch' is in fact deployed by Kuhn (1962: 111–14).

7 As I have been at pains to demonstrate, this claim is entirely compatible with the argument of authors like Marsh, Rhodes and, more recently, Kerr that the break with the past which Thatcherism marked is a consequence less of innate radicalism than of the incremental attrition of almost two decades in office. The logic of their argument is that there is nothing exceptional about the Conservatives' two decades in government in terms of the extent of the transformation of the state and the economy. Whilst this is not a view that I share, it is important to note that the argument that I am making about the considerable nature of the Thatcherite legacy is not dependent on any claim to the exceptional character of the Thatcher years.

8 Though this was precisely the sense of 'Thatcherite revisionism' that I sought to convey in earlier work (Hay 1994), it is interesting to note that this is by no means the only sense of the term attributed to me in the secondary literature. Adam Lent and Matthew Sowemimo are then by no means on their own in taking my reference to Thatcherite revisionism to imply something much closer to sense 5 in the above list (1996: 122).

9 Garrett, for instance, in the most recent (and, arguably, one of the most important) additions to this voluminous literature suggests that 'social democratic corporatist regimes are based on a virtuous cycle in which government policies that cushion market dislocations are exchanged for the regulation of the national labour market by the leaders of encompass-ing trade union movements' (1998: 5). Clearly, this does not accurately describe the British experience at any point in the post-war period, let alone today. Moreover, even if we soften the stipulation of national wage bargaining in such a definition, Britain still comes nowhere close to exhibiting such a virtuous cycle – nor, for the foreseeable future, is it likely to.

10 The oft-cited remark that 'socialism is what a Labour Government does' is generally, though by no means exclusively, attributed to Herbert Morrison. It is, nonetheless, almost certainly apocryphal (see for instance Paterson 1993: 1, 4).

11 I refer, of course, to Black Wednesday and Britain's ejection from the European Exchange Rate Mechanism, on whose political consequences see Gavin and Sanders (1997); King (1998: 185–92); Norton (1998: 79–82); and, especially, Wickham-Jones (1997a).

12 In a very much earlier version of this argument (1994: 700–1), I placed
the emphasis, as in the 'modernisation' thesis, almost exclusively on the
Policy Review process itself and hence on the period 1987–9. As the
literature has developed subsequently, however, important contributions
by Eric Shaw (1994) and Mark Wickham-Jones (1995b) have served to
demonstrate the extent to which the period 1983–7 was crucial, both in
the revision of policy and, more significantly, in providing the institutional context without which the Policy Review would have been
impossible.

13 To appeal to the notion of consensus here is, potentially, to open a
Pandora's box. The idea of a post-war consensus is highly contested and
the notion of a post-Thatcher consensus is likely to prove more contentious still. It is perhaps, then, important to say something further about
the nature of the claim being made here. Consensus is, of course, a
comparative concept in the sense that a particular period or episode is
only more or less consensual relative to another. It is thus important to be
explicit about the specific comparison being made (see also the discussion in Hay 1996b: 47–8). By suggesting a return to consensus, I am
arguing that contemporary British politics is characterised by a degree of
political convergence between the parties unusual in Britain by recent
historical standards and certainly as pronounced as that identified in the
early post-war period. This does not imply that important policy differences between the parties do not exist, but that on a wide range of issues
the proximity between the parties is considerable and, in comparative
historical terms, unusually so. As a study by the National Institute of
Economic and Social Research concluded in 1990 on the basis of a
comprehensive review of Labour policy documents, 'the economic policy
differences between the two major parties are narrower now than they
have been for about twenty years' (National Institute of Economic and
Social Research 1990: 52; cited in Shaw 1994: 107).

14 This is a theme to which we return in much greater detail in later
chapters. If only as an indication of the complexity of such issues,
however, it will suffice for now to note that much of this secular decline
can be traced to under-investment and capacity constraints. At the time of
writing, the trend rate of growth for the British economy (the rate at
which the economy can grow without exceeding its short-run capacity) is,
on the basis of the most optimistic estimates, somewhere between 2 and
2.25 per cent. The growth rate of the economy during the period 1995–8
was over 3 per cent, indicating that it was operating well in excess of
capacity. As Matthew Watson notes, 'the expectation within the market is
that, with the economy being run at unsustainable capacity levels, the
medium term effect of continued consumption growth must be inflationary in the absence of pre-emptive counter movements in interest rates by
the monetary authorities' (personal correspondence, 1998). Such action

on the part of the Bank of England, it is also anticipated, is likely to be both swift and harsh. This, in large part, explains the attractiveness of bonds denominated in sterling. The vicious circle is completed if we note that interest rate rises are likely only to depress further underlying levels of investment, thereby merely exacerbating existing capacity constraints. On capacity constraints within the British economy see Driver (1996); Watson (1997, 1999c); more generally, see Buxton (1998); Driver (1998).

15 Though, at the time of writing (August 1998), the structural weaknesses (particularly the capacity shortfall) of the British economy are hidden to some extent from full view by the stage in the economic cycle, this condition is unlikely to endure for very much longer. The prospect of a full-blown manufacturing recession looms dark and ominous on the not too distant horizon.

16 Were the market quite as self-correcting as some neo-liberal economists would have us believe, perhaps it would make such a case itself.

17 Of course, for proponents of such a view, this was something of a hypothetical and *post hoc* rationalisation. Writing, as most of them were, immediately after the Policy Review, their argument was that this was not only what Labour had to do, but exactly what it had done.

18 As Mark Peffley suggests, 'citizen judgements do not occur in a vacuum, but in a political context that is shaped as much by the actions of strategic elites as by objective material conditions. Most voters are highly dependent upon elites for distilling the complex machinations of the macro-economy to more accessible interpretations' (1984: 289; cited by Shaw 1994: 184–5; see also Peffley *et al.* 1987). As he goes on to argue, 'the judgements of many citizens may be little more than ready-made verdicts, adopted *in toto* from political elites, without any appreciation for the reasoning behind them' (1984: 289).

19 As Eric Shaw notes, amongst Marshall *et al.*'s respondents, over 40 per cent offered explanations of Britain's economic problems consistent with Tory diagnoses (Marshall *et al.* 1988: 159; Shaw 1994: 185).

20 On the dangers of the notion of national competitiveness see Krugman (1996); Ormerod (1996); Rapkin and Strand (1995); Watson (1999b).

21 At this stage, this is a largely an analytical point. Two more substantive comments, however, might serve to indicate the general trajectory of the argument. First, as a growth strategy, neo-liberalism is singularly lacking, being able to conjure only a somewhat naive faith in the ability of the market to generate sustainable growth if only left to its own devices. Second, almost any supply-side interventionist strategy designed to deal with the twin problems of under-investment and capacity constraints and attached even to a fairly orthodox macro-economic stance is likely to prove much more effective in generating higher and sustainable rates of growth in an open economy than neo-laissez-faire (Piven 1997). In subsequent chapters I deal with the suggestion that, in the Policy Review –

if not for much longer – Labour did in fact develop such a 'supply-side socialist' strategy.

22 Quite how the economy's structural competitiveness would be enhanced simply by leaving it alone is, of course, not discussed. No obvious mechanism springs to mind.

23 As I have been at pains to demonstrate, the notion of a neo-liberal modernisation strategy is an oxymoron.

24 It will be the argument of later chapters that the parameters of political and economic possibility have indeed been transformed since the mid-1970s in ways which render strategies premised on 'Keynesianism in one country' problematic. It should be noted, however, that the notion of the British economy as a paragon of 'closure' or, indeed, of 'Keynesianism in one country' throughout the post-war period is largely mythical. With respect to the former, the persistence of a set of macro-economic priorities which prized above all else a stable value for sterling facilitated the overseas orientation of the City of London. With respect to the latter, the British economy was never particularly responsive to injections of domestic demand (which tended to precipitate instead import penetration and balance-of-payments difficulties). Moreover, that the parameters of political and economic possibility have been transformed does not imply that the manner of this transformation is well captured by orthodox accounts of globalisation, nor that the convergence in economic policy that such accounts tend to predict is warranted. On both counts the globalisation thesis is sadly lacking (Hay and Marsh 1999a; Watson 1999a).

25 To say nothing of Thatcher's personal conviction to lay to rest the spectre of socialism once and for all (see Jenkins 1987).

26 It might be objected that such a thesis is refuted by the outcome of the 1997 election. For, since 1992, the Labour Party has moved ever closer to the Conservatives on the majority of issues (see chapter 4). If the electorate were ever to vote for the devil it knew rather than that it didn't, it would surely have done so at the 1997 election. The point is, however, that after at least a decade of 'neo-liberalisation', the Labour Party eventually acquired a reputation for economic competence on such terms and, more significantly, on Black Wednesday the Conservatives lost theirs.

27 Perhaps the boldest and most self-conscious attempt at preference-shaping in the history of British electoral competition.

28 Despite the rhetoric of Thatcher's 'supply-side economics', with its emphasis on the elimination of supply-side 'rigidities' such as labour-market regulation and industrial rights.

3   On New Labour's Ups –
and (Anthony) Downs

It is not from the benevolence of the butcher, the brewer or the baker
that we expect our dinner, but from their regard to their own interest.
(Adam Smith, *The Wealth of Nations*, cited in Downs 1957: 28)

It is a peculiar irony of the literature on New Labour that in searching
for a way in which to describe and account for the qualitative novelty
of contemporary electoral competition in Britain, commentators and
analysts have invariably found themselves drawn to some of the oldest
theories of party competition. Perhaps most frequently cited in this
regard is the 'spatial' theory of voting first advanced by Harold
Hotelling (1929) and most famously elaborated by Anthony Downs in
An Economic Theory of Democracy (1957) (for reviews of this
literature see Dunleavy 1991: chapters 4 and 5; Fiorina 1997; Hinich
and Munger 1997: chapter 2; Ordeshook 1997; Self 1993: 24–7;
Stokes 1963). Embarrassed perhaps by the strange juxtaposition of this
simple, elegant but above all rather dated model with the seeming
complexity, technical sophistication and modernity (however contrived) of contemporary electioneering, references to Downs' work
have tended to remain casual and cursory (see Blyth 1997b; Gavin and
Sanders 1997: 127; Heath and Jowell 1994: 199–201; Heath and
Paulson 1992; Kenny and Smith 1997b: 224–5; Sanders 1998: 216–24;
Shaw 1994: 171–5).[1] A quite startling range of authors have nonetheless been impressed by the similarities between Labour's 'politics
of catch-up', with its studious targeting of the 'median voter', and the
Downsian logic of electoral rationality and/or expediency.

   Yet, to date, no detailed, far less systematic, attempt has been made
to assess either the extent to which the electoral strategy of New
Labour exhibits Downsian tendencies, or, if the similarities are as
considerable as a number of authors seem to suggest, how this might
be accounted for.[2] In this chapter my aim is to elaborate upon the rather
stylistic and schematic depiction of Labour's 'politics of catch-up'

presented in the previous chapter by seeking to provide precisely such an evaluation. The argument proceeds in three stages. In the first section, I attempt to provide a relatively comprehensive yet succinct summary of Downs' public choice model of voting and party competition, before turning in more detail in the second section to the assumptions upon which it is premised and the extent to which they came to be shared by New Labour in opposition. In the final section I turn to the perhaps difficult issue of the implications of this analysis for Downs' theory itself, the nature of and prospects for electoral competition in Britain, and an assessment and evaluation of Labour's 'politics of catch-up'. I suggest that Downs' model of party competition in a (largely) bipartisan system does provide a disarmingly accurate (if nonetheless rather simplistic) *description* both of New Labour's electoral strategy in recent years and, rather more alarmingly, of the assumptions informing Labour's reprojection of itself as a 'catch-all party'. Despite this, however, I argue that we must be extremely wary of treating such evidence as any kind of confirmation of Downs' theory. Its model of bipartisan convergence provides, at best, a useful analogy. Whenever observed economic or political behaviour seems to conform to the predictions of rational or public choice theoretical models, I argue, we need to ask a series of supplementary questions. In particular, it is imperative that we consider under what conditions and in which contexts and environments actors do indeed behave in a manner consistent with the assumptions of such a model – of self-serving, self-interested utility maximisation. Moreover, if we harbour any normative opprobrium for such conduct, it is perhaps also incumbent upon us to ask under what conditions actors may exhibit different forms of rationality. Answers to such questions may tell us much about the character of New Labour and about the nature of contemporary British democracy.

An economic theory of democracy: Downsian Machiavellianism?

> Political parties tend to maintain ideological positions that are consistent over time unless they suffer drastic defeats, in which case they change their ideologies to resemble that of the party which defeated them. (Downs 1957: 300)

Downs' *An Economic Theory of Democracy* has the not inconsiderable virtue of being one of the most clear, unambiguous and least pretentious works of political theory ever written. Its assumptions, logic and conclusions are boldly, even starkly, stated – surely a significant factor in its phenomenal and continuing influence. The boldness of the argument, however, also serves to expose the simplicity and implausibility of many of the assumptions on which the model is premised. Downs, however, is both refreshingly sanguine and un-apologetic about this. His assumptions are chosen neither for their intuitive accuracy nor for their sophistication but for their simplicity and parsimony. As he famously remarks, 'theoretical models should be tested primarily by the accuracy of their predictions rather than by the reality of their assumptions' (1957: 21). Given the assumptions on which his model resides, this is perhaps no bad thing. Yet it does raise an important issue concerning the status of Downs' *heuristic model* as a *theory*, which we shall return to at rather greater length later. It is certainly refreshing that theorists, invariably rational choice theorists, should admit voluntarily the implausibility (even, on occasions, the falsity) of their assumptions.[3] Yet such candid confessions must surely lead us to question the claim that any theory constructed on the basis of such assumptions can, in any meaningful sense, explain those out-comes which do happen to coincide with its predictions (Hay 1998a: 14).

Yet confessions as to the implausibility of his assumptions do not exhaust Downs' candour. For he goes on to draw further attention to the rather pared-down nature of the theoretical model he advances, pointing out that 'it proposes a single hypothesis to explain govern-ment decision-making and party behaviour in general'. On the basis of this, he argues, testable corollaries can be generated and hence the thesis 'submitted to empirical proof' (1957: 33). Again, we can only ask ourselves quite what status might be accorded such 'proof' given that Downs quite clearly regards the assumptions from which any such corollaries might be derived as unrealistic (and admits (p. 4) that they are chosen precisely so as to render political action predictable).

Rational voters, rational parties
The basic premise on which the Downsian model is constructed is simply stated. It is 'that parties in democratic politics are analogous to entrepreneurs in a profit-seeking economy' (p. 295). It is this analogy which allows Downs to import the micro-foundations of neo-classical economics into political science in developing a truly 'economic theory of democracy'. Though he does not play on the semantic

ambivalence of the term, the theory is 'economic' both in the sense that its most basic assumptions are imported directly from the study of economic processes but also in the secondary sense that these assumptions are few and far between and are stretched a very long way. As in neo-classical economics more generally, Downs takes as his starting point the ontological proposition that all behaviour (in this case political behaviour) is ultimately reducible to, and hence explicable in terms of, the rational conduct of individual actors. For the purpose of simplicity (and the ease with which he might generate testable hypotheses), he allows himself the luxury of treating political parties as if they were themselves unified rational subjects. The rest can be derived from this starting point.

Voters, for the purpose of the model, are assumed to be rational with respect to means rather than ends. To explain, Downs does not assume that voters choose their preferences rationally (so as to maximise their utility or welfare function for instance), but that they act rationally in pursuit of those preferences (whatever they happen to be). A rational voter is one who is efficient in adopting strategies (principally either in voting or in abstaining) so as to maximise his/her *perceived* utility. As Downs elaborates:

> a rational man [*sic*] is one who behaves as follows: (1) he can always make a decision when confronted with a range of alternatives; (2) he ranks all the alternatives facing him in order of his preference in such a way that each is either preferred to, indifferent to, or inferior to each other; (3) his preference ranking is transitive [if *a* is preferred to *b* and *b* is preferred to *c*, then *a* is preferred to *c*]; (4) he always chooses from among the possible alternatives that which ranks highest in his preference ordering; and (5) he always makes the same decision each time he is confronted with the same alternatives. (p. 6; see also Arrow 1951: chapters 1 and 2)

Governments and opposition parties, too, exhibit the same qualities. Accordingly, both can be assumed to act rationally in pursuit of a single goal – re-election and election, respectively (p. 11). This, of course, precludes the possibility at a stroke that political parties might engage in a cost–benefit analysis of the price (in terms of political convictions, ethos and tradition) at which electoral victory is bought. That parties behave in this way (and this way alone) is traced back further to the motivations of party members (Downs is principally concerned here with senior party officials). Applying the now familiar axiom of rational self-interest, he suggests that party members (can be assumed to) 'act solely in order to attain the income, prestige and power which comes from being in office' (p. 28). It follows directly from such an assumption that for politicians the reward of office is an end in itself (indeed, both a sufficient and singular end), to which particular policies are merely a means. Of course, for such a strategy to be rationally operationalised, it is imperative that the pretence must be maintained that policies are in fact the ends to which office is the means. In so far, then, as the social function of government (to provide utility and welfare for its citizens and, in so doing, to satisfy their preferences) is performed, it is done so quite independently of any motivation to do so on the part of elected officials and those competing for office. Downs here cites Joseph Schumpeter to the effect that:

> the social meaning of parliamentary activity is no doubt to turn out legislation and, in part, administrative measures. But in order to understand how democratic politics serve this social end, we must start from the competitive struggle for power and office and realise that the social function is fulfilled, as it were, incidentally. (1950: 282; cited in Downs 1957: 29)

Perverse though this may seem in painting what is hardly a particularly edifying picture of candidates for political office, the crucial point for both Downs and Schumpeter is that majority voter preferences are indeed satisfied in such a system. Indeed, arguably, they are rather better satisfied that they would be were politicians modelled instead as enlightened and altruistic paternalists (p. 52). The mechanism is one of competition and it serves to ensure, for instance, that 'the government is likely to adopt any act of spending which, coupled with its financing, is a net addition of utility to more voters than it is a subtraction, i.e., it pleases more than it irritates' (p. 70). In this way, at least in a two-party electoral system, policies tend to converge on the median voter's position. As Patrick Dunleavy and Brendan O'Leary note in an admirable summary:

> On certain assumptions the median voter's position may be the best single representation of what a majority of the citizens want. The process of 'median voter convergence' is seen as an ideal result, which maximises the welfare of citizens, since whichever party or candidate wins the election will implement policies that are the best feasible approximation to majority views. (1984: 28)

This may seem like an elaborate hoax, and in one sense it is. If we assume, theoretically, the worst of our politicians, we get the best outcomes – provided, of course, that when it comes to voting we continue to believe their mythical claims to be concerned genuinely and directly for our interests and preferences.

Again, in order to simplify the model as a means of generating general and testable hypotheses, Downs assumes that there are fixed-term elections (p. 12), that party officials will not seek to benefit themselves at the expense of other party officials (p. 30) and that parties will remain within the bounds of legality. Nonetheless, the governing party 'manipulates its policies and actions in whatever way it believes will gain it the most votes without violating constitutional rules' (p. 31).

This array of assumptions allows Downs to formulate, indeed to derive, an initial hypothesis which summarises his entire approach to electoral competition:

> Since none of the appurtenances of office can be obtained without being elected, the main goal of every party is the winning of elections. Thus all its actions are aimed at maximising votes, and it treats policies as means towards this end. (p. 35)

If Downs here emphasises the cold calculating rationalism of political parties in this pared-down model, then it is important to note that voters are no less instrumental in their deliberations. The rational voter will always opt for the alternative that she/he believes will yield the highest personal utility. The citizen's motivation to vote is thus reduced to a simple function of the algebraic difference in the projected utility incomes arising from the election of each party (in a two-party system). This can be represented as follows:

$$M_{v,a} = Pref_a - Pref_b = E(U_{a, t+1}) - E(U_{b, t+1})$$

where:

$M_{v,a}$ is the degree of motivation of voter v to vote for party 'a';
$Pref_a$ is the voter's preference for party a;
$E(U_{a, t+1})$ is the expected utility arising from the election of party a over the duration of the electoral cycle $(t + 1)$.

Up until this point, Downs has assumed that the voter is relatively well informed and that the cost of acquiring the information needed to engage in such electoral calculus is negligible. Thus, although projections of expected utility can remain only that – projections – they can be assumed to be based on the best available evidence. This, however, is one implausible assumption that Downs does choose to correct (see especially chapter 14). Though information may not be costly in purely financial terms, its acquisition may nonetheless consume considerable amounts of time and effort. Moreover, the probability that the actions of any one individual will prove significant to the outcome of the election is extremely low; the difference between the expected utilities of the two parties – $E(U_{a, t+1})$ and $E(U_{b, t+1})$ – is often fairly marginal and it is difficult to acquire reliable and independent information on which to base such expectations. Given such considerations, it is a wonder that anyone votes at all. Nonetheless, people do vote, so in one sense this may seem like a purely abstract and trivial point. Yet, in another sense, it cuts to the core of the rational theory of voting. As Dunleavy notes:

> A rational voter should first work out her 'party differential' (the benefit she will receive if one party rather than its rivals wins the election). This stake is then multiplied by the likelihood that her own vote will be decisive in determining which party forms the government. This probability is almost always minute ... however large her party differential a rational voter cannot receive discounted benefits sufficient to offset the costs of acquiring political information or travelling to the polling station to vote. (1991: 80; see also Aldrich 1997: 387)

The problem this poses for Downs' economic theory of democracy is simply stated. If, strictly speaking, it is irrational to vote, then it does seem rather perverse to develop a rational theory of the conduct of those who have already revealed themselves irrational by their very decision to make the trip to the polling station![4] Downs fails to deal with this problem at all adequately, pointing merely to the means by which voters may minimise the cost to themselves of acquiring information (relying on experts, choosing their party on the basis of ideology and ethos rather than a detailed consideration of policy, and so forth). Whilst this may indeed seem rational *given the decision to vote*, it hardly renders that decision rational in the first place (for a discussion of alternative attempts to avoid this paradox see Aldrich 1997; Dunleavy 1991: 80–3). Downs seems, tacitly, to acknowledge this and is ultimately forced to fall back on the argument that voters invariably decide to cast their vote out of a general concern to maintain the health of their democratic system. Once again, however, whilst this may very well be true, it is hardly consistent with a purely instrumental conception of rationality, falling foul as it does of the 'free-rider problem'.

Notwithstanding the problems of attributing rationality to actors who behave irrationally by voting in the first place, Downs proceeds to model the consequences of rational voting in both two-party and multiparty democratic electoral systems. In so doing, however, he is forced to make one further and fundamental background assumption – that voters' preferences are fixed, providing effectively a static context within which electoral competition occurs (p. 47).[5] This, as we shall see, is a crucial step, the most obvious consequence of which is that Downs cannot model (nor even consider) attempts by political parties to shape the distribution of preferences within the polity. Quite simply, if preferences are assumed to be fixed, then any such strategy is clearly irrational. In fact, whilst acknowledging that this is a simplifying assumption, Downs indicates that he does not consider political strategies of preference-shaping to be a significant factor in political competition, commenting:

> Even though [political] tastes often change radically in the long run, we believe our assumption is plausible in the short run, *barring wars or other social upheavals*. (p. 47, emphasis added)

A spatial theory of electoral competition

Thus far, Downs has merely sought to construct abstract models of the behaviour of rational voters on the one hand and rational parties in a polity of rational voters on the other. It is in bringing them together and, specifically, in considering the competition between political parties in such a context that Downs introduces the distinctively spatial dimension to his analysis. Here he draws upon and develops the pioneering work of Harold Hotelling (1929) and, if to a somewhat lesser extent, Arthur Smithies (1941).

As noted above, Downs' most basic assumption is that political parties can be assumed to compete in a manner analogous to capitalist entrepreneurs. It is perhaps somewhat ironic, then, that the spatial model of voting tends to take as its starting point not capitalist entrepreneurs but petty bourgeois shopkeepers or ice-cream sellers. Consider, for instance, a rural village comprised essentially of a main

street along which the majority of the population resides. Houses are
distributed fairly evenly along the street with, perhaps, a higher density
in the centre and lower densities at the village's fringes. If this village
is served by a single butcher's shop, then the butcher has a clear
monopoly in the market for, amongst other things, sausages.[6] Accordingly, it matters little where along the main street her shop is located
as, we can assume, residents will be prepared to walk the length of the
village to sate their craving. The considerable appetite of the villagers
for sausages may, however, tempt a chain of butcher's shops to open a
store on the main street (or, indeed, for an existing store to diversify
into this lucrative market). The result is competition. At this point, the
spatial location of both the original and new outlet for sausages
becomes highly significant. Were both shops mobile, there would be a
clear tendency for each to move towards the other in the middle of the
village in an effort to protect and maximise their potential market (on
the basis of the assumption that consumers will, all other things being
equal, prefer the supplier closest to them). In this particular example,
however, the new butcher's shop has a significant advantage in that it
can choose its location (provided suitable accommodation is available)
so as to maximise its potential market, safe in the knowledge that the
original butcher's shop is unlikely to be able to relocate its premises
(because of the considerable costs involved).

According to the spatial theory of democratic politics, the electoral
competition between two parties can be assumed to be analogous to
this process. The only difference is that rational parties will choose not
to encumber themselves with the bricks and mortar of elaborate
ideological commitments which may hinder significantly their mobility along the political spectrum. This gives a clear potential advantage
to parties prepared to act in a manner consistent with Downs' assumption that policies are a means to the end of political office, rather than
office a means to the realisation of political ends. If we assume that
this is indeed the case – that parties will move freely along the political
spectrum – then the analogy with the competition between butcher's
shops on the high street begins to break down. Rather more appropriate is that between (mobile) ice-cream sellers on the beach. As
Dunleavy succinctly notes:

> Parties alter their position in electoral space to attract the maximum
> number of votes, and voters choose the party closest to their personal
> position on key issues – just as ice-cream stalls position themselves on

the beach to attract the maximum custom, and holiday-makers collect their ice-cream from the nearest stall. (1991: 79)

Clearly, the distribution of bodies along the beach will influence the positioning of purely sales-maximising ice-cream vendors. If bathers tend to congregate over time on the right-hand side of the beach, then a vendor dedicated to serving her customers on the left-hand side of the beach is likely to be penalised for her loyalty. So too, by analogy, a party which proves itself unresponsive to the changing tides of political preference will be penalised. Under conditions of rationality, however, the ice-cream sellers and, by extension, political parties will act so as to maximise their utility (sales and votes, respectively).

If we return, momentarily, to the sale of sausages, we can see that, as in the case of the beach, in positing a single street (running, say, north–south) along which potential customers are distributed we have, effectively, assumed a one-dimensional model. Clearly, things are complicated if we introduce a second dimension, by positing a network of streets running at right angles (east–west) to the main street. The decision as to where best to locate a new outlet for sausages is now rather more complex. In just the same way, if voters are differentiated amongst one another not merely with respect to a left–right axis, but also with respect to their relative preferences for, say, environmentalism or economic growth, the nature of the competition between the parties will change as a consequence (on two-dimensional and multidimensional models of voting behaviour see Hinich and Munger 1997: chapters 3 and 4; Ordeshook 1997). The more dimensions we consider, the more complicated the model becomes and, consequently, the more difficult the mathematics. The predicted outcome of electoral competition on the basis of assumed rationality thus comes to depend upon three factors: (i) the number of parties competing for office; (ii) the number of policy dimensions or axes (left–right, authoritarian–liberal, environmentalism–economic growth, and so forth) considered; and (iii) the distribution of voter preferences with respect to each axis. Unsurprisingly, the simpler the assumptions we make about the shape of the distribution, the number of axes and the number of parties, the simpler the calculation of expected outcomes.

Hotelling, as befits the founder of the spatial model of voting behaviour, chooses the simplest possible assumptions – that only one axis is relevant, that this axis can be assumed to be linear and that voters are distributed equally along it (such that the probabilities of a citizen's views lying at any point along the axis are identical). He also assumes that all citizens will vote and that they will vote for the party closest (numerically) to their position along the axis. On the basis of such assumptions, it is simple to derive the hypothesis than in a two-party electoral system, the parties will tend to converge on the median voter.

Take the example depicted in figure 3.1. Party 'a' lies at position 25 (P_a) towards the left side of a left–right axis running from 0 to 100. Party 'b' lies at position 85 (P_b), rather further to the right side of this axis, along which voters are distributed equally. In this situation (at time t), the difference between the two parties (D_{b-a}) is 60 units (P_b – P_a). Accordingly, voters at position 55 [P_a + (D_{b-a}/2)] find themselves equidistant from the two parties. All those to the right of this position vote for party b, all those to the left vote for party a. Consequently, party a wins with 55 per cent of the vote, with party b gaining the remaining 45 per cent. If party b is to do anything about this situation in subsequent elections (at t + 1, t + 2, etc.), it can do so rationally only by moving to the left and towards party a. In anticipation of this, party a may seek to take pre-emptive action by moving towards the right and towards party b. The result is a race to the centre – to the position of the median voter (at position 50). In what is now in effect a multi-round game, electoral outcomes at future elections are determined by the pace at which the parties accommodate themselves to the median voter – the party that is likely to become the 'natural' (indeed permanent) party of government being that which gets to the median position quickest.

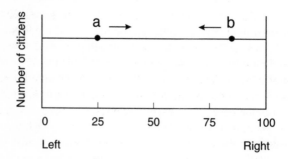

Figure 3.1   Hotelling's spatial model of bipartisan (electoral) competition

Smithies (1941) revises Hotelling's assumptions somewhat and introduces the possibility that not all citizens will choose to vote in a situation where there is a large disparity between their views and those of the parties competing for their vote. In particular, he notes, demand for the utilities offered by a party may, like demand for consumption goods, be *elastic*. Just as the consumer may decide that the sausages are not worth the trip to the butcher's shop at the other end of the village, so the citizen may decide that it is simply not worth voting for a party whose policies are quite so far from those which would maximise his/her perceived utility. The 'leakage' of voters disgusted by their party's drift towards the centre may then halt, or at least mediate, the tendency of parties to convergence on the median voter.

Consider the example in figure 3.2. Here we adapt the assumptions governing the voting behaviour of citizens in the previous example. Citizens will abstain from voting if *both* the following pertain: (i) the party closest to them is over 20 positions away; *and* (ii) their own preferences are nearer to the end of the left–right axis than the party closest to their preferences. Thus, for instance, a citizen at position 4 will not vote for party a at position 25 (and will in fact abstain), but (whilst party b remains at position 95) a citizen at position 50 would vote for party a. The second additional assumption can be dropped if we assume 'symmetrical elasticity' (that the median voter will abstain if either party is over 20 points away). However, if we are seeking to model the leakage of dissatisfied extremists with a party's drift towards the centre, then the second assumption is required. In figure 3.2, the lightly shaded area represents those who vote for party a, the darker shaded area those who vote for party b and the unshaded area those who abstain.

In the first scenario (at time t), party a is at position 25, party b at position 95. Those at position 60 $[P_a + (D_{b-a}/2)]$ find themselves equidistant from both parties (although the number of citizens *exactly* at position 60 and *exactly* equidistant approaches zero). Accordingly, those to the right of position 60 vote for party b, which thereby secures 40 per cent of the vote. Those to the left of position 60 vote for party a, except those to the left of position 5 (for whom the party is simply too far to the centre). Accordingly, party a secures 55 per cent of the vote and wins the election. Five per cent abstain.

This creates a clear incentive for party b to move towards party a and the centre. However, any tendency for party a to take pre-emptive action by itself moving to the centre is tempered significantly by the

Situation I (at time t):
party a at position 25; party b at position 95

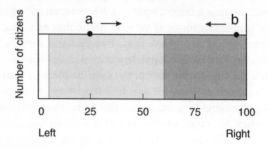

Situation II (at time t + 1):
party a at position 25; party b at position 80

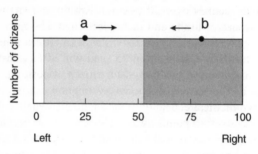

Situation III (at time t + 2):
party a at position 25; party b at position 75

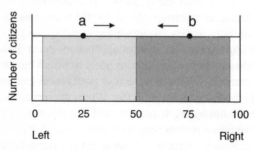

Figure 3.2 Bipartisan competition with elastic demand

(rational) fear of vote leakage. In fact, in this particular example, party a is best to stay where it is (or to move to any position between 20 and 25). In the second situation (at time t + 1), party a has remained at position 25 whilst party b has moved to position 80. Here, any voter to the right of position 52.5 will vote for party b, whilst any voter to the left of position 52.5 and to the right of position 5 will vote for party a. The result is a tie, in which both parties secure 47.5 per cent of the vote. Again, 5 per cent abstain.

In the third scenario (at time t + 2), party b moves further to the centre, to position 75, in an attempt to improve further its share of the vote. The cost of so doing, however, is that those to the right of position 95 now rationally abstain. Here, then, those between positions 5 and 50 vote for party a, whilst those between positions 50 and 95 vote for party b. The result is, again, a tie, but one in which both parties' share of the vote falls to 45 per cent as 10 per cent of the electorate now abstain. In fact, a dynamic equilibrium has now been established. If party a limits any movements it might make to those between positions 20 and 25 and party b restricts itself to movement between positions 75 and 80, no party can win. To maximise their share of the vote, however, party a and party b will in fact diverge, moving to positions 20 and 80, respectively.

The specific details are relatively insignificant, dependent as they are largely on our choice of initial assumptions (especially those governing demand elasticity and voter leakage). Yet what this example does serve to establish is that if we assume elastic demand, then any rational movement of parties in a bipartisan system towards the median will be halted by leakage effects. Nonetheless, as Downs himself notes, 'at exactly what point this leakage checks the convergence of A and B depends upon how many extremists each loses by moving towards the centre compared with how many moderates it gains thereby' (p. 117).

At this point it is somewhat chastening to recall the crass simplicity of the assumptions governing the models of both Smithies and Hotelling. In particular, both assume that preferences can be distributed evenly along a single, linear scale. Whilst the premise that only one axis is relevant to voting behaviour and that this axis is linear can be nothing other than a distorting simplification, it may well be a plausible assumption to make in certain situations (especially those in which class is not thought to influence significantly voting behaviour). The assumption of an equal distribution of preferences along, say, a

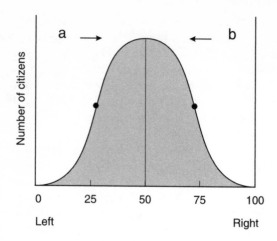

Figure 3.3   A normal distribution of preferences: bipartisan convergence

left–right axis is, however, grossly implausible. Enter Downs, whose major contribution is to contemplate and to consider the consequences of a variable distribution of voters along the scale. As he shows, the precise shape of the distribution of preferences now determines to a significant extent the behaviour of the parties and, hence, tendencies to convergence or divergence (compare figures 3.3 and 3.4).

In figure 3.3, there is a normal distribution of preferences about a mean of 50. If parties a and b are placed at positions 25 and 75, respectively, there is a clear tendency for them to converge over time towards the centre. Moreover, even if we allow for elastic demand, the convergence tendency will hardly be tempered at all, since voters lost at the margins (where the density of preferences is low) are likely to be more than compensated for by those gained at the centre (where the density of preferences is much higher). Electoral competition on the basis of such initial conditions is thus likely to be characterised by a rapid race to the position of the median voter.

In figure 3.4, by contrast, the tendency will be for the parties to stay apart or even diverge (depending on the precise starting points of the parties). Here the distribution of preferences is bimodal (with twin peaks). The rational course of action for each party is to ensure that it maximises the votes it might obtain from one of the two peaks in the distribution. It might be thought that if one peak is larger than the

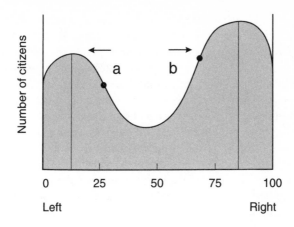

Figure 3.4   A bimodal distribution of preferences: bipartisan divergence

other, there would be a tendency for the party closest to the smaller peak (in this case party a) to gravitate towards the centre. However, under conditions of elastic demand, such a move would be checked rapidly by the disaffection of voters at the extreme. The effect of any such leakage from the extreme (where the density of preferences is now high) is likely to outweigh considerably the potential gain from converts at the centre (where the density of preferences is now far lower). In such a situation, if the distribution of preferences remains constant and party b behaves rationally, it simply cannot lose.

In examples like this, Downs demonstrates that the expected outcomes of his spatial theory of electoral competition are extremely sensitive to changes in the initial assumptions concerning the preferences distribution of potential voters. In many respects this is a very significant concession, since Downs provides neither a theory which would allow us to derive the preference function of the electorate (on the basis, say, of assumed rationality), nor a methodological discussion of the means by which to establish empirically the shape of the distribution. We are, then, forced to fall back on assumptions as to the pattern of citizens' preference functions which are, at best, intuitive and, at worst, completely arbitrary.

In fact, for the purposes of most of his analysis, Downs simply assumes a unimodal and near-normal distribution of preferences along a single (left–right) axis.[7] Accordingly, despite acknowledging that 'a basic determinant of how a nation's political life develops is the distribution of voters along the political scale' (p. 140), he can, nonetheless, conclude that 'in two-party systems, each party will try to resemble its opponent as closely as possible' (p. 127). The consequence of this is that if preferences prove stable over time, it is likely to be a condition of any change in government that it is not accompanied by a significant change in policy. There are only two factors, he goes on to note, which mediate this consensual tendency within a bipartisan political system. The first is the fear of voter leakage. Yet this, as discussed above, is likely to be of fairly minor significance if preferences are indeed stable and normally distributed. The second is the fear that if parties threaten to converge completely – their policy programmes becoming identical – then at some stage in this process a point must surely be reached at which electoral turnout will plummet dramatically and the polity will effectively cease to function as a democracy (there being no possible reason why anyone should vote). This is an interesting and important point, all the more so when it is considered that although it is in the long-term collective interest of both parties to preserve reasonable levels of political participation, it is unlikely to be in the immediate interest of either party to take the unilateral action required to address this pathology. In most rational and public choice theoretical models, the identification of the very possibility of such a 'free-rider problem' is sufficient to ensure that the worst case scenario is indeed realised. Downs' faith in the willingness of parties in this situation to sacrifice their own potential advantage appears, then, by the standards of rational choice theory, somewhat naive.

Either way, the logic of Downs' analysis of electoral competition within two-party democratic systems is to establish a seemingly inexorable tendency towards bipartisan convergence. It is this conclusion that has motivated a certain return to Downs by analysts and commentators on electoral competition in contemporary Britain.

On Downs' ups and downs: is New Labour 'Downsian'?

It is somewhat perverse, if not perhaps particularly surprising, that the currency of Downs' spatial theory of party competition – at least amongst British political scientists – tends to wax and wane roughly in proportion to the extent to which its predictions seem to be borne out by contemporary developments. It was fashionable in the late 1950s and for much of the 1960s, less so in the 1970s and 1980s, and is now undergoing something of a renaissance as we approach the millennium. For proponents of a theory (if that is indeed what it is) which would claim to be general and trans-historical, this is hardly comforting. Nonetheless, as a theoretical device, Downs' model retains a certain heuristic value and an intuitive appeal. Moreover, that a considerable number of commentators in recent years have been struck by the similarities between contemporary British political competition and that described in rather more abstract terms in Downs' model is not merely testament to the timelessness of the latter's appeal. It also indicates much about the character of contemporary British democracy and the competition between the parties which animates it.

This presents us with a certain evaluative paradox. How do we assess both the contemporary condition of British political competition and Downs' economic theory of democracy in the light of the (suggested) affinities between the two? Two questions naturally present themselves. Though related, I want to suggest that it is imperative that we keep them separate. They are:

1 To what extent, if any, can electoral competition in contemporary Britain be *described* adequately and usefully in terms of a Downsian economic theory of democracy?
2 To what extent, if any, can electoral competition in contemporary Britain be *explained* and *accounted for* adequately in terms of a Downsian economic theory of democracy?

My reason for keeping these questions distinct is simple. I want to suggest that although the Downsian model of electoral competition might indeed provide a useful and, above all, a suggestive *description* of contemporary British democracy, it can in no way *explain* the nature of party competition in this context. We will come to the descriptive accuracy (or otherwise) of Downs' model presently. But it is important to establish (indeed, to re-establish) at the outset precisely why Downs' economic theory of democracy is no contender as a *theory* of party competition in Britain today (or, for that matter, at any other point in its recent past). Whilst a number of points could be made here, two are of particular significance.

First, as argued in the introduction to this chapter, the status of a theory constructed on the basis of assumptions whose implausibility (even inaccuracy) is freely admitted by the theorist must surely be questioned. Accordingly, even if such a theory could predict with unerring accuracy the outcome of every electoral competition in every polity over a given (and extensive) period of time, I do not see how one could legitimately claim to explain any one of those results with respect to such a theory. Yet this is not the predicament with which we are faced. Quite simply, the predictions of the Downsian theory of electoral competition – a general theory, we should recall – fail to correspond with empirical outcomes in many more situations than they are confirmed. Given, then, that we are not likely to find ourselves particularly impressed by the weight of confirming evidence, the interesting question becomes this: *under what conditions do parties and voters behave in a manner consistent with Downsian assumptions?*

In posing this question I am not seeking a general answer. Clearly, a whole variety of different social, political and economic contexts might generate electoral behaviour consistent with a Downsian theory. What is of interest to the present study are the specific conditions under which New Labour has come to play the 'politics of catch-up' in a seemingly Downsian manner. What I will argue is that such conditions are in fact largely ideational and contingent: New Labour has learned to play the politics of catch-up by Downsian rules largely because it has come to accept (for a variety of reasons) many of the assumptions which inform such a theory of electoral competition. That this is so, as I will attempt to demonstrate, should, however, be taken neither as evidence of the validity of such assumptions (nor of the theory to which it gives rise), nor of the direct influence of Downs' theory on the party's strategic thinking.

New Labour's assumptions about the immediate electoral context within which it had to compete for office can be grouped, usefully, into four categories: (i) those relating to the relative fixity or flexibility of societal perceptions and preferences; (ii) those relating to the shape of the distribution of societal preferences; (iii) those relating to the dangers of leakage effects and extremist disaffection; and (iv) those relating to the strategies and techniques appropriate for electoral competition in such a context. In each category, there is considerable overlap between the assumptions informing the Downsian economic theory of democracy and New Labour's politics of catch-up. I consider each in turn.

(1) Preference fixity: a 'new model party' with
a new model of party competition

The debate on the relative merits of preference-shaping and preference-accommodating electoral strategies for Labour following the
party's fourth consecutive electoral defeat in 1992 exposed a series of
fundamental disagreements between the protagonists (see for instance
the exchange between Hay 1994; Smith 1994 and Wickham-Jones
1995a). On one thing, however, the authors were united – Labour had
in 1992 and, arguably in 1987, adopted a principally preference-
accommodating strategy. In so doing, it had either discounted the
possibility of shaping preferences or had simply assumed that such
preferences were, at least for the purposes of electoral strategy, fixed.
Accordingly, if the party were indeed out of tune with the aspirations
and expectations of the electorate (as its ever fading recollections of
office would seem to suggest), then it was presented with a stark
choice: adapt or perish.

As the recent political history of the party demonstrates, from 1983
onwards and perhaps with greater alacrity and effect from 1987, Labour
sought to accommodate and temper its more radical instincts to the
extant preferences of the electorate. In so doing, as Eric Shaw notes, it
underwent something of a 'strategic paradigm shift' (1994: 55–60),
becoming, in the process, a 'positioning' as distinct from a 'programmatic' party (Epstein 1980). This transformation was accompanied by
an expansion and, above all, professionalisation of the party's cam-
paigning and communications strategy. With the establishment of the
Campaign Strategy Committee in October 1983, the party now came to
adopt, with growing frequency, advertising and marketing strategies.
These were deployed as a means not only of 'getting its message
across' but, increasingly, of refining, defining and redefining that
message in tune with evidence of voter preferences. Nonetheless, at this
relatively early stage, the emphasis was still upon presenting the party
in such a way as to maximise its existing affinities with the electorate,
rather than responding directly to the electorate's preferences with
policy modifications. Given the still rather diffuse nature of policy-
making within the party, this was simply the best that could be
achieved. The strategy is well summarised by Shaw in the following
terms:

> The party should, in the main, concentrate its communications effort
> on maximising the saliency of those matters where it was most in line

with popular sentiment, such as health and education, and strive as far
as possible to neutralise or exclude from the agenda issues such as
industrial relations and defence, where it had few hopes of evoking a
supportive response. (1994: 61; see also Hewitt and Mandelson 1989)

With the growing, if initially incremental, centralisation of policy-
making within the party under Kinnock's leadership, this would
change. Thus, by the Policy Review, the possibility existed for the first
time of gauging voter preferences as a relatively direct means to the
revision of policy (Hughes and Wintour 1990). The party would now
come to employ and deploy, with ever greater frequency and with ever
growing political significance, the services of dedicated market research
specialists such as Philip Gould. The latter's focus groups – conducted
with carefully selected (former) Tory voters in marginal middle-
England constituencies – became a thing of legend in the run-up to the
1997 election campaign, contributing significantly to Labour's revision
of policy in that period.[8] As Leo Panitch and Colin Leys note, the
influence of such new professional strategists served further to re-
inforce two crucial shifts in the party's electoral politics.

First, electors were now seen primarily *as consumers of party programmes, with already-given attitudes and interests,* rather than as
people who could be persuaded to find their needs and aspirations met
in the party's projects for social change.... Second, editors and journalists were treated as the arbiters of what it was sensible for the party to
advocate, in a way that even National Executive members were not.
(1997: 221; emphasis added)

By 1997, then, Labour had developed a highly sophisticated repertoire of techniques for assessing public opinion (particularly that of
'floating voters' in the marginal electoral battleground of middle
England) and for revising policy in the light of such assessments. A
more distinctly Downsian strategy could scarcely be imagined.

(2) The distribution of voter preferences
If New Labour's assumptions regarding the essential (or at least effective) fixity of voter preferences were, by the mid-1980s, in essence
Downsian, then its assumptions about the distribution of such preferences were no less so. Two points are, perhaps, of particular significance
in this respect. First, Labour clearly came to believe in the wake of its
1983 election debacle that, whatever the specific distribution of voter

preferences, the party was far to the left of the median (for evidence to the contrary see Heath *et al*. 1985: 89; Wickham-Jones 1996: 189–91). Assuming preference fixity, there could only be one explanation for this – in response to electoral defeat the party had simply lurched in the wrong direction. Between 1979 and 1983, the party had pitched leftwards, thereby alienating its more moderate supporters, who flocked in droves to the Conservatives and the Social Democratic Party. Such an analysis might not, at first, appear to imply much about the specific shape of the distribution of voter preferences in this context – merely that Labour was far to the left of the median and would be rewarded by moving towards it. Yet that Labour could believe this to be the case, in and of itself, implied a quite fundamental rethinking of the party's traditional conception of the distribution of voter interests (and hence preferences).[9] This may seem counterintuitive and requires some explanation.

Traditionally, Labour was a class party. As such, in so far as it subscribed to a view of the distribution of voter interests and preferences, it did so in terms of a class-divided society and in terms of a conflict of interest (and hence preferences) between the working class on the one hand and the bourgeoisie (in its various guises) on the other. Such a conception logically implied (without ever explicitly positing) a bimodal distribution of (potential) voter preferences (such as that in figure 3.4). If we assume this to be the case, whilst Labour in 1983 might indeed have moved well to the left of the median voter, it is not at all clear that this electoral misfortune could simply be turned around by a quick jump to the right (to a position of lower preference density on the graph). An alternative diagnosis of the party's predicament, consistent with the persistence of a class-divided society, would be that the overall size of the working class had diminished and was, perhaps, insufficient to secure a majority on its own. Under such painfully familiar conditions, social democratic parties have traditionally sought to shape the preference function of the electorate by building alliances with fractions of the middle classes (offering various incentives and hence transforming interests and, in turn, preferences) in the attempt to reconstitute an electoral majority (or winning minority).

In establishing for itself the electoral expediency of cultivating the median voter ('Mondeo man'?), Labour from the mid-1980s onwards came to reject such a bimodal view of the distribution of voters' preferences. In so doing it came instead to rely on a rather more Downsian conception – of a unimodal and normally distributed pattern of preferences. Arguably, it did so not because it became converted to a Downsian view of electoral competition under the influence of a new clutch of psephologists, but because it came to accept the class dealignment thesis. Quite simply, if class was no longer a significant determinant of voting behaviour, there was no reason to suppose that the distribution of voter preferences should be bimodal. Accordingly, as a matter of self-preservation, the party would have to reproject itself as a catch-all party and begin a studious courting of the median voter.

(3) The dangers of disaffection
If Labour came to assume, as I suggest it did, that the preferences of the electorate were, with respect to electoral strategy, essentially fixed and that they were normally distributed about a median some way to its right, then its strategy of preference-accommodation was, of course, entirely rational. According to Downs, then, only two factors could serve to slow or even halt its rightward drift: (i) the fear of left dis-affection and voter leakage; and (ii) the fear that by aping the policies of the Conservatives, voters would come to perceive no difference between the parties, calling the very nature of British democracy into question as electoral turnout would plummet.

Whilst we might take the significant drop in turnout in the 1997 election (the lowest in any modern general election) as evidence of precisely this latter perception on the part of the electorate, we would, I think, be profoundly mistaken to do so. Although the fall in turnout is certainly alarming, there is little evidence to suggest that voters perceived no difference between the parties. Moreover, and perhaps more significantly, they anticipated rather different outcomes from the two parties in power even on issues where there was no ostensible policy difference between them at the election. It is more likely, then, that in so far as the drop in turnout reflects the conduct of electoral competition in contemporary Britain (rather than any longer-term secular trend), it can best be accounted for in terms of voter leakage. Thus, as David Denver and Gordon Hands note in a careful analysis of turnout at the 1997 election:

> the evidence does suggest that there was a tendency for past and potential Labour supporters to stay away from the polls in larger numbers ... there is a substantial section of the electorate – concen-trated in poor, inner city areas but not confined there – [whose] engagement with democratic politics is slight. Whether this indicates disaffection, lack of interest or a pragmatic response to the alternatives

offered is not clear, but this is certainly an issue to which the parties ought to give some attention. (1997: 224)

The Downsian model would suggest that a 'rational' party, such as Labour, would indeed give some attention to this potential outcome *before* the election – and discount it. For, as Labour's landslide would certainly suggest – and as any more detailed scrutiny could hardly fail to confirm – Labour did not (nor was it ever likely to) lose out on the basis of working-class and left disaffection. Quite apart from anything else, those electoral constituencies in which turnout declined most precipitously (in particular those in the north-east of England) were invariably those with the most insurmountable Labour majorities (a factor which may, in turn, have contributed to citizens' decisions not to exercise their vote). Accordingly, in purely instrumental terms, if Labour could adopt policies which would appease the median voter in middle-class, middle England, at the cost of irritating to the point of disaffection its most loyal and traditional supporters in seats it could scarcely fail to win, this was likely to prove a positive-sum game. Labour could, again in a manner entirely consistent with Downsian assumptions, happily discount voter leakage or left disaffection as a price it was very willing to pay for the instrumental gains it might buy.

(4) Strategies of electoral competition:
bypassing the median voter?
This brings us finally, and fairly directly, to the strategies appropriate to electoral competition in a context in which preferences are understood to be fixed and normally distributed and in which the effects of 'extremist' disaffection can be discounted.

In particular, it allows us to deal with the observation – made recently and on the basis of detailed empirical evidence by John Curtice (1997) – that, in seeking to accommodate electoral preferences, Labour had moved some time before the 1997 election to a position significantly to the right of the median voter. How can we account for this seemingly bizarre anomaly?

The answer is, in fact, fairly simple and, once again, largely consistent with Downsian assumptions. Three separate factors need to be noted. First, as a 'rational' (for which read 'instrumental') vote-maximising party, yet one which until recently claimed for itself a working-class social base, Labour may well suffer the consequence of the associations and connotations its very name conjures. As Andrew

Gamble notes, shedding policies is one thing, shedding images is an altogether more difficult and, generally, a more lengthy process (1992: 61). Accordingly, then, for voters to believe that Labour in government would not revert to its traditional policies – and, in particular, to the 'profligacy' with which it became symbolically (however unfairly) associated during the late 1970s – the party may have moved rather further to the right (in policy terms) than the median. If Labour was naturally seen as party of the left, it may well have overshot the median to be seen even as a party of the centre.

Second, Labour can (and could throughout the 1980s and early 1990s) fairly safely assume that it will not be challenged to any significant extent in Britain's first-past-the-post electoral system by either new or revitalised parties of the left. Accordingly, particularly given the geo-graphical distribution of its traditional constituencies (discussed above), it could simply assume that the majority of the left would vote Labour almost regardless of the policies for which the party came to stand. As a consequence, Labour could effectively recalculate the median having discounted all those on the left with nowhere else to turn. The revised median to which New Labour sought to accommodate itself was thus somewhere to the right of the median of the total population.

Finally, and relatedly, since 1987 the party has increasingly sought to accommodate itself not to the preferences of the electorate as a whole, but to those of floating voters in marginal constituencies. In so doing, it has come, quite rationally, to define the electoral battleground extremely narrowly. This sub-population (of floating voters in middle-class, middle-England marginals) is hardly representative of the population and its median is likely to lie somewhere to the right of that for the electorate as a whole.

All three factors would suggest that it is indeed rational, in purely instrumental terms, for a party, like Labour, pursuing a preference-accommodating strategy, to adopt a policy stance somewhere to the right of the median voter. Whether it is rational for a party which would claim to be anything other than an opportunistic instrument of vote maximisation is another matter altogether.

Conclusions: the dangers of Downsianism

In this chapter I have sought to examine why quite so many authors should have been quite so impressed to remark on the similarities between electoral competition in contemporary Britain and the Downsian economic theory of democracy. I have argued that the Downsian theory of electoral competition can in no sense be held to explain or account for Labour's modernisation nor the politics of catch-up in which, in recent years, it has indulged. At the same time, however, it offers a disarmingly accurate (if clearly somewhat simplified) description of that politics. As such, it provides an extremely useful heuristic device, suggestive of the assumptions informing Labour's electoral strategy in recent years.

That Labour has behaved in a manner seemingly consistent with Downsian assumptions clearly requires some explanation. Three potential answers naturally present themselves:

1 that the Downsian theory of electoral competition is in fact correct and New Labour behaves in a manner consistent with its predictions and assumptions because it is a rational party;
2 that whether the Downsian theory of electoral competition is correct or not, Labour believes it to be correct and, as a 'rational' party, constructs its rationality in the image of that presented in the theory;
3 that Labour strategists are largely unaware of the Downsian theory of electoral competition but have nonetheless come to embrace assumptions which are broadly congruent with it – accordingly, they 'act Downsian' without necessarily 'thinking Downsian'.

As I have been at pains to demonstrate, the first answer can be readily dismissed. The second is, I think, largely implausible. Whilst Labour has certainly drawn upon the advice of a number of political scientists and psephologists operating with (modified) Downsian assumptions, arguably Labour's electoral strategy in recent years owes rather more to professional market researchers and advertising executives than it does to psephologists. Yet herein lies the irony. For both political advertising and political market research, unremarkably, rely upon an implicit economic theory of democracy. Indeed, their most fundamental premise is that electoral competition is analogous to the competition for market share amongst capitalist entrepreneurs. This, we should recall, is Downs' starting point; we have come full circle. Labour may well have imported a (quasi-Downsian) economic theory of democracy into its electoral practice by drawing on the services of those who increasingly come to define what capitalist entrepreneurialism means to capitalist entrepreneurs. Colin Leys' description of Labour's new electoral politics as 'market-research socialism' (1990) could scarcely then be more apt.

If much of the analysis of this chapter has been concerned to demonstrate the extent to which New Labour's electoral politics might be regarded as Downsian, this should not lead us to overlook the dangers of such a strategy. A few cautionary remarks may serve to provide an appropriate conclusion. The dangers of Downsianism are, basically, fourfold:

1 As noted by Eric Shaw (1994: 174–80), such a strategy tends to a certain defensiveness, even fatalism, which may serve to validate and thereby legitimate the policies of the incumbent administration whilst effectively precluding a principled critique of the policy paradigm adopted by the latter.
2 Accordingly, such a strategy tends to yield electoral benefits at precisely the point at which it proves impossible for the incumbent administration to continue to demonstrate competence within the existing policy paradigm – a paradigm which may now also come to ensnare the incoming government.
3 In serving to bring the parties together, the studious courting of the median voter may also serve to amplify the significance of potentially minor policy differences on relatively inconsequential issues, as well as minor gaffes and strategic errors of judgement during election campaigns. Kinnock's unfortunate and rather misinterpreted remarks during the 1987 election campaign on the possibilities of occupation by Soviet troops provide an obvious example (Hughes and Wintour 1990: 28–9; Shaw 1994: 77–9).
4 It is far easier for the incumbent administration to gain, maintain and, indeed, to lose perceived competence for political and economic management than it is for an opposition party espousing very similar policies to do so. Consequently, parties deploying Downsian strategies may well have to wait for the incumbent administration to prove itself incompetent before the benefits of preference-accommodation are likely to be rewarded by office. The significance of Black Wednesday to Labour's election victory in 1997 should not, in this context, be underestimated.

Whether, in the end, it is rational to be Downsian, and hence rational to be 'rational', is a debatable point and relies on an essentially

normative judgement. Yet, whatever one might think of it, the Downsian analogy would seem to provide an interesting and potentially
suggestive perspective on New Labour's ups and downs.

Notes

1 Interestingly, in their useful review of the literature on New Labour,
   Michael Kenny and Martin Smith (rightly) identify as a distinct approach
   the Downsian perspective (1997b). They can, however, find only two
   sources in which, they suggest, it has been applied. One of these is an
   American study published in the 1960s (Kirscheimer 1966); the other
   makes no (explicit) reference to Downs at all (Hay 1994).
2 The recent discussion by David Sanders is perhaps the most comprehensive in this regard to date (1998: especially 216–17).
3 Nobel Laureate Douglass North's comment that 'very few economists ...
   really believe that the behavioural assumptions of economics [and, by
   extension, rational choice theory] accurately reflect human behaviour' is,
   in this context, not only remarkable but surely highly significant (1990:
   17; see also Ward 1995).
4 Or, indeed, to be well enough informed to know where it is.
5 As Dunleavy notes, this assumption of fixed preferences, though clearly
   limiting, is imported directly from neo-classical economics, where it is
   almost invariably adopted (1991: 99). For a rare attempt to model
   changes in preferences and hence to endogenise them within an economic analysis see von Weizsacker (1971).
6 We will assume, for now, that there is no out-of-town hypermarket, nor a
   black market in sausages produced by the villagers themselves.
7 Downs seeks to escape the charge that in so doing he is making an
   arbitrary judgement by pointing (in a footnote) to what he sees as the
   political instability likely to result from a bimodal distribution of preferences such as that depicted in figure 3.4. Since, he argues, no democracy
   exhibiting such a preference distribution can function effectively for long
   as a democracy, it is fair to assume that preference distributions in
   actually existing democracies are rather closer to that in figure 3.3.
   Suffice it to note that this strangely convoluted and functionalist logic
   does not bear terribly close scrutiny.
8 Gould is reputed to have responded to criticisms that such a strategy
   represented something of a capitulation to the rather reactionary nature of
   public opinion after almost two decades of Conservative government in
   the following terms: 'this is democracy – asking the people what they
   want and giving it to them'. The rather specific socio-economic profiles
   of those *chosen* to participate in Gould's focus groups would suggest that

such a conception of (elite) democracy may serve to disenfranchise rather more citizens than it incorporates.

9 The party had, traditionally, assumed a simple correspondence between preferences and interests in a class-divided society.

4 That Was Then, This Is Now: the politics of conspicuous convergence

In the previous two chapters, my aim has been to establish the political conditions, motivations and perceived exigencies of Labour's modernisation and the Downsian logic of political convergence that they have served to consolidate. In this chapter, I turn in rather more detail to the consequences – in particular, to the nature and extent of the resulting bipartisan convergence.

With the landslide electoral triumph of Tony Blair's New Labour, the question of the degree of convergence between Labour and the outgoing Conservatives in opposition takes on even greater strategic and political significance. It is generally undisputed that the terms of political debate in contemporary Britain have been altered markedly in recent years, and that this is not unrelated to Labour's self-styled 'modernisation' in the face of four consecutive election defeats. More contentious, however, is the interpretation of this trend. Has Labour abandoned its socialist and social democratic traditions, and reprojected itself as an essentially Conservative, even Thatcherite, party, or has it managed to develop a novel, dynamic and modernising social democracy for new times? In this chapter, I seek to provide an empirical benchmark of sorts against which such propositions can be evaluated and to assess the extent of bipartisan convergence since 1992. On the basis of comparisons of policy commitments at the 1992 and 1997 general elections, I argue that there has indeed been significant convergence between the parties, that this convergence has been driven principally by Labour and that Britain is witnessing the emergence of a new bipartisan consensus. Such an interpretation is further reinforced by a consideration of revisions to policy since the Tories' electoral debacle, which would merely seem to confirm the ascendancy of neo-liberalism in contemporary Britain. I conclude by considering the likely trajectory of social and economic policy under a New Labour administration with a seemingly unassailable parliamentary majority.

Mapping the contours of convergence

The interpretation of the British Labour Party's self-styled 'modernis-ation' since its 1987 election defeat continues to divide commentators, analysts and political scientists alike – as indeed it does many of the protagonists themselves. With Labour's first election victory in twenty-three years and its largest ever proportion of parliamentary seats, the stakes of this particular debate have been raised considerably. At issue is our assessment of the very nature and trajectory of the British state and economy and, indeed, the very future of social democracy as a political project in western Europe, North America and the antipodes. Are we witnessing a convergence between the parties that is in fact symptomatic of the consolidation of a new political settlement, replac-ing the ascendant 'Keynesian welfarist' paradigm of the post-war years? Or do a certain stylistic convergence and the somewhat contrived novelty which has tended to characterise New Labour's new-found appeal to the electorate merely serve to hide a basic divergence between underlying policy regimes? Moreover, does the unprecedented scale of Labour's recent landslide electoral victory serve to liberate the party *in government* from the self-imposed shackles of a neo-liberal economic and political paradigm that it has done much to espouse in opposition? Alternatively, does a reorientation of the global political economy in an era of financial liberalisation, capital flight and an at least putative globalisation usher in a new phase of capital ac-cumulation, circumscribing the parameters of the politically and economically possible – constraints to which both parties have in recent years simply accommodated themselves?[1]

In the context of such debates, the contribution of this chapter is a modest one. Its aim is neither to explain the distinctive character of political debate and competition in contemporary Britain (whether this is held to be consensual or adversarial), nor to engage in a normative evaluation of Labour's chosen electoral strategy – issues I have attempted to leave to other chapters. Rather, my aim is to provide some basic parameters within which such a debate can occur. Accordingly, I assess the proposition that British politics is characterised by an emergent consensus, by identifying the extent of the convergence between the parties between 1992 and 1997. I go on to assess the strategic implications of Labour's unprecedented electoral triumph for the trajectory of institutional and constitutional reform under the new administration and consider the extent to which Labour is likely to remain within the (restrictive) bounds mapped out for itself in opposition. I argue that despite some significant revisions to manifesto pledges since 1 May (*New* Labour Day?), the first few months of Blair's presidential prime ministership merely provided further evidence of bipartisan convergence.

Bipartisan convergence? The evidence

On the basis of manifesto commitments, supporting policy documents and conference speeches, I identify clear policy differences between Labour and the Conservatives at the 1992 general election in a range of policy areas. These provide an (admittedly crude) baseline from which to assess the proposition that there has been a significant policy convergence between the parties *since 1992* and that this convergence is largely the consequence of revisions *by the Labour Party* to preexisting policy commitments.[2] On each of the issues that divided the parties in 1992, I consider Labour's proposals at the 1997 general election, categorising any policy shifts in terms of convergence and divergence. The results are presented and interpreted in the sections which follow. They are summarised in tables 4.1–4.8 and 4.10–4.14.

Before turning to a detailed analysis of these results and an assessment of their significance for the 'convergence hypothesis', however, a couple of brief methodological qualifications are perhaps in order.

First, to assess the proposition that there has been a convergence between political parties over a given time frame requires a consideration of revisions to policy on *both sides* of the political spectrum. To produce evidence of policy change by one party to positions formerly associated with its political opponents need not imply convergence in a context of policy flux on both sides. Nonetheless, in the contemporary British context a concentration on the revision of Labour's policies in opposition can be justified. For, arguably, the key developments in policy terms since the Conservatives' fourth consecutive election victory have been made by Labour. While the Major government concerned itself with the management of the Thatcher legacy, Labour engaged in a systematic and 'modernising' review of policy, reprojecting itself as 'New Labour'. The party's relaunch under the increasingly presidential (even messianic) leadership of Tony Blair certainly suggests the value of an analysis of the extent of New

Labour's (much vaunted) novelty. Whilst the rhetoric of novelty was examined in chapter 1, it is the substance of that claim which is examined here.

Second, in its concentration on issues dividing the parties in 1992, such an analysis (on its own) gives limited attention to newly emerging policy differences. Such a bias is likely to exaggerate the extent of any convergence and resulting consensus between the parties. To compensate for this, policy differences between the parties that have emerged since 1992 will be considered separately.

In the sections which follow, the analysis of the British Labour Party's changing electoral commitments is grouped into five policy areas which are considered in turn: (i) labour-market regulation; (ii) education and training policy; (iii) welfare reform and social policy; (iv) economic and industrial policy; and (v) constitutional reform.[3]

Labour-market regulation: trade union reform and employment policy

The extent of convergence between the parties since the 1992 general election, and in particular in the extended run-up to the 1997 election, is striking and considerable. As argued in chapter 1, however, such changes must be situated in terms of a far longer process of reform, in which the party has slowly accommodated itself to the new and distinctly post-corporatist capital–labour relation that is a distinctive feature of the Thatcher legacy (see Dorey 1995; Howell 1995/6; Marsh 1992). Thus, Labour's 1992 election manifesto, *It's Time to Get Britain Working Again*, already forcefully proclaimed, in a theme reiterated throughout the campaign, 'there will be no return to the trade union legislation of the 1970s. Ballots before strikes and for union elections will stay. There will be no mass or flying pickets' (Labour Party 1992: 13).[4] Similar sentiments were echoed in New Labour's *Road to the Manifesto* document, *Building Prosperity: Flexibility, Efficiency and Fairness at Work*: 'the old approach of trade union immunities as the basis for legislation has gone.... There will be no blanket repeal of the main elements of 1980s' legislation' (1996a: 1). Again, in the 1997 election manifesto, *New Labour: Because Britain Deserves Better*: 'there will be no return to flying pickets, secondary action, strikes with no ballets or the trade union law of the

Table 4.1 Bipartisan convergence in Britain, 1992–7: trade union reform

	1992	1997	
Employees' charter	Labour: right to trade union representation	Both parties – no such right	+
Trade union recognition	Labour, yes; Conservatives, no	Labour, recognition dependent on majority workplace vote	+
Secondary picketing	Labour, legal under some circumstances; Conservatives illegal under all circumstances	Both parties – secondary picketing illegal	+
Strikers' rights	Labour, right to be reinstated if dismissed	Labour, right to take cases of unfair dismissal to tribunal	±
Rights of non-union members	Labour, rights through union membership; Conservatives, rights independent of membership	Labour, rights independent of membership	+
Public sector disputes	Labour, restoration of the right to strike, repeal of offending legislation	Labour, proposals to outlaw strike action in essential public services	+

+, policy convergence; –, clear policy difference; ±, qualified difference.

1970s ... we will leave intact the main changes of the 1980s legislation' (1997: 3, 15).[5] There is little to choose between these passages. In terms of Labour's acceptance, then, of the broad thrust of trade union reform in the Thatcher years, there would appear to be near consensus *by 1992*, a consensus merely further consolidated in the intervening years. Yet while this may well be the case, in 1992 there were nonetheless certain clear differences in the *texture* and, on occasion, substance of policy between the parties, reflecting some residual (if diminishing) loyalty on the part of Labour to its traditional allies in the labour movement (see, especially, Rosamond 1992).

These differences are starkly revealed if we consider modifications to Labour's stance on existing trade union legislation *since* 1992 (table 4.1). Indeed, the story of Labour's revisions to trade union policy under Blair's leadership in particular provides a powerful empirical reminder that no consensus is ever absolute and that policy convergence may continue in a context already characterised by underlying consensus.

Where Labour had, at least in principle, been committed to the universal right of the individual to be *represented* by a trade union, it was by 1996 committed only to the nominal right of that individual to *belong* to a union, where the capacity of that union to represent her was now rendered conditional upon a majority workplace vote. Where Labour had been committed to a reinstatement of the right of workers to engage in secondary picketing[6] (albeit under certain atypical conditions),[7] it was by 1996 unambiguously committed to the *status quo ante*. By the time of the 1997 general election, Labour had also withdrawn its unequivocal commitment to reinstate the right of public sector workers to engage in strike activity, in favour of compulsory and binding arbitration for all (legal) disputes concerning public sector employees in essential services. Where, moreover, the 1992 election manifesto had promised a restoration of the right of strikers to be reinstated if dismissed, the draft manifesto for the 1997 election merely promised that dismissed strikers would have the right to take their grievances to an industrial tribunal (a commitment dropped from the manifesto itself). More significantly perhaps, where Labour was still committed in 1992 to the principle that employment rights should in part be conferred through union membership, by 1997 this was replaced by a clear commitment to the principle of 'individual rights' which do not 'discriminate' between union and non-union members. As Tony Blair would himself boast in an interview given to Naomi

Klein of the *Toronto Star* less than a month before the election, 'the changes that we propose [to trade union legislation] would leave British law the most restrictive on trade unions in the Western world' (7 April 1997, cited in Panitch and Leys 1997: 254).

Finally, it is important to note New Labour's scarcely veiled warnings to the unions in the extended 1997 election campaign itself. If repeated hints to the media and a series of very public exercises in 'thinking aloud', most notably by Kim Howells,[8] were indicative of Labour's strategy for government,[9] one can only surmise that the new Labour administration will respond to any wave of union militancy by threatening to sever formal links between the party and the unions. This was, at least, the impression which the leadership apparently wished to convey to the electorate and the unions alike. If the events of the Winter of Discontent[10] (which, it should be recalled, hastened and heralded Labour's last departure from office) were to repeat themselves, New Labour would make sure that the boot would be on other foot this time around. Blair's Labour thus threatens to 'hold the trade unions to ransom', allowing a continuation of formal relations with its former fraternal allies only in return for good behaviour.

It is only in the light of such developments, and with the benefit of the hindsight that this affords, that the existence of a bipartisan consensus on trade union legislation in 1992 could be questioned.

If the legacy of Labour's 'modernisation' has been a clear convergence between the parties on trade union reform in the context of an already considerable bipartisan consensus, then its consequences for employment policy have been somewhat more ambiguous. Here, at least, significant policy differences can still be detected between the parties (table 4.2). These principally concern Labour's attitude to Europe.

Throughout the election campaign, New Labour remained committed to the Social Chapter of the Maastricht Treaty[11] and to the comparative labour-market re-regulation that this would entail (a commitment reflected in government by the speed with which Britain became a signatory of the Social Chapter). Nonetheless, even this seemingly unequivocal commitment and the (rare) continuity in policy it represents must be interpreted cautiously. In the party's 1992 manifesto, the Social Chapter was accepted enthusiastically as providing a much-needed European 'safeguard' against the worst ravages of unfettered competition (Labour Party 1992: 27). Yet, in a more recent statement of policy, *New Opportunities for Business*, as indeed in the

Table 4.2 Bipartisan convergence in Britain, 1992–7: employment law

	1992	1997	
Charter of rights	Labour, for all workers from start of employment	–	Both parties – no charter, unequal status for full- and part-time employees (unless through Europe)	+
Dismissal of part-time workers	Labour, right to tribunal hearing after six months; Conservatives, after one year	–	Labour, workers' access to tribunal after first year; Conservatives, after two years	±
Maastricht Social Chapter	Labour, unconditional acceptance	–	Labour, signatory, with selective opt-out	–
Labour-market regulation	Labour, committed to re-regulation; Conservatives, committed to further deregulation	–	Labour, 'no new rights for workers' (Blair); Conservatives, further labour-market deregulation	+

+, policy convergence; –, clear policy difference; ±, qualified difference.

manifesto itself, this enthusiasm was qualified somewhat (Labour Party 1996b, 1997). In a detailed statement of policy which consistently stressed the 'dangers of over-regulation', Labour proposed what was, in effect, a selective opt-out of Union-wide legislation passed in the name of the Social Chapter. Thus, although (at the time) committed to those (two) measures that had already been agreed within the framework of the Social Chapter, the document emphasised the need to overturn the Conservative government's 'empty chair policy' in order to maximise Britain's influence over European legislation in this area. The subtext to such a position (a subtext make explicit elsewhere)[12] was that it was only by taking a direct role in the shaping of future Social Chapter legislation that the 'social costs' of 'European-style' over-regulation of the labour market could be averted. Should this fail to secure the desired outcome, 'a Labour government would rigorously examine any proposals for further measures to ensure that they would not damage our competitiveness and support only those that bring real benefits and are appropriate to Britain' (Labour Party 1996b). This hardly represented an unequivocal acceptance of the spirit of the Social Chapter. Moreover, Blair's statement, following the election, of his principled objections to the extension to Britain of European-style works council legislation under the provisions of the Social Chapter would seem to compromise fundamentally the policy with which Labour approached the election – extending, as it does, the principle of a selective opt-out to legislation already approved.[13]

Yet despite such machinations, the Social Chapter does continue to divide the parties. The same cannot be said, however, for other aspects of Labour's revised and 'modernised' employment policy. Where once the party was committed to a 'charter of rights' for all workers, enshrining an equal status before the law for full- and part-time employees, such a re-regulation of the labour market can now come only by way of European legislation – legislation which a Labour government seems likely to oppose in the name of 'competitiveness'. The party that in 1992 wished to restore the rights of part-time workers employed for a minimum of six months to appeal their dismissal could, in the 1997 election campaign, only state its opposition to Tory plans to extend to two years the period within which employers could dismiss their employees with impunity. Where once Labour was committed to the principle and politics of labour market re-regulation, New Labour is committed, in Tony Blair's own memorable terms, to 'no new rights for workers' and to not allowing Britain to be 'bullied

by Brussels' into 'automatically accepting Continental-style employment policies'.[14]

Bipartisan convergence would, once again, appear to capture the
mood of the times.

Education and training policy

Revisions and modifications to Labour's education (table 4.3) and
training policies (table 4.4) since 1992 have also been significant,
reflecting the full gamut of changing principles, priorities, means and
ends. Echoing developments in western Europe and the advanced
capitalist economies more generally, Labour has replaced its emphasis
upon the need for an integrated 'national strategy for training' with a
more regionally and locally differentiated conception (on which see,
inter alia, Amin and Robins 1990; Amin and Thrift 1992; Best 1990;
Sabel 1994). Yet this is not the only modification to principle in recent
years. Since 1992, Labour has revised its commitment to training as a
primary responsibility of the state, joining with the Conservatives in
placing an ever growing emphasis upon the individual's civic duty to
avail herself of existing training opportunities. Arguably, New Labour
goes further even than the Conservatives in placing the burden on the
individual in its suggestion that state sponsorship of individually
targeted training programmes should be made conditional upon financial contributions by the trainee. This does, however, reveal a central
difference in the parties' positions: where New Labour is committed to
funding for training premised upon an individuated citizenship contract between the individual and the state, the Conservatives continue
to place their emphasis upon public–private partnerships and less
personalised training initiatives. Given its stress on the reciprocal
obligations and duties of the state and the individual, and its disavowal
of a nationally co-ordinated training strategy, it is perhaps unsurprising
that Labour abandoned its proposals for a national training fund based
on a 0.5 per cent payroll tax some time prior to the election. Yet in the
absence of such commitments and despite much rhetorical posturing
about the need to build a 'skills superpower' for an 'age of achieve-
ment',[15] it seems clear that neither party has yet proposed substantive
measures capable of raising significantly the skills base of the British
economy and of projecting a tech-rich, high-skill trajectory for Britain
on a European, far less world, stage. In the absence of such a strategy,

Table 4.3 Bipartisan convergence in Britain, 1992–7: education policy

	1992		1997	
Primary school class sizes	Labour, maximum 40; target maximum 30	–	Labour, target maximum of 30 for 5–7-year-olds only	±
Assisted Places Scheme	Labour, to be scrapped	–	Labour, to be scrapped	–
School maintenance	Labour, immediate public funding	–	Both parties, public–private partnership; school building prioritised by Labour	±
Selection at age eleven	Labour, end to selection at eleven; Conservatives, maximise 'consumer' choice	–	Both parties, selection to be retained	+
Control of grant-maintained schools	Labour, restore local authority control	–	Labour, may opt for partial local authority control (as foundation schools)	±
Tax on school fees	Labour, introduction of tax on school fees (a proposal only introduced after 1992 general election defeat)	–	Labour, no extension of value-added tax	+

+, policy convergence; –, clear policy difference; ±, qualified difference.

Table 4.4 Bipartisan convergence in Britain, 1992–7: training policy

	1992		1997	
National strategy for training	Labour, yes; Conservatives, no	–	Both parties – none; greater emphasis on local initiatives	+
National training fund – payroll tax	Labour, national training fund and payroll tax at 0.5 per cent	–	Both parties – no national fund, no payroll tax	+
Responsibility for training	Labour, state; Conservatives, private sector	–	Both parties – increasing emphasis on individual responsibility	+
Responsibility for funding	Labour, state; Conservatives, public–private partnership	–	Labour, state (conditional on individual's contribution); Conservatives, public–private partnership	±

+, policy convergence; –, clear policy difference; ±, qualified difference.

Britain would seem consigned to compete, as it does at present, on the basis of a comparatively unregulated labour market and correspondingly low wages.

Labour's proposals for the reform of primary and secondary education at the 1992 election, though themselves modest, also came in for significant dilution in the long lead-up to the 1997 election. Though New Labour remains resolutely committed (in government as in opposition) to reductions in primary-school class sizes, funded by the phasing out of the Assisted Places Scheme (itself an item of unambiguous policy continuity since 1992), these are now to be more selectively targeted at five- to seven-year-olds. Though Tony Blair restated during the campaign his pledge that there would be 'no return to the eleven plus',[16] New Labour nonetheless came to accept the principle of selection at eleven. It will not remove grammar school status from a single educational institution except under the (perhaps unlikely) circumstance that a majority of the pupils' parents vote for such a course of action.[17] Moreover, although Labour has proved consistent in its prioritisation of school-building and renovation, it was not, at the time of the election, committed to 'immediate public funding', and stressed instead the need to assemble public–private partnerships over a somewhat longer time frame. In seeming confirmation of this gradual convergence between the parties on education and training policy, Labour abandoned previous proposals to introduce value-added tax (at the current rate of 17.5 per cent) on school fees and to restore grant-maintained schools and city technology colleges to local authority control (allowing them instead to opt to become hybrid 'foundation schools').

Again, the evidence of this comparison would appear to suggest significant convergence since 1992, though in a policy area that had previously been somewhat more adversarial than most.

Welfare reform and social policy

It is perhaps fair to suggest that welfare reform and social policy (tables 4.5–4.8) have been depoliticised to some extent in recent years (for a similar, if much earlier, observation of this tendency see Alcock 1992). Both parties have acknowledged publicly (along with Christian democratic and nominally social democratic parties across western Europe as well as conservative and labour parties in the antipodes) what they perceive to be the threat posed to a comprehensive welfare

Table 4.5 Bipartisan convergence in Britain, 1992–7: pension provision

	1992		1997	
Public pension linkage	Labour, earnings linkage to be restored	–	Both parties, price-linked pensions	+
Public–private balance	Labour, preference for publicly funded pensions; Conservatives, preference for privately funded pensions	–	Both parties, preference for private pension schemes	+

+, policy convergence; –, clear policy difference; ±, qualified difference.

Table 4.6 Bipartisan convergence in Britain, 1992–7: family policy

	1992		1997	
Scope/scale of child benefit	Labour, child benefit to be increased; scope the same	–	Labour, child benefit to be replaced by means-tested allowance for 16–18-year-olds in full-time education	+
Ministry for Women	Labour, new Ministry and Cabinet post	–	Labour, no new Ministry; new unit within the Cabinet Office	±

+, policy convergence; –, clear policy difference; ±, qualified difference.

Table 4.7 Bipartisan convergence in Britain, 1992–7: National Health Service reform

	1992		1997	
Hospital trusts	Labour, responsibility to be restored to district health authorities	−	Labour, all local health services to manage own affairs; financial control to revert to Health Service, but not to district health authorities	±
Bureaucracy	Labour, review and reform of 'unnecessary' bureaucracy	−	Labour, £1.5 billion from scrapped bureaucracy to cut waiting lists	−

+, policy convergence; −, clear policy difference; ±, qualified difference.

Table 4.8 Bipartisan convergence in Britain, 1992–7: welfare/workfare

	1992		1997	
Personalised social security	Labour, general entitlement to social security	−	Labour, personalised 'career development plans', 'welfare-to-work'	+
Welfare or workfare?	Labour, principled objection to workfare	−	Labour, commitment to welfare-to-work programmes	±

+, policy convergence; −, clear policy difference; ±, qualified difference.

system by the liberalisation of capital flows, financial globalisation and the competitive imperative. Welfare expenditure is here conceived of as a drain on the competitive economy that can simply no longer be afforded at the levels to which we became accustomed in the post-war period.[18] This has produced some rather bizarre reversals of prior positions, with the spectacle of Harriet Harman (then shadow Social Security Secretary) denouncing the government for raising the level of public expenditure at a time of falling unemployment.

Within this broader context, recent revisions to Labour's former social policy commitments seem merely to confirm the impression of a more general 'welfare retrenchment consensus'. Yet this consensus is somewhat more complex and contradictory than it might first appear, as it involves a clear disarticulation of rhetoric and reality. For it seems to consist in both parties proffering the *rhetoric of retrenchment* (within whose chilling embrace the comprehensive welfare state must be sacrificed on the altar of international competitiveness) at a time when public expenditure continues to rise.[19]

If this somewhat schizophrenic consensus has become well established, this should not lead us to overlook perhaps the single most significant revision to Labour's welfare policy in recent years. Where the party was, in 1992, committed to the effective restoration of earnings-linked public pensions,[20] it approached the 1997 general election with no proposals to modify the Conservatives' price-indexation formula (see table 4.5).[21] On other areas of welfare and social policy, Labour's revisions to policy have been less significant, though once again their general direction has been one of convergence with the Conservatives (see also Sanders 1998: 234–5). New Labour now publicly declares its preference for private over public pension schemes, overturning a long-standing and principled commitment. Proposals for a Ministry for Women have now been downgraded as, by the time of the election, New Labour merely committed itself to the establishment of a 'dedicated unit' within the Cabinet Office. Child benefit for sixteen- to eighteen-year-olds in full-time education is now to be replaced by a means-tested education maintenance allowance, the specific details of which remained (as they remain today) 'under review' at the time of the general election. Despite the equivocation, however, this still overturns the party's previous commitment to preserving the scope and increasing the scale of such benefits.

With respect to the National Health Service (NHS), Labour remains committed to the reform of 'unnecessary' and 'inefficient' bureaucracy, promising at the election (and subsequently) to redeploy projected savings of £1.5 billion to cut waiting lists and improve patients' access to consultants. Yet where Labour was committed to returning NHS hospital trusts to district health authorities (DHAs) in 1992, it now proposes that all local health services will manage their own affairs. Though financial control will revert to the NHS, it will not be restored to DHAs.

On the question of the welfare–'workfare' balance, both parties now advocate some form of workfare or, in New Labour's rather euphemistic terms, 'welfare-to-work'.[22] Within such a framework, welfare is made conditional upon the recipient's conduct and, in many cases, menial work. This reflects a more general subordination of welfare programmes to economic imperatives (on which see Jessop 1995). Having reaffirmed its commitment to a general entitlement to social security and its resistance to any individuation of benefits at the 1992 election, New Labour in 1997 advocated the gradual replacement of 'blanket benefits' with personalised 'career development plans'. It proposed the introduction of welfare-to-work schemes for those aged between eighteen and twenty-five and the tightening of the criteria of eligibility for unemployment benefit (proposals specified in much fuller detail in Labour's first 'emergency' budget). Under a Labour government, benefit recipients of six months' standing *were* to lose 40 per cent of their benefit indefinitely if they refused to accept one of the welfare–workfare options presented to them (these include voluntary work and training).[23] However, the surprisingly punitive reforms announced by the Chancellor represent a significant tightening of these pre-election proposals, reiterating the now familiar refrain 'no rights without obligations'. Thus, in a measure which arguably goes further than anything attempted by the Conservatives, those aged between eighteen and twenty-five claiming dole for more than six months will now lose *all* entitlement to benefit as and when they refuse to take up one of the options presented to them within the government's welfare-to-work 'deal' (a job with an employer; work with a voluntary organisation; work on an environmental task force; or, for those without basic skills, full-time education or training).[24] As under the Conservatives' controversial 'job seekers' allowance', those deemed 'vulnerable' (those either pregnant or with dependants) would still lose 40 per cent of their benefit entitlement were they to fail to comply with their part of this 'welfare-to-work contract'. In seeming confirmation of Labour's workfare drift, a clear commitment to the repeal of the job

Table 4.9 Consolidating welfare retrenchment: Labour's changing attitude
to welfare reform

Retrenchment zone	Extent of retrenchment since 1979[a]	Labour manifesto, 1992	Labour manifesto, 1997
Pensions	High	Reversal[b]	Acceptance
Housing	High	Acceptance and encouragement	Acceptance and encouragement
Income support	Low	Token resistance[c]	Acceptance[d]
Health care	Low/medium[e]	Partial resistance[f]	Tinkering within the system[g]
Disability/ sickness	Low/medium	Reluctant acceptance[h]	Reluctant acceptance[h]

[a]Adapted from Pierson (1994: figure 4.1) and assessed in terms of the 'extent to which reforms seem likely to produce long-term changes in benefits and on the balance between public and private sectors' (p. 142).
[b]Commitment to restore earnings or price indexation, whichever was higher.
[c]No proposals to restore previous levels and eligibility criteria for unemployment and child benefit.
[d]Principle of benefit targeting accepted; proposals to restrict eligibility criteria for child benefit.
[e]Pierson regards the extent of reform as 'low' due to institutional inertia. Allowing for the specificity and complexity of the NHS system, however, such reform might better be regarded as 'low/medium'.
[f]NHS hospital trusts to be restored to DHAs.
[g]Savings from NHS bureaucracy to be used to cut waiting lists; all local health services to manage their own affairs.
[h]Despite protestations, no proposals to restore earnings indexation on disability benefits, or to lift the tax on sick pay.

seekers' allowance was withdrawn by Labour prior to the election. This should come as no great surprise. For, as Seumas Milne and Richard Thomas noted in their commentary on the 1997 budget in the *Guardian*, 'the sanction regime for the under 25s who refuse to take part in the [so-called] New Deal programme is essentially the same as that introduced as part of the Tory government's job seekers' allowance last year' (1997).

In assessing the consequences of such policy revision for the proposition of a growing 'welfare–workfare' consensus, we can usefully draw on Paul Pierson's (1994) analysis of the transformation of the welfare state in Britain since the late 1970s. Pierson identifies five key areas of welfare retrenchment and restructuring and assesses the degree of change in each domain. His analysis can be adapted and extended (by considering Labour's changing attitudes to welfare reform) to reveal the extent of any emerging bipartisan consensus and hence any emergent 'welfare–workfare' political settlement. Such an analysis is presented in table 4.9. It suggests that although there was already considerable acceptance by Labour of the new institutional architecture of the reformed welfare state by 1992, this accommodation to the legacy of the Thatcher years has merely been confirmed and entrenched by policy revisions since 1992 (and indeed subsequent to the 1997 election). If the British welfare state cannot be considered to have undergone a systematic *retrenchment* in the Thatcher years, as Pierson powerfully demonstrates, it has nonetheless been subject to significant and, in the context of the post-war period, unprecedented restructuring. The trajectory of Labour's 'modernisation' would then appear to indicate that Britain's emergent welfare–workfare regime is here to stay. It will continue to circumscribe the parameters of what is considered politically possible for both parties for the foreseeable future.

Economic and industrial policy

If there was already evidence of a considerable convergence *on welfare* prior to the 1992 election, then it is important that this does not lead us to lose sight of crucial revisions to the party's position in other policy domains since 1992. Arguably, the most significant modifications to Labour's proposals in recent years have come in the areas of economic and industrial policy (tables 4.10 and 4.11) – or, perhaps more precisely, revisions to Labour's policy in these areas are likely to prove most significant, heralding perhaps the emergence of a new political and economic settlement.

Labour's industrial policy has undergone significant revision and an effective emasculation in recent years – a process accelerated since 1994 by the resolution of a growing conflict between the teams at the shadow Treasury and shadow Department of Trade and Industry (DTI) in favour of the former. Thus, despite continued reference to the structural weaknesses of the British economy – the shortfall of dedicated capital and long-term strategic investment in particular – New Labour

Table 4.10 Bipartisan convergence in Britain, 1992–7: economic policy

	1992		1997	
Purpose of economic policy	Labour, increase investment, boost productivity, reduce unemployment; Conservatives, monetary stability, control inflation	−	Both parties, macro-economic stability, control of inflation	+
Taxation	Labour, top rate to rise to 50p in the £1, end to 'ceiling' on national insurance contributions	±	Labour, target bottom rate taxation of 15p (and ideally 10p) in the £1, no end to national insurance ceiling	+ +
Means to secure investment	Labour, reform of financial institutions; Conservatives, inward investment, partnerships	−	Labour, public–private partnership, inward investment	+
Public spending	Labour, prioritise increased public spending	−	Labour, no new public expenditure	+
Purpose of competition policy	Labour, protect employees from unfair competition; Conservatives, protect consumer interest	−	Both parties, protect consumers, promote competitiveness	+
Means of economic management	Labour, supply-side intervention; Conservatives, control of inflation	−	Labour, strict monetary and fiscal discipline	+

+, policy convergence; −, clear policy difference; ±, qualified difference.

Table 4.11 Bipartisan convergence in Britain, 1992–7: industrial policy

	1992		1997	
Role of DTI	Labour, DTI as 'super-ministry' on par with Treasury; Conservatives, subordination of DTI to Treasury	–	Labour, subordination of DTI to Treasury	+
National investment bank (NIB)?	Labour, NIB to supply investment capital	–	Labour, proposal for NIB withdrawn	+
Regional investment banks (RIB)?	Labour, RIBs to supply dedicated regional capital (proposal introduced after 1992 election defeat)	–	Labour, proposal for RIBs withdrawn	+
Regional development agencies (RDAs)?	Labour, committed to RDAs in England	–	Labour, proposal for RDAs maintained (after review)	–

+, policy convergence; –, clear policy difference; ±, qualified difference.

retains little in the way of concrete proposals which might address this distinctively British pathology (Hutton 1996; Watson and Hay 1998). As noted in chapter 2, following the Policy Review the party continued to emphasise the crucial strategic role that the DTI would have to play in the rejuvenation of Britain's manufacturing economy, requiring its elevation to 'super-ministry' status. Yet in the run-up to the 1997 election, it underwent a complete *volte face*, proposing instead to expand the role of the Treasury such that it would encroach significantly into the remit of the DTI. Proposals for a national investment bank that might provide investment capital on competitive terms to British industry were dropped. Proposals for regional investment banks, introduced in 1994 and based on similar principles, were shelved at the same time. By 1997, this left New Labour with no proposals to address what it still identified as the principal structural weakness of the British economy – its investment shortfall.[25] At the time of the 1997 election, then, the sole remaining aspect of the regional industrial strategy developed under the tutelage of Bryan Gould and subsequently Robin Cook (as shadow Secretaries for Trade and Industry) was its commitment to regional development agencies. Yet in so far as these merely build upon and institutionalise existing arrangements, Labour seems effectively to have vacated the industrial policy arena, emphasising instead macro-economic conservatism and fiscal stability (for a more detailed exposition, see Watson and Hay 1998).

Here, too, the general trajectory of Labour's reforms in opposition was one of convergence on an agenda increasingly circumscribed by the tenets of neo-liberal economics. By the 1997 election, Labour's economic policy was a catalogue of abandoned commitments and political U-turns. As recently as 1992, the party identified the principal means of economic management as supply-side intervention, in clear contrast to the Conservatives' fiscal conservatism and control of inflation. Yet, less than three years later, it conceived of economic management as the means of securing 'a robust and stable framework of monetary and fiscal discipline' (Labour Party 1995).[26] Competition policy, once justified principally in terms of its contribution to the protection of employees from the consequences of unfair competition, was now recast in terms of its role in protecting consumer interests, promoting flexibility and enhancing competitiveness. Where in 1992 Labour identified increased public expenditure as a top priority, by 1996 it would come to chastise the government for an increase in welfare spending at a time of falling unemployment. It now pledges itself in government to 'no new public expenditure' without corresponding reductions in existing departmental budgets. Where Labour sought significant reform of Britain's financial institutions and the development of, first, a national investment bank and, subsequently, a network of regional investment banks as the means by which investment in the domestic productive economy could be raised, it could by the election only echo the Conservatives' faith in private–public partnership and foreign direct investment. As recently as 1994 the party proposed an increase in the top rate of taxation to 50 pence in the pound and an end to the 'ceiling' on national insurance contributions (effectively raising the top rate of taxation from 40 to 59 pence in the pound); in government it now sets as its long-term goal a reduction of the bottom rate of taxation to 15 (and ideally 10) pence in the pound, while quietly dropping any commitment to reform of the national insurance system. Where, in 1992, Labour's principal economic goals were to raise investment in the domestic economy, to boost productivity and to reduce long-term unemployment, its primary aims had, by 1997, become the control of inflation and the promotion of macroeconomic stability.[27] The Keynesian consensus of the post-war period would appear to have been replaced by the neo-liberal consensus of the post-Thatcher period.

This new consensus is reflected in Labour's changing commitments on privatisation, the public sector and the regulation of the mass media (tables 4.12 and 4.13). Where, at the date of privatisation, Labour stood clearly opposed to the private ownership of rail, coal and Her Majesty's Stationery Office (HMSO), and committed (if only in an attempt to 'derail' privatisation) to the renationalisation of Railtrack, it had, by the election, dropped all plans for the renationalisation of coal and the HMSO and would maintain Railtrack within the private sector (albeit with a majority share to be held by a new, state-owned, Strategic Rail Authority). On more general matters of principle, where Labour previously set itself the clear long-term priority of restoring all essential services to the public sector, it could now only commit itself in government to increasing the public accountability of such services within the private sector and to a one-off 'windfall' tax on the profits of the privatised utilities to fund training and job-creation programmes for the young. In 1992, Labour promised to initiate an immediate enquiry (by the Monopolies and Mergers Commission) into what it saw as the 'unacceptable' concentration of media ownership in Britain.

Table 4.12 Bipartisan convergence in Britain, 1992–7: privatisation and the public sector

	1992	1997	
Primary policy goal	Labour, return essential services to public sector (as and when funds allow)	Labour, essential services to be made accountable in the private sector	±
Privatised utilities	Labour, return to the public sector	Labour, 'windfall tax' to be levied on the profits of the privatised utilities	±
National rail service	Labour, privatisation fought, proposed renationalisation of Railtrack	Labour, Railtrack to remain in the private sector, majority share to be held by a new (public) Strategic Rail Authority	+
Coal industry	Labour, privatisation fiercely resisted	Labour, no plans for renationalisation	+

+, policy convergence; –, clear policy difference; ±, qualified difference.

Table 4.13 Bipartisan convergence in Britain, 1992–7: media regulation

	1992		1997	
Media monopolies	Labour, unacceptable concentration of ownership, immediate enquiry	−	Labour, calls for enquiry dropped, no proposals for reform	+
Media regulation or deregulation	Labour, need for stricter regulation; Conservatives, committed to deregulation	−	Labour, plans to lift restrictions preventing large newspaper groups buying into the television market	+

+, policy convergence; −, clear policy difference; ±, qualified difference.

In a quite remarkable U-turn it has come to embrace the further deregulation of the media market – proposing to lift the restrictions which currently prevent large newspaper groups from buying domestic television companies, whilst conspicuously courting the international media barons.[28]

Such policy modifications, revisions and U-turns may be born of a combination of pragmatism and astute political strategy. Yet their consequences are surely to reaffirm and consolidate an emergent bipartisan consensus on economic, industrial and competition policy which will, for the foreseeable future, remain couched within, and circumscribed by, the now dominant neo-liberal paradigm.

Constitutional reform

Even in the area of constitutional and governmental reform – in many respects. Labour's flagship policy arena over recent years – there has been a seemingly inexorable dilution of previously unambiguous and quite radical proposals for institutional overhaul (table 4.14). The debacle over the issue of Scottish devolution during the campaign itself and the considerable political fallout this has generated north of the border have only served to highlight New Labour's rather frantic efforts to shore up what it surely came to perceive as a potential electoral liability. New Labour's invocation of a 'one-nation' communi-tarianism and its proposals for devolution in Scotland in particular are shot through with irreconcilable tensions and contradictions. Despite his Scottish schooling, Blair seems to exhibit a remarkable disdain and ambivalence towards the Celtic periphery, manifest most famously in his insistence that, whatever the specific nature of the constitutional settlement in Scotland after the election, 'sovereignty' would remain in the hands of English MPs such as himself. Preaching, as he was, to marginal constituencies south of the border, his comments could scarcely have been better chosen to inflame Scottish political opinion. Blair's politics, whether a reflection of perceived psephological im-perative or a more deeply ingrained Anglo-Philistinism, are the politics of middle English sentiment. This is likely to make it very difficult to negotiate a stable British constitutional settlement (Blackburn 1997: 6–7; Nairn 1997).

In this area as elsewhere, revisions to party policy since 1992 are legion. Where until recently the party pledged itself to the abolition of

Table 4.14 Bipartisan convergence in Britain, 1992–7: constitutional reform

	1992		1997	
House of Lords	Labour, to be replaced by elected second chamber	–	Labour, to be retained, though voting rights of hereditary peers to be removed	+
Scottish Parliament	Labour, to be created immediately with taxation powers	–	Labour, twin referendums on Parliament and taxation power	±
Welsh Assembly	Labour, created within first 5 years (no taxation powers)	–	Labour, single referendum on Assembly	±
Regional government for England	Labour, regional chambers to be created and, in time, to become elected regional authorities	–	Labour, regional chambers to be established, regional government dependent on regional referendums	±

+, policy convergence; –, clear policy difference; ±, qualified difference.

the House of Lords and its replacement by an elected second chamber, it now merely proposes to remove the voting rights of hereditary peers (themselves largely Conservative), whilst 'considering further reform'. Where Labour was passionately committed to the immediate creation in office of a Scottish Parliament with (albeit limited) taxation powers, it came rapidly to lose the courage of its former convictions, promising instead a two-part referendum on a Scottish Parliament and its *potential* taxation powers as it came to fear the consequences of a militant-Labour-dominated Scottish Parliament. The initial proposals for a Welsh Assembly (without taxation powers) suffered a similar dilution. As for the English regions: where Labour was in 1992 committed to the establishment of elected regional authorities (then an integral aspect of its reform of regional institutions and its promotion of regional industrial strategies), it now merely intends to introduce regional chambers which may – in time and on the basis of regional referendums – become democratically elected and accountable.

Policy differences between the parties do remain and they should not be under-emphasised. Yet the broad trajectory, accelerated significantly in the long run-up to the 1997 election and consolidated subsequently, has been one of clear convergence between the parties – a convergence, once again, initiated by Labour.

New departures: divergence or diversion?

As suggested at the outset, a comparison of Labour's changing electoral promises and pledges, though a useful heuristic, cannot provide us with an unambiguous and definitive evaluation of the extent of bipartisan convergence, far less bipartisan consensus. Such an assessment requires, at minimum, a consideration of the emergence of policies which divide the parties today but did not do so in 1992. Though these are in fact few, they do nonetheless exist.

Labour had pledged itself, when in government, in Margaret Beckett's terms, to 'offer small firms who take on a long term unemployed person under 25 a £60 tax rebate a week – provided they offer approved training for a day'.[29] It has, at the direct instigation of Tony Blair, signed an agreement with British Telecom to provide cable and Internet connections to schools, colleges, universities and libraries at no cost to the taxpayer. It also pledged itself during the election campaign to the creation of a new University of Industry, though its precise form and function remain somewhat shrouded in mystery. It promised (or promises) in office to halve the time it takes for young offenders to get to court; to ban the private ownership and possession of handguns; to reform Prime Minister's question time; and to fund environmental, educational and public health projects through the proceeds of the National Lottery. At the time of writing, each of these pledges has been fulfilled, though with varying degrees of commitment and success.

More tentatively, Labour promised during the election campaign to consider: (i) an amalgamation of the functions of the Monopolies and Mergers Commission and the Office of Fair Trading in a unitary Competition and Consumer Standards Office; (ii) a reform of the regulations governing take-overs to place the onus of proof on the bidding company to demonstrate the public good of its proposed acquisition; (iii) the appointment of leading figures from businesses with high export profiles as ambassadors; and (iv) reviews of both the Export Intelligence Service and of Export Credit Guarantee Departments. Again, to a greater or lesser extent, each of these tentative proposals has resulted in action by the Labour government.

Though many of these proposals would represent important policy changes in specific areas and although they do indeed indicate some clear space between the parties, they hardly constitute grounds for rejecting the convergence thesis. Were New Labour in power to enact each and every one of these policies and proposals (itself somewhat unlikely), this would clearly mark no decisive break with the legacy of the outgoing Major government. Indeed, such measures can really be viewed as only *tinkering* within the broader architecture of an institutional, political and economic settlement that the incoming Labour administration inherited from the Conservatives – a settlement whose basic parameters are outlined in chapter 2.

Ironically, then, a consideration of New Labour's policy departures from the Conservatives merely serves to emphasise the full extent of the convergence between the parties since 1992.

Convergence vindicated? The limits of electoral expediency

Tony Blair had two objectives during the election. The first was to win, the second was to minimise every expectation of what would happen then. He wanted to over-perform, but under-promise, and thought the first depended on the second. (Hugo Young, *Guardian*, 3 May 1997)

The above analysis clearly demonstrates the considerable extent of bipartisan convergence in Britain in the five years leading up to Labour's election – a convergence it is crucial to recall taking place within a context already widely regarded as consensual at the outset. Before concluding that, in the light of such convergence, the election of Tony Blair represents the return of consensus politics in Britain, it is nonetheless important that we reconsider this evidence with the benefit of the hindsight afforded by New Labour's electoral landslide. For there are a number of rather different interpretations which might be placed on the electoral politics of convergence with Tony Blair now resident in Downing Street.

Labour's unprecedented share of the seats (though by no means of the votes cast)[30] would perhaps first suggest that the strategy of convergence (whether intended, intuitive or unintended) has indeed been vindicated. If Labour's strategy was to convince the electorate of its studious moderation and competence whilst toiling tirelessly to diminish (inflated) expectations for government, as it appears it was, then, as an electoral strategy, it surely proved highly successful. Yet however obvious this may seem, a certain degree of caution is required in assessing the political consequences of convergence. First, and though somewhat tangential to the concerns of this chapter, the role of the Conservatives' visible disintegration before the media's glare from 'Black Wednesday' onwards should not be under-emphasised. The Conservatives lost the 1997 general election (and before that the will to govern) more than Labour won it (see also Blackburn 1997; Harrop 1997). Moreover, it is important to note that, as argued in chapter 2, Labour has, in effect, been engaged in the psephologically inspired 'politics of catch-up' and convergence since 1987 and, arguably, 1983.[31] As the above analysis reveals, Blair's New Labour has gone far further down this 'Downsian' road than the party under the leadership of either Neil Kinnock or John Smith, studiously targeting and courting the median voter in the marginal constituencies of middle England in a manner difficult to contemplate even in 1992. None-theless, the trajectory of Labour's 'modernisation' was established some time after the 1983 general election fiasco and reinforced and reinvigorated after further defeats in 1987 and 1992. Cast in such a light, and projected over this more extended time frame, the strategy appears less obviously successful. Here is not the place to review the (now purely historical) alternatives (though see chapters 2, 5 and 6). Suffice it to say that from 1987 (if not before), Labour consistently engaged in the politics of *preference-accommodation* rather than that of *preference-shaping* – adapting and revising its policies on the basis of a strategic assessment of the sensitivities and aspirations of the electorate as evidenced in previous elections (in which the governments of Thatcher and Major were elected and re-elected). The Downsian road to government has then proved both long and winding, its sides littered with the discarded remains of Labour's former social democratic, labourist and socialist convictions.

Yet there are those commentators for whom such an interpretation mistakes, even conflates, contingent electoral strategy and political pragmatism *in opposition* for the realities of government. Having achieved governmental power on the basis of preference-accommodation, expectation suppression and studious moderation, the argument runs, Labour is now in a position to dust off the true convictions it had previously learned to silence and to unveil its radical manifesto for the millennium. Such an argument is certainly enticing and the scale of Labour's parliamentary majority, combined with the opposition's disarray, serves to render it rather more plausible than it might otherwise seem. Nonetheless, there are several very good reasons for rejecting it as the product of wishful thinking rather than a more dispassionate analysis. First, as Robert Reich noted in some open advice to Tony Blair immediately prior to the election, 'to govern well you need a public well-versed in where you want to lead them' (1997). Labour is all too well aware of this and is not prepared to sacrifice impressions of managerial competence, discretion and restraint that it has taken years to cultivate by unmasking a radical agenda that it was, presumably, too timid to present to the electorate. Second, this is to assume that such an agenda in fact exists. The sad reality for the left in Britain – as in western Europe, North America and the antipodes more generally – is that there is no evidence that it does. Moreover, there is precious little in the way of coherently and consistently developed social democratic (far less socialist) alternatives to which a government such as Blair's might turn *were it committed to the need for an alternative vision* anyway.[32] Yet even this is to beg the question. For, quite simply, and with very few exceptions,[33] the Labour government conceives neither of the need for, *nor indeed the possibility of*, such an alternative to the ascendant neo-liberalism of the times.

This is a crucial point and takes us to the crux of the matter. It demonstrates that it is not purely (perceived) electoral expediency that has dictated Labour's neo-liberal conversion and convergence. Along with almost all of the (former) social democratic parties of western Europe and, indeed, the labour parties of Australia and New Zealand, New Labour now accepts that there is simply no alternative to neo-liberalism in an era of heightened capital mobility and financial liberalisation – in short, in an era of globalisation. In so doing, it subscribes to something akin to a revised and updated version of Przeworski and Wallerstein's 'modified structural dependence thesis' that we consider in more detail in the next chapter (1988). The state and, hence, parties vying for state power are dependent upon capital in that they must prove themselves capable of securing conditions conducive to continued investment. In an era of enhanced exit options, capital mobility and potential flight, this means that social democratic parties such as Labour must effectively abandon their social democratic credentials, accommodate the perceived interest of capital for fiscal and monetary conservatism and low taxation, whilst promoting labour-market flexibility and enhanced competitiveness, if their election (or even the likelihood of their election) is not to precipitate disinvestment and economic crisis.[34] Within the constraints such a thesis implies, there is simply no alternative within the contours of contemporary capitalism to neo-liberal economics, welfare retrenchment and labour-market deregulation. This would in turn suggest that the *perceived* exigencies of globalisation may have at least as much to do with bipartisan convergence on macro-economic, fiscal, industrial and employment policy and the staged management of welfare retrenchment and workfare encroachment as the Downsian logic of electoral expediency. This is the central theme of the following chapter. It would also suggest that a dispassionate assessment of the (supposed) limits imposed by globalisation – such as that begun by authors such as Berger and Dore (1996), Boyer and Drache (1996), Garrett (1998) and Hirst and Thompson (1996) – is both long overdue and a condition of the ability 'to think that things might be different', upon which a reinvigorated social democracy must depend. Finally, it would suggest that the unprecedented scale of Labour's landslide electoral victory may well fail to liberate the party in government from the self-imposed shackles of a neo-liberal economic and political paradigm that it has done much to espouse in opposition.

That was the election ... this is now

If the above analysis, however schematic, suggests a pervasive logic of convergence established in opposition that Labour has taken with it into government, then further evidence for such a proposition can be found if we examine the record of the Blair administration in its first few months in office.

The extent to which Labour in government has revised the policy commitments with which it fought the 1997 election is quite remarkable and might lead one to suggest that its (original) 179-seat overall majority in the House of Commons has indeed liberated the government from the moderation and restraint it cultivated in opposition. Equally remarkable, however, is that each of these policy revisions (with perhaps one exception) merely confirms, as it adds to, the extent of bipartisan convergence, providing yet further evidence of the extent to which the parameters of political and economic possibility are now circumscribed for both parties by the seemingly unassailable paradigm of neo-liberal economics. A few brief examples will perhaps suffice.

Within a week of Labour's electoral triumph, the new Chancellor, Gordon Brown, announced, to the amazement of journalists, analysts and commentators alike, that operational responsibility for the setting of interest rates would be ceded to the Bank of England. This was certainly a radical measure, all the more so given that there had been no hint of such a proposal in the manifesto or supporting documents.[35] The clear intention was to demonstrate that Labour was indeed to be a radical government – radical in its desire to project for itself an image of fiscal and monetary conservatism and, wherever possible, to depoliticise macro-economic policy-making. As a shocked Larry Elliott observed in the *Guardian* the next day, within the parameters of a neo-liberal conception of economic policy:

> it makes perfect sense to hand over interest rate policy to the Bank of England and its governor, Eddie George, and to call in the head of BP [Lord Simon] as minister for export promotion. They are, after all, likely to make a better fist of things than elected politicians.... Labour doesn't want to take the big decisions: it wants them taken off its hands so that it can concentrate on micro-changes and be blame-free when things go wrong. (1997)

The consequence of ceding operational independence to the Bank of England, however, was to compromise further Labour's avowed (and, one can only surmise, largely rhetorical) aim of promoting productive investment in the domestic economy – and hence, perhaps, its sole remaining difference with the Conservatives on economic policy. For, as the *Financial Times'* editorial argued the day after the Chancellor's momentous decision, '[the Bank] is still viewed as the spokesman [*sic*] for the City' (7 May 1997). The fear is that the combination of the Bank's new role and its old image will be taken by productive interests as a sign that they should expect no downward pressure on the cost of borrowing. In short, the depoliticisation of interest rate policy can only be expected to institutionalise further the primacy of financial over industrial interests. It is precisely this expectation that already undermines productive investment in the domestic economy, as the Labour Party until recently clearly acknowledged. The economic 'stability' which Gordon Brown so clearly espouses can, then, be interpreted as stability only on financial capital's terms. For the tight monetary stance which the Bank of England has repeatedly indicated will be necessary to ensure 'financial stability' can only further destabilise indigenous investment potential.

New Labour's new-found radicalism in government (the radicalism to contemplate proposals that not even the Tories considered) has not, however, been restricted to economic policy. Far from it. Leaked confidential policy documents indicate that Labour's comprehensive review of NHS expenditure will exclude nothing – perhaps most contentiously health 'rationing' as well as charges for visits to the doctor, food and accommodation in hospital, and pensioners' prescriptions. This has produced the rather surprising spectacle (one to which we will soon, no doubt, become accustomed) of Frank Dobson, the Minister for Health, being grilled by his Conservative predecessor, Stephen Dorrell, for betraying the historical principle of the NHS – 'care based on need, not on ability to pay'. That the expenditure review should exclude nothing is ultimately not that surprising, given that the Chancellor could only find £1.3 billion in extra funds for the NHS in his first budget speech. This figure represented only a 2.25 per cent increase in its budget for the following fiscal year, compared with an average annual increase of 3 per cent under the Conservatives. This, combined with an estimated £10 billion backlog in essential building maintenance, has conspired to produce the financial crisis to which the review is merely a first and preliminary response.

Elsewhere, further confidential policy documents leaked to the BBC's *Panorama* programme disclosed that the government was considering some form of privatisation for the London Underground, by selling off its controlling stake, in clear violation of a manifesto commitment. A rather shell-shocked John Prescott, the Deputy Leader of the party with responsibility for transport policy, was forced to concede that the government was indeed examining 'ways of bringing in the private sector to improve services'. These might involve 'public–private partnerships', possibly along the lines of British Rail privatisation, with separation of control of infrastructure and services.[36] The government is also drawing up plans for the privatisation of the Benefits Agency medical service (which examines some 600,000 claimants per year).[37] Moreover, in a clear reversal of previous party policy, the Home Secretary, Jack Straw, ordered two privately operated prisons to be built in Salford and Bristol. He also announced that he was considering the commissioning of further prison ships, less than two months after publicly chastising the then Home Secretary, Michael Howard, during a televised election debate for this precise policy and threatening in government to moor the sole existing floating prison, HMS *Weare*, off Howard's own coastal constituency.

If the above examples all provide clear evidence of further policy convergence *after* the election, and even perhaps of a radicalisation of Labour's neo-liberal agenda since 1 May 1997, then there is at least one area of *potential* policy revision which might serve to complicate this picture. Yet another confidential report leaked from Whitehall (*Options on How to Raise Pensions Beyond Inflation*) showed that the Department of Social Security was costing measures to restore (over a period of time) earnings indexation for state pensions. Yet, with the Labour government committed to the strict spending targets it *chose* to inherit from the Conservatives, earnings indexation could be restored only if the cost (an estimated £550–£775 million in the first year alone) could be met from other sources. Three options were considered: (i) ending the £10 Christmas bonus for pensioners (to raise £137 million); (ii) abolishing the 25 pence per week bonus given to those aged over eighty (to raise a meagre £28 million); and (iii) abolishing the upper earnings threshold on national insurance contributions (to raise up to £4 billion). The immense media and public outcry at the suggestion that either of the first two options could even be contemplated, together with the unpopularity of the third option among Labour's newly recruited middle-class voters (who would be penalised disproportionately by such a measure), conspire to render the restoration of earnings indexation at best unlikely.

Conclusions: the politics of conspicuous convergence

The implications of such an analysis for the convergence and consensus theses are, I think, significant. Since the 1992 election, itself regarded by most commentators as one in which there was a rare proximity between the parties (Butler and Kavanagh 1992; Heath and Jowell 1994), Labour has undergone a significant and comprehensive review of policy in almost all areas. Moreover, as the last section reveals, this review has if anything been stepped up in government – a consequence in large part of choosing to accept (for its first two years in office) the punitive public spending targets set by the outgoing Conservative administration. As this chapter demonstrates, the trajectory of change for Labour has been overwhelmingly in one direction – that of convergence with the Conservatives on the basis of the dilution, weakening and selective abandonment of prior commitments.

The last vestiges of Labour's 'old' Keynesian, welfarist and social democratic sensitivities would seem to have been displaced by a pervasive spirit of 'new realism'. This has manifest itself in terms of macro-economic conservatism, fiscal fortitude and an increasing disavowal of both labour-market re-regulation and consistent demand- or supply-side intervention. Labour, like many of its (former) social democrat allies in western Europe and North America, and its antipodean namesakes, has lost any remaining confidence in the ability to retain a comprehensive welfare state in an era of capital flight, financial liberalisation and burgeoning globalisation. On this understanding it must now accommodate itself to the task at hand – the more or less equitable management of welfare retrenchment in the name of competitiveness.

It is this agenda that defines the new bipartisan consensus in Britain. It has emerged in circumstances very different from those of the early 1950s, and the principal agent of revision this time around is clearly Labour and not the Conservatives. Yet in both contexts we see an accommodation and internalisation in opposition of the new governing paradigm: a paradigm, in both cases, taken to circumscribe the parameters of the politically and economically possible. The bipartisan consensus of the 1950s was to remain relatively unchallenged until the rise of the new right in the mid-1970s. With, as yet, no sign of a resurgent and renewed left whether in Britain, on the Continent or in North America, it is difficult to see where the challenge to today's emergent neo-liberal consensus will come from.

Notes

1 For varying interpretations see Coates (1996); Kenny and Smith (1997b); Leys (1990); Perryman (1996); Shaw (1994); Smith (1994); Toulouse and Worcester (1995/6); Wickham-Jones (1995a, 1995b, 1997b). For post-election assessments, see Blackburn (1997); Brivati and Bale (1997); Fielding (1997); Leys and Panitch (1997); Marquesee (1997); Rose (1997); Seyd (1998).

2 As discussed in some detail in chapter 2, many commentators have suggested that significant policy convergence between the parties had already occurred by 1992, describing the election in more or less consensual terms. In his comments on the election, for instance, Kenneth Newton argued that 'if the two parties had everything to fight for [in 1992], they also fought over very little.... In this sense it was a "valence-issue", not a "position-issue" election'. He goes on to elaborate, 'the latter involves parties putting different issues at the top of the agenda or applying different policy solutions to the same problems. In contrast, valence-issue elections involve general agreement about the urgent problems and the best policy "solutions" for them. The winning party is the one that manages to persuade voters that it can handle matters better than the other parties' (1993: 135; see also Crewe 1993; and chapter 2 in the present volume).

3 For a similar analysis, reaching remarkably similar conclusions, yet which chooses as its point of reference a rather different range of policy areas, see Sanders 1998 (231–7).

4 'Flying pickets' are mobile bands of strikers, brought in to picket particular strategic plants and places of work in which they are not employed. Flying picketing became a favoured and much-publicised strategy of public sector trade unionists during the 'three-day week' of 1972–3, the 'Winter of Discontent' of 1978–9 and, more recently, the year-long miners' strike of 1984–5.

5 See also Tony Blair's speech to the Labour Party annual conference, Blackpool, 1 October 1996.

6 'Secondary picketing' refers to the picketing of another employer or place of work.

7 Secondary picketing, as Ben Rosamond noted at the time, would be reinstated as a worker's right only where 'a second employer [is] directly assisting a first employer in the frustration of a legitimate industrial dispute' or in which 'the primary employer [has] contracted out work to avoid strike action; the outcome of the primary dispute will affect the terms and conditions of another employer's employees; [or] where corporate legal identity is manipulated to make secondary action unlawful' (1992: 93; see also Labour Party 1990: 11–13, 32–5; Marsh, 1992: 160).

8 At the time, the party's shadow spokesperson for home affairs.

9 Blair's refusal to chastise the MPs concerned would perhaps indicate that they were.

10 In which a wave of both public and private sector industrial disputes erupted, coincident with the worst winter in living memory, shattering the incumbent Labour administration's 'Social Contract' with the trade unions and precipitating a palpable sense of state crisis that would see the Conservative Party (in the form of Margaret Thatcher) restored to Downing Street (see Hay 1996a).

11 The Social Chapter is an annex to the Treaty on European Union signed at Maastricht on 7 February 1992. It relates to social policy within the Union and was not included in the overall Treaty at the insistence of the then Conservative government of the United Kingdom. This allowed the UK to sign the Treaty whilst opting out of the Social Chapter. As Linda Hantrais notes, 'by including a separate Protocol on Social Policy the other eleven member states could proceed with the Community Charter and make decisions without taking account of the views of the United Kingdom' (1995: 12–13; see also George and Haythorne 1996; Leibfried and Pierson 1995).

12 See for instance, Tony Blair's speech to the *Keidanren*, Tokyo, 5 January 1996, on 'The Global Economy'.

13 *Financial Times*, 5 June 1997; for a similar interpretation see Marquesee (1997: 128).

14 Tony Blair, speech to the biennial conference of the Federation of German Industry, 18 June 1996; as reported in the *Daily Telegraph*, 19 June 1996.

15 The terms are Tony Blair's and come from his speech to the 1996 Labour Party conference in Blackpool.

16 A competitive entrance examination at the age of eleven to determine the type (and quality) of secondary education a child would receive.

17 Blair's speech to the Labour Party conference, Blackpool, 1 October 1996.

18 Though such a position has a certain academic currency, it has also been exposed to significant critique in recent years. See, in particular, Berger and Dore (1996); Boyer and Drache (1996); Hay and Marsh (1999a); Hirst and Thompson (1996); Rieger and Leibfried (1998); Watson, (1999a). On New Labour's deployment of the rhetoric of globalisation see Hay and Watson (1998).

19 If only in an aggregate sense.

20 It was in fact committed to earnings or price indexation, whichever proved the higher. In fact, had earnings indexation not been abolished by the Conservative government of Margaret Thatcher in 1980, the value of the single person's pension would be an estimated £82.45 per week rather than £62.45 at the time of the election, a couple's pension £129.80 as

opposed to £99.80. These figures come from Labour's own leaked confidential *Options* paper on pension reform (*Guardian*, 20 August 1997).

21 That Labour did not commit itself *explicitly* to preserving this price indexation formula in fact owes much to Old Labour. After a rousing speech to the 1996 Labour Party conference by Dame Barbara Castle (the very personification of 'Old' Labour?) in defence of earnings indexation, the party leadership announced a (somewhat cosmetic) review of Labour's policy on pensions. This is a theme to which we return in discussing the likely trajectory of social policy under the Labour administration. Suffice it to note that the considerable cost of restoring earnings indexation must render this an unlikely revision of policy (though one that has certainly been considered in some detail).

22 There is very little evidence to suggest that existing 'workfare' schemes have contributed much to the employment prospects of those they have kept from registering on the unemployment statistics (see for instance Dolowitz 1998).

23 For a trenchant critique of such measures by a Liberal Democrat peer, see Russell (1996).

24 Gordon Brown's budget speech, 3 July 1997 (HM Treasury: paragraphs 105–9).

25 Labour had tentatively, and with the backing of the Confederation of British Industry (CBI), advocated a two-tier capital gains tax to reward longer-term investment in the domestic economy. Yet with the CBI's change in directorship and subsequent pre-election withdrawal of support for such a measure, Labour was quick to emphasise the highly provisional nature of this always vaguely stated policy proposal. As a consequence, Labour presented itself to the electorate at the 1997 general election with no single policy proposal either designed or likely to raise the level of productive investment in the domestic economy, despite continuing to identify this as the principal structural weakness of the domestic economy.

26 These sentiments were echoed powerfully in Gordon Brown's 1997 budget speech and in his decision to cede operational independence to the Bank of England for setting interest rates.

27 For clear statements of these new priorities see Labour Party (1995, 1996a, 1996b) and Tony Blair's speeches to the Singapore business community (8 January 1996), the Federation of German Industry (18 June 1996) and the 1996 Labour Party annual conference. For evidence of the complete absence of substantive measures designed to promote investment in the productive economy see Labour Party (1996c).

28 It is surely no coincidence that the *Sun* newspaper (owned by media mogul Rupert Murdoch) should announce its historic decision to 'back Blair' in the 1997 election campaign only days after the party's

announcement of its commitment to further deregulation of the media market and only a matter of months after Blair was himself flown, at Murdoch's expense, to the latter's island 'retreat' for a private 'conference' (McSmith 1996: 318).

29 Margaret Beckett (shadow Secretary of State for Trade and Industry), speech to the Labour Party conference, Blackpool, 30 September 1996.

30 With the fall in electoral turnout between 1992 and 1997, it is interesting to note that the Conservatives achieved a higher total vote in 1992 than the Labour Party managed in 1997. Labour was a significant beneficiary of the distortions of the first-past-the-post electoral system, recording the highest ratio of seats won to votes cast of any party at any election in the post-war period (winning 64 per cent of the seats for just 44 per cent of the votes cast). For a more detailed analysis see Harrop (1997).

31 For a critique of this interpretation see Kenny and Smith (1997b).

32 Here it is surely telling to note Robin Cook's call to academics and think-tanks of the centre-left to develop the ideas that might animate a 'millennial' vision for Labour in power. The clear implication of this is that Labour currently lacks such a vision and that candidates are currently rather thin on the ground. Yet should this be taken as evidence of Labour's desire to fashion a genuinely radical manifesto for the new century, it should also be noted that Cook is in a minority (possibly of one) among his Cabinet colleagues in his desire to reproject Labour in government as a visionary administration animated by a consistent and coherent modernising project (Cook 1996).

33 Robin Cook, the Foreign Secretary, being by far the most obvious and prominent one.

34 For an admirable (and sympathetic) summary of this position see Wickham-Jones (1995b).

35 Such a proposal had, nonetheless, been contemplated publicly by analysts and advisors close to Brown (see for instance Layard 1997: 126–7).

36 John Prescott, quoted in the *Guardian*, 17 June 1997.

37 As reported in the *Times*, 1 June 1997.

5 Studiously Courting Capital: the economic politics of accommodation

In the previous three chapters, we have tended to focus on what might be termed the 'political logic of modernisation'. Accordingly, we have concentrated primarily on Labour's (developing) conception of the immediate political context in which it found itself in the 1980s and the party's subsequent diagnosis of its electoral and psephological predicament. Of at least equal, and arguably ever greater, significance, however, has been a parallel 'economic logic of modernisation'. The party has come to understand the nature of its predicament and the conditions of its reacquisition of electability in not purely political terms. Modernisers within the party came to reconceive the parameters of political possibility in terms of the imperatives imposed by economic integration, financial liberalisation and heightened capital mobility – in short, globalisation. The party's adaptation to the 'harsh economic realities' of 'new times' and, in particular, its accommodation to the preferences of capital in such a context increasingly came to be seen as a condition of political rejuvenation and electoral success.

The precise process by which this economic modernisation has been achieved is complex and convoluted. It is well summarised by Wickham-Jones (1995b, undated). Yet however nuanced and differentiated, what is remarkable is that the process of economic modernisation (or, at least, the economic logic of political modernisation) parallels that of political modernisation extremely closely. If New Labour, in Downsian terms, found itself drawn some way to the right of the median voter by the political logic of modernisation, then arguably it also found itself drawn by the economic logic of modernisation to a position close to the preferences of the median industrialist (if not, perhaps, quite to the position of the median institutional investor).

It is to the logic of this process and to the mechanisms sustaining it that we turn in this chapter. My argument in some respects mirrors that of chapter 3. Just as New Labour has come to behave in a manner seemingly consistent with the Downsian economic theory of democracy, so too it has come to act in a manner consistent with the 'modified structural dependence thesis' of Adam Przeworski and Michael Wallerstein (1988; see also Lindblom 1988; Przeworski 1990; Swank 1992). As argued in chapter 3, however, evidence of behaviour consistent with such a theory should not be taken as confirmation of that theory. Though New Labour's conduct – its proffering of prawn cocktails to domestic industrialists, financiers, institutional investors and, eventually, international brokers and bankers for instance – can usefully be redescribed in terms of the structural dependence thesis, the latter does not provide an adequate explanation of that conduct.

The chapter proceeds in five parts. In the first section, I provide a relatively succinct statement of the modified structural dependence thesis and consider its applicability to the contemporary British context. In the second section, after a few preliminaries, I critically review those attempts to qualify the thesis further, as a means to account for Labour's modernisation and its studious courting of capital in the late 1980s and early 1990s (see especially Wickham-Jones 1995b, 1997b). In the remaining sections, I argue that just as Labour might have considered as an alternative to preference-accommodation the politics of electoral preference-shaping, so might it have considered the politics of capital preference-shaping as an alternative to capital appeasement. I present a diagnosis of the British affliction before considering what a preference-shaping alternative strategy might have looked like and assessing its feasibility in the current context.

The structural dependence thesis

The structural dependence thesis, in its purest form, rests upon a central premise of both neo-classical economics and Marxist state theory (not perhaps the most likely of bedfellows) that the (capitalist) state in a capitalist society must respect, protect and secure the interests and claims of capital (see for instance Offe 1975; Offe and Ronge 1975; Pashukanis 1978). As Przeworski and Wallerstein suggest, 'the effective capacity of any government to attain whatever are its goals is circumscribed by the public power of capital' (1988: 11). The state, so the argument goes, is dependent on capital (if only in the sense that its very existence relies in a dynamic way upon the extraction of a portion of capitalist profits in the form of taxation). As such, it must seek to secure conditions conducive to the continued ability of capital to maintain levels of investment and accumulation (Block 1987a; Lindblom 1988; Swank 1992; Taylor 1960; for a useful review see King and Wickham-Jones 1995). In an era of enhanced exit options, heightened capital mobility and potential capital flight this places considerable (if hardly unfamiliar) constraints on the political latitude of parties vying for state power. At pain of a haemorrhaging of investment, parties (especially those that have traditionally sought to project themselves as parties of the working class) must convince capital prior to their election of their prudence and moderation. This is the modified structural dependence thesis.

The logic of inevitability and inexorability that it seems to conjure can be derived quite simply on the basis of a few initial premises. Thus, Przeworski and Wallerstein begin their analysis by pointing to the potential conflict between, on the one hand, a capitalist economic system of accumulation founded on private ownership, allocation and prerogative and, on the other, a democratic political system founded on rather different premises – such as a direct relationship between citizen preferences and the allocation of resources. This raises a perennial theme of both Marxist theory and neo-classical economics – to what extent (if any) can (and, in the case of the latter, should) the state serve to regulate the capitalist economy (see Hay 1996b: chapter 5; 1999c)? Interestingly, if hardly surprisingly, whereas the neo-classicists tend to fear the crisis-inducing subordination of capitalism to democracy (see for instance Crozier *et al.* 1975), Marxists have tended to point to the limits of democracy under capitalist conditions (Przeworski 1985; Przeworski and Sprague 1986; Wood 1995) and to the inability of the capitalist system to secure the conditions of its own reproduction in the absence of a significant degree of regulatory intervention (Block 1987a; Habermas 1975; Offe 1984). These are themes to which we return. Suffice it for now to note that any shift from (relatively) closed to (more) open economies, raising the spectre of heightened capital mobility, may alter significantly the balance between the conflicting imperatives of accumulation and regulation/legitimation.

The point, however, for neo-classical economists and Marxist state theorists alike is to emphasise the limits of capitalist regulation in a functioning capitalist economy and to emphasise that, irrespective of the specific nature of the government, the state is structurally dependent upon capital. The state, under capitalist conditions, simply cannot 'organise production (Offe 1975), mandate investment (Lindblom

1977) or command consumption' (Przeworski and Wallerstein 1988: 12). For these are the exclusive prerogatives of the owners of private property. In its most deterministic and functionalist form, as Przeworski and Wallerstein note:

> it does not matter who the state managers are, what they want, and whom they represent. Nor does it matter how the state is organised and what it is legally able or unable to do. Capitalists do not even have to organise and act collectively: it suffices that they blindly pursue narrow, private self-interest to sharply restrict [*sic*] the options of all governments. (1988, p. 12)

Przeworki and Wallerstein's modified variant of the structural dependence thesis is essentially an attempt to provide – or rather import (from neo-classical economics) – the micro-foundations underpinning this bottom-line functionalism. In so doing, they are, in effect, suggesting that the myth of a functional state operating over and above the heads of state managers, and independently of their will, need not be conjured or invoked to account for the state's seeming subordination to capitalist imperatives. All that is required, certainly in a context in which capital flight is a possibility, is that politicians (social democratic or otherwise) seek to maximise their utility (for which read votes) and that capitalists blindly (i.e. 'rationally') pursue their own self-interest.

Their thesis, then, is a simple one. Politicians seeking re-election – and, indeed, parties seeking election – 'must anticipate the impact of their policies on the decisions of firms because these decisions affect employment, inflation, and the personal income of voters: vote-seeking politicians are dependent on owners of capital because voters are' (1988: 12). Consequently, social democratic parties must seek to accommodate the preferences of capital, or at least reassure investors of the safety of their investments, if their election or even the prospect of their election is not to precipitate a flurry of disinvestment. Social democrats, according to this view, would be well served by abandoning publicly and prominently their remaining commitments to radical reform – particularly (re)commodification or redistribution – well in advance of any election they wish to win (Wickham-Jones 1995b: 467). As Przeworski himself suggests, 'given the costs of anticipations, left-wing governments may best promote the interests of their constituencies by assuring capitalists that they would not pursue such policies' (1990: 95). This, as Przeworksi and Wallerstein are not embarrassed to admit, is but a small step from the neo-liberalism of the Chicago School itself. For this latter group of neo-classical economists, redistribution and political utility maximisation (vote seeking) are anathema; rational capitalists will simply withdraw (or relocate) their productive investments as taxes rise (and hence the projected return on that investment falls) (see Bates and Lein 1985; Becker 1983; Peltzmann 1976).[1]

In an era of much-vaunted globalisation, the logic of the argument might be taken one step further. For, if we can assume that capital is likely to associate the election of a social democratic administration with higher levels of domestic taxation and, in an integrated global economy, enjoys near perfect mobility (the assumptions that make the model possible), then the merest whiff of a hint of the election of a social democratic government is likely to be accompanied by a rapid and destabilising exodus of capital. Quite simply, then, this means that social democratic parties (and parties, such as Labour, which retain even residual social democratic associations) must effectively abandon their remaining social democratic credentials and accommodate themselves to the perceived interest of capital (for low taxation, labour-market deregulation, welfare retrenchment and fiscal austerity) if the very suggestion of their election is not to precipitate disinvestment, currency speculation and subsequent economic crisis. Within the parameters of such a thesis, whatever label one might choose to affix to one's party ethos, there is simply no alternative to neo-liberalism within contemporary capitalism.

What is so remarkable about such a thesis is the extent to which it seems to capture New Labour's strategic assessment of the context within which it finds itself – an assessment it seems to share with its antipodean namesakes and former social democratic allies across western Europe (see the various contributions to Glyn 1998; Sassoon 1997). New Labour has behaved in a manner entirely consistent with how a utility-maximising (former) social democratic party *would* act *were* the structural dependence thesis valid. This, as Wickham-Jones' careful and important analysis makes clear, can be seen in its studious courting, since 1992, of domestic industry, the City ('prawn-cocktail offensive' and all) and, eventually, international investors from Wall Street to Singapore (1995b; undated). What this suggests, in turn, is that Labour does indeed accept and embrace the logic of structural dependence and the logic of no alternative that it conjures. This makes a more dispassionate analysis of the structural dependence thesis all the more pressing. Before embarking upon such an exercise, a few preliminaries are perhaps in order.

Anticipating accommodations, accommodating anticipations
There can be little doubt that Mark Wickham-Jones' detailed analysis of Labour's economic modernisation and his attempt to demonstrate the relevance of the modified structural dependence thesis to such a project represent to date the most sophisticated and perceptive account we have of this process. In a seminal article in *Politics and Society* and in a series of papers, he provides a cogent, detailed and sophisticated account of the evolution of Labour's economic policy between the election defeats of 1987 and 1992 and, indeed, subsequently (1995b, undated, see also 1995a, 1996, 1997b). In so doing, he fills a considerable gap in our understanding of the political economy of New Labour (though see also Coates 1996; Panitch and Leys 1997; Thompson 1996) and, in particular, our understanding of the mechanisms of Labour's transformation in this respect. He also adapts and develops the modified structural dependence thesis of Przeworski and Wallerstein.

The result is an original and convincing periodisation of economic policy formation within the party after 1987, distinguishing between the Policy Review period, in which electoral considerations predominated, and the post-Review period, in which Labour sought to project itself to the City and the CBI as more representative of the interests of industrial and financial capital alike. This significant intervention in the debate on Labour's 'modernisation' raises a number of crucial questions regarding the prospects for social democratic parties in the post-Keynesian era and hence the range of alternatives that now present themselves (or might be presented) to a New Labour government.

His provocative, if perhaps rhetorical, conclusion – that social democratic parties may well be incapable of winning elections in today's advanced capitalist societies – is, I suggest, remarkably close to that the party has come to embrace tacitly in the post-Policy Review period as in government. As such, it is an argument whose significance can scarcely be overstated. Given the magnitude of its implications, it is, moreover, an argument which must be exposed to the most intense theoretical and empirical scrutiny.

In what follows, I suggest that whilst the cost of Labour's chosen strategy for securing electability may well have been its social democratic credentials, this does not entail Wickham-Jones' more general conclusion. Social democracy need not necessarily be sacrificed on the altar of economic or electoral expediency. I argue that Wickham-Jones' over-generalised conclusion can be traced to the limitations of the modified structural dependence thesis: its historically undifferentiated conception of the relationship between the state and capital; its assumption that social democratic governments act in the interest of labour to the detriment of capital (in, what is in effect, a zero-sum game); and its failure to assess either the strategic alternatives to, or the consequences of, preference-accommodation for social democratic parties. When these weaknesses are considered, it becomes apparent that it is the political logic of preference-accommodation, and not that of capital accumulation, which dictates that social democratic parties cannot win elections. Moreover, if Labour in government continues to consign itself to the politics of preference-accommodation (whether directed at capital or at the electorate), then it can only be to the long-term detriment of British capital, the competitiveness of the British economy and Labour's traditional constituencies alike. For it is only by acting against the short-term interests and immediate preferences of capital (as currently conceived) that governments (of whatever political complexion) can secure the conditions for long-term economic competitiveness. In the final sections of the chapter, I argue that there is an alternative to the politics of capital appeasement, making a distinctive case for the politics of preference-shaping and the projection of an alternative to the ascendant neo-liberal economic paradigm.

Modifying and qualifying the structural dependence thesis
In restating the structural dependence thesis, Wickham-Jones presents us with the central strategic dilemma of social democratic parties: 'all governments, left-wing or not, are constrained in what they can do by the need to sustain economic conditions that promote investment' (1995b: 466). Yet, as he notes, even this is to paint an unduly optimistic picture. For the assumption which informs the thesis is that it is only when left-wing parties find themselves in government that capital flight and disinvestment begin. Przeworski and Wallerstein's *modified* structural dependence theory suggests instead that it is in the very moment of *anticipation* of such an electoral victory that the torrent of capital flight will commence (1988; Przeworski 1990). The challenge, then, for parties of the left is to convince capital of the fiscal probity and responsibility of their measures before election, whilst sustaining a popular political project capable of providing a sufficient

electoral base. To juggle these often conflicting imperatives is no mean feat, as the recent history of the British Labour Party testifies.

This is an important argument, one that clearly has highly significant strategic implications for social democratic parties and one which deserves closer scrutiny. At first sight it would appear obvious enough that if capital is mobile, parties of the left must indeed sustain and promote conditions conducive to continued investment. Yet it is important to note that this is primarily a discursive bind. The assumptions of the modified structural dependence thesis are: (i) that capital will invest where it receives the greatest rewards on that investment; (ii) that capital is blessed with perfect knowledge of the conditions likely to maximise returns on investment; and (iii) that social democratic parties tend not to act in the 'objective' interest(s) of capital (Przeworski and Wallerstein 1988: 14–15, 20–1). Within this framework, what is required of parties of the left is that they demonstrate – to the satisfaction of capital – that they will indeed act in its interest(s), while abandoning all (social democratic) measures that threaten to advance interests not held (by capital) to be conducive to profit maximisation (over capital's preferred time horizon).

The problem here is (primarily) one of perceptions.[2] Capital invests where it _perceives_ and _projects_ the greatest likelihood of a return on that investment. Yet it has no privileged vantage point from which to cast its gaze into the future, no privileged perspective from which to make such projections. Accordingly, its investment and disinvestment decisions are often informed by (more or less) conventional mappings of the terrain of the global political economy that are, or may prove to be, demonstrably false. Once it is recalled that (i) capital has no single universal interest (as distinct from a series of divergent and conflicting interests projected over different time horizons), that (ii) it tends to act in pursuit of short-term gain often to the detriment of longer-term advantage, and that (iii) the capitalist class, far from actively sponsoring major reforms in its long-term collective interest, often provides the most vociferous opposition to such measures (Block 1987a; for a commentary, Hay 1999d) the argument that parties of the left should seek to accommodate the preferences of capital in economic policy formation appears less appealing. Tempting though it might seem, however, this cannot be the end of the story. For, to the extent that social democratic administrations are dependent upon the investment decisions of capital, as Przeworski and Wallerstein rightly note, the perceived interest(s) of the latter cannot simply be ignored. The dilemma deepens.

The problem can be restated – in this now doubly modified structural dependence thesis – as follows. Accommodating one's strategy to the preferences of capital by seeking to incorporate the *perceived* interests of capital into an accumulation strategy may well have the (unintended) effect of undermining the long-term stability and/or competitiveness of the economy. For, as Block notes, capital is (generally)[3] incapable of acting in its own long-term collective interest (1987a: 55–7; 1987b: 62, 66–7; Finegold and Skocpol 1995: 196–9) – as, presumably, is a government that simply accommodates itself to the preferences and perceived interests of capital. If capitalist reproduction at a national level is to be secured successfully within a competitive global market economy, then the state must act as a collective *custodian* of capital – as if an 'ideal collective capitalist'.[4] This it simply cannot do if it seeks merely to ascertain, anticipate, accommodate and appease (as distinct from, say, shape, educate and transform) the preformulated perceived interest of capital. Yet, as Wickham-Jones powerfully demonstrates, this was precisely Labour's principal ambition in economic policy formation between the publication of the Policy Review in 1989 and the general election of 1992 (1995b: 487). Had Labour succeeded in winning that election, the clear danger was that it would have done so merely to contribute further to the undermining of the long-term competitiveness of the British economy in the name of the parochial and conservative interests of capital. This it would have done having already dispensed with those more positive aspects of its strategy (well documented by Wickham-Jones 1995b: 468–70) that might have begun to address the persistent and institutionally inscribed structural frailty of the British economy. By seeking to internalise the perceived interest of capital, then, Labour threatened to militate against the realisation of its 'real' interest.[5]

Was there an alternative? The pessimism of Wickham-Jones' account – in many respects mirroring that of Przeworski and Wallerstein – derives from the premise that social democratic governments cannot manage capitalism without effectively internalising and acting upon the (existing) preferences of capital. The consequence of any failure *either* to demonstrate to capital's satisfaction the projection of its interests in the framing of economic policy, *or* to realise such interests in substantive policy initiatives once in government, is capital flight and inevitable economic crisis. Social democratic parties thus find themselves precariously positioned between the horns of a particularly intractable dilemma. For the aim of social democratic parties (one might surmise) must be to achieve governmental (and state) power in order to realise and institutionalise a social democratic project. Yet the very condition of achieving governmental power is that such parties must first sacrifice most (if not all) of their social democratic credentials. It is to Wickham-Jones' credit that he does not shy away from the logical conclusions of this argument. Indeed, despite the profound pessimism it must surely engender, he bravely concludes, 'The crux of the revised structural dependence thesis may be, not that social democrats will inherit an economic crisis, but that they will not be able to win elections at all' (1995b: 488). To be elected, and effective in government, social democratic parties must abandon their social democracy.

However, before trooping off to jump on our swords, it is worth considering the theoretical and empirical limitations of this argument – if only to inspire, in Gramsci's terms, a little 'optimism of the spirit' to temper the gathering 'pessimism of the intellect'. Three principal weaknesses of the modified structural dependence thesis (as advanced by Wickham-Jones) can be identified. In the sections that follow we consider each in turn.

The historical specificity of structural dependence
Perhaps the most immediately obvious limitation of the modified structural dependence thesis is also, ironically, the basis of its appeal – its generality. The thesis rests on an historically undifferentiated model of the relationship between the state and capital. This model is premised upon a series of assumptions which may be held to pertain to any western European society in the post-war period. These are the existence of: (i) a democratic polity; (ii) a social democratic party seeking electoral gain; and (iii) a (national) capitalist economy characterised by a rigid demarcation between wage earners and the owners of capital. Thus if, as Wickham-Jones contends, the model generates the prediction that social democrats 'will not be able to win elections at all', the model is indeed historically undifferentiated as argued above *and* an example of a social democratic party winning an election in post-war western Europe can be found, then the model is presumably refuted by its own criteria.

Of course, Przeworski and Wallerstein do not predict that social democratic parties cannot win elections. On the basis of their model, they do nonetheless suggest that 'social democrats seeking power will moderate their proposals wholesale before the election (to meet the policy desires of capitalists) or they will risk precipitating an economic crisis' (Wickham-Jones 1995b: 467). Again, if an example of a social democratic government can be found which did not manage to allay the fears of capital prior to its election and whose term in office was not truncated by economic crisis, then the thesis would appear to have been refuted on its own terms. Numerous examples (in a number of European contexts) spring to mind, though that of the Attlee government in Britain will serve for current purposes (on capital's fear of 'socialism' in 1945 see for instance Miliband 1970; Morgan 1984; Tiratsoo 1991; Tiratsoo and Tomlinson 1993).

Though the thesis need not be dismissed entirely on the basis of this critique, a significant qualification is surely called for. For, as the example of the Attlee government reveals, social democratic administrations have indeed been elected which did not successfully appease capital (at least to capital's satisfaction), which managed to enact significant social and economic reform and which did not precipitate economic crisis (at least, not by Przeworski and Wallerstein's standards). At minimum, then, an extra proposition is required which might indicate how the situation facing aspiring social democratic administrations has changed over the last fifty years.

In fact, such a proposition is not that difficult to find. Arguments are frequently made to the effect that the current context is, when set in historical terms, qualitatively distinctive and that there is a higher price to be paid for social democratic political aspirations today than, say, in 1945. Wickham-Jones hints at precisely such an argument when he suggests that, in the 1990s, 'with far fewer restrictions on the movement of capital, the bind on Labour is tighter still' (1995b: 466; see also Cerny 1995; Cohen 1998; Moses 1994; Schmidt 1995). In so doing, he invokes a conception frequently deployed by New Labour modernisers – in opposition as in government. Two mechanisms by which this (putative) effect might be realised can be differentiated. The first is the 'exit' of footloose foreign direct investment; the second, the ease and speed with which financial capital (as distinct from place-bound 'locational' investment) may flow on the foreign exchange markets out of currencies whose governments reveal themselves 'incompetent' or 'profligate'. Both processes are invoked in New Labour's new political economy.

In a recent unpublished paper, Wickham-Jones is quick to acknowledge this, citing a number of interviews to this effect with Labour advisors and politicians. As John Eatwell, former economic advisor to Neil Kinnock, himself remarks:

> Credibility has become the keystone of policy-making in the nineties.
> A credible government is a government that pursues a policy that is
> 'market friendly'; this is a policy that is in accordance with what the
> markets believe to be sound. (Eatwell 1996: 12; cited in Wickham-
> Jones undated: 6)

This is not merely the personal view of former advisors, however. For
even if we restrict ourselves to public statements by Cabinet (or
shadow Cabinet) members, the message is a clear one. Thus, in his
shadow budget statement in November 1995, Gordon Brown claimed
that 'business will never have the confidence to invest for the future,
unless they [*sic*] believe that the macroeconomic environment will
remain stable' (1995a). As Chancellor, Brown's views have not
changed. Financial capitalists, he has observed, now have 'more choice
and freedom than ever before, and day to day flows of capital are
greater and faster than ever before.... Today, the judgement of the
markets – whether to punish or to reward government policies – is as
swift as it is powerful' (cited in Shaw 1997). This orthodoxy is well
captured by David Andrews in the following terms: 'when capital is
highly mobile across international borders, the sustainable macro-
economic policy options available to states are systematically
circumscribed' (1994: 193). Similarly, Eric Helleiner notes, the threat
of capital flight and currency crisis 'has given those who control
internationally mobile funds ... an increasingly powerful tool of "exit"
with which to encourage changes indirectly in government policy
towards their preferences' (1994: 173). If we are to take such comments at face value, then there may be good reasons for expecting the
burden of structural dependence to be all the more considerable in an
era of heightened capital mobility and financial deregulation.[6]
    The implications of such a qualification are themselves very
interesting. For, if correct, this *modified* and *qualified* structural
dependence thesis would imply that, where once states (and governments giving effect to state power) retained a degree of autonomy from
capital that was sufficient for them to act as custodians of the general
interest of capital, with financial globalisation and the greater mobility
of capital that this has engendered this is no longer the case. The
consequence may well be the accumulation of capitalist contradictions
at a national level as governments are increasingly constrained to act in
the short-term *perceived* interests of particular capitals to the detriment
of the long-term collective interest of capital *per se*. Yet this would be

to share with Przeworski, Wallerstein and Wickham-Jones the assumption that parties (of whatever complexion) must indeed internalise the preferences of capital in formulating economic policy (a point to which we return below). Moreover, it implies a singular and unanimous *interest* of capital which can be gauged, accommodated and appeased.

What price governmental power?

A second problem with the modified structural dependence thesis concerns Przeworski's assertion that 'left wing governments may best promote the interests of their constituencies by assuring capitalists that they would not pursue such [radical and redistributive] policies' (1990: 95). This is a slightly ambiguous passage and one which could be read in two rather different senses. It is certainly tempting to interpret Przeworski as hinting that social democratic governments might reinterpret (if not totally abandon) their pre-election pledges, promises and assurances once in power. This is certainly how some disillusioned, frustrated, but nonetheless exceedingly optimistic Labour activists liked to interpret New Labour's apparent accommodation to much of the Thatcherite legacy in opposition. Yet given Przeworski's broader (if qualified) sympathy for the (unmodified) structural dependence thesis, this reading is probably inaccurate.

Indeed, what is most problematic here is the suggestion that social democratic parties which assure capitalists that they will not pursue radical and/or redistributivist policies, and which do not renege on such pledges, are capable in any meaningful sense of acting 'in the interests of their constituencies'. Surely there must be some cut-off point at which we no longer regard nominally 'social democratic' parties as acting in the interests of 'their constituencies' (presumably the broader labour movement). This point, I would contend, comes at precisely the moment when redistribution is sacrificed on the altar of political and economic expediency (see the discussion of social democracy in chapter 2). As the recent history of the Labour Party demonstrates only too well, aspiring governments set on appeasing capital often find it hard to remember what their 'true' or at least historical constituency is. Though Labour has thus far resisted the temptation to dispense with the proletarian connotations of its name, it is at least debatable that it continues to warrant the label 'labourist', or for that matter 'social democratic'. Much of the party's 'modernisation' has been a scarcely veiled attempt to reconfigure its 'natural constituency', albeit driven by the (laudable) imperative of achieving governmental power. This raises perhaps the most significant objection to the modified structural dependence thesis, namely its failure to consider alternatives to preference-accommodation.

Alternatives to preference-accommodation

Wickham-Jones' article presents a detailed and sophisticated account of the trajectory of Labour's 'modernisation' between 1987 and the 1992 election and the party's projection of a novel construction of itself to the electorate and to capital alike. Whilst the period of the Policy Review (1987–9) can be seen as one of *electoral* preference-accommo- dation, 'market-research socialism' (Leys 1990), or the psephologically inspired 'politics of catch-up' (see chapter 2), the period after 1989 can similarly be characterised as one of accommodation to the preferences of *capital*. This raises the question of *alternatives to* preference- accommodation. The fundamental premise of the structural dependence thesis (however modified, however qualified) is that social democratic parties cannot win elections, or if elected cannot remain in power, whilst they fail to accommodate themselves to the preferences and perceived interests of capital. Disinvestment and economic crisis will surely follow.

Need this be so? The logic of the argument developed thus far is that an alternative does, indeed, exist. Moreover, if capital is in fact incapable either of perceiving, far less acting in, its own collective interest (or at least, if there can be no guarantee of this happy conformity of preference, interest and action), then an alternative is required if an accumulation of economic contradictions is to be averted. Put simply, if the British state under Labour management is not to heap further dereliction upon the structures of an ailing British economy, it must regain sufficient autonomy to act in the longer-term collective interest of capital at the expense of the more immediate and parochial considerations of specific capitals and sectors thereof. This is surely one of the lessons of the Thatcherite project.

If Labour is to overturn its complicity in the consolidation and attempted management of a deeply contradictory political and econ- omic settlement that is the legacy of Thatcherism, it must first abandon the politics of *preference-accommodation* (whether directed at capital or the electorate) in favour of that of *preference-shaping*. This, as was suggested in chapter 3, was no small task in opposition and is likely only to prove considerably more difficult in government (see also

Lindblom 1977: 135–7; for an alternative view, see Smith 1994: 711). Yet it is only if it can (re)discover the voice and conviction in government to project an alternative conception of a dynamic and competitive British economy (freed from the imperative to compete on the basis of a hire-and-fire, low-wage, low-skill strategy) that social democracy and economic competitiveness can indeed be salvaged. So long as Labour *in opposition* continued to play the 'politics of catch-up' by the rules of preference-accommodation and capital appeasement, it could only continue to sacrifice social democratic values on the altar of electoral expediency; so long as Labour *in government* continues to abide by the terms of the resulting political and economic settlement, it can only serve further to consolidate a post-social-democratic polity and a post-industrial economy. As Wickham-Jones' depressing tale of Labour's trajectory from electoral defeat to electoral defeat suggests, Labour's social democracy was effectively emptied of all content long before its electability was achieved via this route. It is the restrictive logic of preference-accommodation, then, that dictates that social democrats cannot win elections.

If what (little) remains of Labour's positive agenda for economic and political reform is not to go the way of its former proposals for a reinvigorated DTI, a central British investment bank, regional investment banks, effective regional institutions for economic development, pension law reform to promote long-term capital investment, and so forth, it is to preference-shaping on all fronts that the party must turn. Preference-shaping, however, is no easy task (Smith 1994; Wickham-Jones 1996: 189–91; 1997b). New Labour certainly has the opportunity in government to prove Wickham-Jones' version of the structural dependence thesis wrong. Yet, as its years in office provides ample testimony, it seems more likely that it will provide some form of seeming confirmation.[7] For now, at any rate, it would seem that electoral triumph was bought at a high (perhaps even the ultimate) cost to Labour's former social democracy.

Lacing the poison chalice: New Labour and
the Thatcherite inheritance
In 1997, and arguably in 1992 and even 1987, Labour presented itself to the electorate on the basis of its relative competence in the management of the Thatcherite legacy. Lacking a clear diagnosis of the British affliction and the confidence or vision to project a distinctive alternative, this might have appeared, as it appears today, both expedient and

unremarkable. Yet it does not exhaust the party's contemporary conservatism. For, in accommodating itself to the terms of the Thatcherite
legacy, the party has chosen to restrict itself to a repertoire of
managerial techniques and resources heavily circumscribed by a neo-
liberal economic imagery. Though reinflected in more communitarian
rhetoric, the ascendant paradigm of free-market liberalism has thus
come to demarcate the boundaries of the politically and economically
possible for both parties. This new economic convergence effectively
precludes the degree of supply-side intervention that is a condition of
the restoration of an indigenous growth dynamic to the British
economy (Hirst 1994: 94; Reynolds and Coates 1996: 259–60).

Implicit in this paradigm was an understanding of the Major
government as unlucky, and at worst incompetent, in economic matters. For if Labour's macro-economic policy is merely a variant on a
Conservative theme, then to accuse the then incumbent government of
macro-economic mismanagement was, frankly, disingenuous.[8] It is not
surprising, then, that Labour shied away from the more dispassionate
(and ultimately more convincing) analysis: that the Major government
was attempting the impossible – the management and attempted
consolidation of the structures of a deeply contradictory post-Thatcher
settlement that was the Thatcherite legacy; and, moreover, that it was
attempting the impossible with a range of strategic resources heavily
depleted by the anti-statism of its economic convictions. Sadly, given
the macro-economic convergence between the parties, for Labour to
have admitted this would have been tantamount to an exercise in auto-
critique.

The clear danger was that Labour would achieve governmental
power at the cost of consigning itself to futile attempts to manage the
contradictions of a political and economic legacy in an advanced state
of decay. Accordingly, it may have come to inherit not only the crisis
tendencies of the Thatcherite inheritance but also, by virtue of its own
failure to identify and narrate such contradictions, responsibility for
their management.[9] New Labour's laudable (if touchingly naive) aim to
reconcile its newly ascendant economic liberalism with a more inclusive conception of social justice may merely serve to lace with
hemlock the poison chalice of its inheritance (see also Thompson
1996). Far from exorcising the 'ghost of winters past', Labour's
pursuit of governmental power may merely serve to resurrect it,
implicating the party in the disintegration of a deeply contradictory
settlement.[10] This may present a Tory opposition (if one can be found

and resuscitated) with an opportunity to reimagine, reposition and renew its political project, presenting itself once again as the only party capable of the degree of decisive intervention required in a situation of economic and political crisis. Although New Labour is anxious to present itself as the natural heir to the spirit of 1945 (Blair 1994, 1995), comparisons with 1974 threaten to prove somewhat more realistic (though cf. Tomlinson 1997).

Was there an alternative in the mid-1980s? Is there an alternative now? My answer to both these questions is a qualified and somewhat equivocal 'yes'. As I have been at pains to emphasise, however, the political conditions of making the transition from where Labour was – and remains – to such an alternative are rather more exacting now than they were with Labour in opposition. In opposition, as I attempt to demonstrate in the pages that follow, preference-shaping (whether directed at the electorate, capital or both) is facilitated in a context in which the incumbent administration has demonstrated itself incompetent and/or crisis prone. Under such conditions, it is a relatively simple task for the opposition to distance itself from the governing economic and political paradigm, whose obsolescence it may loudly and publicly proclaim.[11] By so doing, the opposition may pose (however opportunistically) as the government in waiting, blessed (if only in its own terms) with a rather more sophisticated analysis of the contemporary predicament and of the measures appropriate to its remedy. In government, the situation is rather different – indeed, the tables are, in certain respects, reversed. For quite apart from the fact that the new opposition may present itself in precisely such terms, it is also altogether more difficult for an incumbent administration to distance itself from the very ideas it so recently came to espouse and embrace and which were central to its appeal to the electorate. Were this not yet difficult enough, even if such a distancing could be accomplished, it is extremely difficult to develop in government an alternative economic and political paradigm, far less to admit the obsolescence of the old paradigm, which is the very condition of the transition to the new. Arguably, this is precisely the predicament that New Labour now faces in government – or, at least, will face once the contradictions of its 'softened neo-liberalism' are exposed by rather less propitious economic circumstances than those it currently enjoys.

If it is altogether more difficult to undergo an economic conversion in government than in opposition, then it is nonetheless important that we consider the viability of New Labour's alternatives to neo-liberal economics, both in opposition and with Tony Blair as Prime Minister. In the remainder of this chapter, I consider the now largely historical alternatives which might have been available in the run-up to the 1997 election, before turning in the final chapter to a consideration of the options (if any) now available to New Labour in government.

In the context of the above discussion, the challenge for Labour in the run-up to the 1997 election was considerable. Were Labour to avoid inheriting responsibility (and culpability) from the Conservatives for the looming crisis (as it did in 1974), it would have had to offer not only a compelling diagnosis of the current British affliction (and its origins), but also to convince capital and the electorate alike that a resolution of that affliction (and Labour's chosen resolution at that) was an immediate concern overriding more parochial and short-term considerations of vested interest and material gain. In short, Labour would have had to recast the preferences and perceived interests of capital and the electorate (or at least broad sections thereof) on the basis of its assessment of the 'state we're in'. New Labour would thus have had to project, to both capital and the electorate in equal measure, a genuinely novel conception of the state, economy and society, and their mutually reinforcing and growth-sustaining symbiosis. Such an alternative projection would, in turn, have required: (i) a clear and resonant depiction of 'where we are' – a diagnosis of the contemporary British affliction; (ii) an attractive yet realistic conception of 'where we might be' (a projected end-state); and (iii) a clearly delineated account of how to get from one to the other.[12]

In the following section, I begin to suggest how the British Labour Party might have presented itself to the electorate and capital alike as offering a decisive intervention – the basis for a 'rectifying economic revolution' – in a situation of secular economic deterioration, social dislocation and political stagnation.

Renewing Labour: towards a rectifying revolution?

It is perhaps the central contention of this book that a radical departure from the economic nostrums of neo-liberalism, and from the institutional architecture of a deeply contradictory post-Thatcher settlement, is a necessary (though not in itself sufficient) condition of restoring an investment-led growth dynamic to the British economy. This was as true in 1992, 1995 or 1997 as it is today. Ironically, then, the politics of capital appeasement may well lead – indeed, may well *have led* – Labour to internalise a set of preferences (for fiscal conservatism and institutional stability) that were, as they remain, deleterious to any more dispassionate conception of the 'genuine interest' of British capital. Indeed, the more general logic of Wickham-Jones' argument might suggest that in an era of globalisation – in which the enhanced 'exit options' for capital threaten to engender a game of deregulatory arbitrage – parties (of whatever political complexion) are driven (at pain of capital flight) to internalise the perceived interest of capital to the ultimate detriment of capital's 'real' interest. If true, this would suggest a tendency (coupled to that of globalisation) for the exacerbation of capitalism's long-term contradictions as the state increasingly loses the autonomy it requires to act as the 'custodian of the general interest of capital'.[13]

Yet there are reasons for thinking that this is perhaps an unduly catastrophist image. For the threat of capital flight can be, and has tended to be, somewhat exaggerated. Though capital may have a strategic stake in emphasising its mobility, and in playing up the likelihood of its imminent departure in the run-up to an election in which a genuine social democratic alternative is perceived to exist, this hardly guarantees a mass exodus of capital in the post-election period (see Drache 1996; Garrett 1998; Hirst and Thompson 1994, 1995, 1996: 115–20; Wade 1996: 80–1).[14] New Labour's new-found macroeconomic conservatism would appear to demonstrate precisely the effectiveness of such pre-election bravado on the part of capital.

It is tempting, then, to conclude that Labour in power should call the bluff of so-called 'footloose' multinational corporations and investors, and advocate instead, say, an expansive social democratic programme oblivious to the likely protestations from domestically located capital. Yet there are at least two good reasons for holding back on such wilful antagonism (however tempting it might seem). First, though capital is by no means 'footloose', financial globalisation has served to lubricate its flows – capital flight in the form of currency speculation is a genuine threat.[15] Second, and more significantly, *threatened* capital flight (however hollow the threat) and the *perception* of its likelihood *in the event of the election of a social democratic government*, may militate severely against such an outcome. Applied to the current British context, the lesson is once again that Labour (whether in opposition or government) must take the interests (short term, long term, perceived and substantive) of capital seriously – more seriously perhaps than it has (or has had to) in the past. In so doing, it must seek to persuade potentially mobile capital in particular that its economic policies, precisely by virtue of their departures from neo-liberal ortho-doxies, will strengthen the productive capacity of the British economy, thereby contributing to economic growth and securing higher rates of return on capital investment. The politics of persuasion and preference-shaping are thus placed once again at centre stage.

Whilst the *general* case for the politics of preference-shaping can be made and defended on its own, what a renewed Labour Party requires is a conception of preference-shaping *in the particular*. Though such a framework cannot be formulated overnight – indeed, the time for developing such a new political imagery to animate a political project for Labour's first term has long since passed – the analysis cannot be allowed to terminate here. Yet before proceeding to outline the broad parameters of an alternative economic and political strategy for New Labour, one proviso is in order. The more general argument for a decisive break with a state and economic inheritance that is un-manageable (and hence the more general argument for an end to the politics of capital appeasement and electoral accommodation) should not, indeed cannot, be dismissed simply on the basis of a rejection of one particular reform strategy. For, once liberated from the shackles of a restrictive neo-liberal paradigm, the boundaries of political and economic possibility (however constrained by global economic dynam-ics) can sustain a great variety of alternative diagnoses, accumulation strategies and political projects. The suggestion that globalisation necessitates neo-liberalism reveals not only a fatalistic economic determinism but, more importantly, a profound failure of political imagination.[16] The left in Britain (as elsewhere) must (re)gain the courage to challenge the near-hegemonic association of globalisation and transnational neo-liberalism, and must suggest that not only is there an alternative, but that the restoration of a growth trajectory to British capitalism is conditional upon the ability to find one.

In developing a schematic outline of one such alternative, I will follow the strategy outlined above and consider in turn: (i) where we are (the diagnosis of the contemporary impasse); (ii) where we might get to (the projection of an alternative future); and (iii) how we might get there (the political strategy to effect the transition from 'here' to 'there'). These are themes to which we return in much greater detail in the final chapter.

Where we are: diagnosing the British affliction

There are perhaps two principal ways in which the contemporary British impasse might be narrated. The first is more historical and relates the contradictions of the current period to the persistent structural weaknesses of the British economy (the principal theme of the next chapter). These can be traced in particular to its 'capital market-based' financial system (Pollin 1995). The result is Britain's distinctive 'exit-weighted' political economy (Hirschmann 1970; Zysman 1983). This is characterised by short-term time horizons, fragmented investment portfolios, fitful as opposed to dedicated capital, a propensity for mergers and take-overs as opposed to long-term productive investment and, in recent years, a haemorrhaging of institutional investment in domestic industry altogether (Albert 1993; Anderson 1992; Cowling and Sugden 1990; Gourevitch 1996; Hirst 1989; Hutton 1996; Pollin 1995; Woolcock 1996; Zysman 1983). It is dominated by 'exit' (as opposed to financial intervention) as the principal means of exercising influence. Despite the post-war rhetoric of Keynesianism and corporatism, and despite the significant extension of the welfare state in the initial post-war period, the peculiarly British dislocation of financial and industrial capital was merely reinforced in this period and the over-determining influence of the 'City–Bank–Treasury nexus' on economic policy reaffirmed (Ingham 1984; Leys 1986). In this sense, the economic settlement of the post-war period, with its emphasis upon a stable value for sterling, was inherited broadly intact from the inter-war years – its contradictions merely exacerbated by the simultaneous commitment to a universal welfare state (initially) free at the point of access to all. The immediate casualty was industrial modernisation, for which there was little enthusiasm; the long-term casualty was the ability of the British economy to sustain a comprehensive welfare state on the basis of its manufacturing capacity.

The initial post-war economic boom would serve to protect this fragile institutional compromise well into the 1960s, when the full extent of its latent contradictions was eventually revealed. Yet, once again, systematic industrial modernisation, though much vaunted, was persistently deferred. Corporatist institutions were now turned to as crisis management became the order of the day. Predictably enough, it was the ability of the Tories to manage the contradictions of the state by deploying corporatist techniques that was exhausted first as Heath was forced to declare a 'three-day week' in 1974. Thus it was a Labour administration that was to preside over the last rights of the post-war settlement as the 'social contract' disintegrated in the 'Winter of Discontent' of 1978–9 (Gamble 1994; Hay 1996b; Jessop 1980; Pollard 1980).

This was to provide the context within which a Thatcherite narration of the 'crisis' of an 'overextended' state 'besieged by the trade unions' was to find resonance, recruiting personal experiences of the Winter of Discontent to its call for a decisive break with the institutional compromises of the post-war 'consensus', whilst appealing to the paranoid anti-statism of British capital (financial and industrial alike) (Hay 1996a). Yet far from addressing the persistent structural weaknesses of the British economy, the Thatcher governments merely served to deepen them – strengthening the position of the financial sector at ever greater cost to the productive economy. The result, as oft remarked upon, has been the institutional and cultural entrenchment of an anachronistic and increasingly pathological tradition of 'gentlemanly capitalism'. Manufacturing industry has thus become dependent upon 'dividend-hungry, arms' length financial institutions and a stock market that all too easily facilitates external and hostile take-over bids if the share price slips' (Hirst 1994: 130–1).

The lessons of such an economic history need to be heeded if New Labour in power is not to reproduce the errors of its social democratic forebears. Yet despite the resonance it might find with British industrialists, a populist political diagnosis of the British affliction it is not. The political problem with such an analysis is its tendency to reduce Thatcherism to a factor (albeit an exacerbating one) in the preservation of the *status quo ante* – merely the latest chapter in an uninterrupted (if uneven) trajectory of decline established in the 1870s, if not before. The specificity of its contribution to the competitive deficit of the British economy is singularly downplayed.

Yet if this should make Labour wary of a populist political strategy based exclusively upon such an analysis, the importance of the *long durée* should not – indeed cannot – be understated. If Labour is to reverse the long trajectory of British decline, then it must be capable of recognising its own culpability in 1945, 1964 and 1974 (and, indeed, in 1924 and in 1929) in the silent reaffirmation of the hegemony of financial capital and the indefinite postponement of industrial modernisation. An account of the historical trajectory of the British state and economy since the late nineteenth century must then be complemented by a passionate and unashamedly populist *exposé* of the contradictions of Thatcherite neo-liberalism and its social and economic pathologies (addressed once again to capital and the electorate in equal measure).

The economic pathologies of the Thatcherite legacy are legion (see chapter 2). Nonetheless, there is one theme which might unify this disaggregated array of 'morbid symptoms', providing the basis for the mobilisation of a popular crisis narrative. This is the perversity of a neo-liberal disavowal of state intervention at a time of economic obsolescence, uncompetitiveness and structural weakness (Cowling and Sugden 1994: 39; Reynolds and Coates 1996: 260). If the crisis of the late 1970s was one of 'overload' (King 1975) – of an overextended and unwieldy state – that of the 1990s is one of 'under-load' – of a state absolved of the responsibility and stripped of the strategic capacity for the promotion of investment-led economic growth.

Where to next? Projecting an alternative

Such a diagnosis of the contemporary British affliction might have provided (as it still might provide today) New Labour with the space in which to project a distinctive vision of an alternative future capable of recruiting the support of domestic industrial capital and broad sections of the electorate alike. This would in turn have allowed the party to distance itself from the economic nostrums of neo-liberalism, to apportion responsibility for its contradictions and to present itself to the electorate (as the Conservatives did at the 1979 general election) as offering a decisive intervention in a condition of economic and political crisis – a break with the redundant orthodoxies of free-market liberalism. In so doing, Labour might learn much from the Conservatives' 1979 manifesto and, indeed, their strategy in the ensuing election campaign. The Thatcherites' emphasis in 1979 was on the outdatedness of the ruling ideas, the necessity of an economic paradigm shift and, above all, the need for a government with the conviction to effect a decisive break with the decaying institutional compromises of the post-war period. The Conservatives' manifesto was rhetorically rich and philosophically portentous, mapping out a broad trajectory of change and giving coherent expression to a distinctive 'Thatcherite instinct'. Yet it was extremely thin on policy commitments and almost completely silent on substantive policy detail.[17]

If the search for the vision to animate such an alternative political project has hardly been extensive, then part of the responsibility must surely lie with New Labour's principal think-tanks (the Institute for Public Policy Research, the Institute for Fiscal Studies and the more independently minded Demos). They did not serve the party well in its long period of electoral exile. Indeed, though keen to proclaim themselves think-tanks of the 'centre-left', they have been exceedingly reluctant to act as organic intellectuals for a New Labour (counter-) offensive. The comparison with the think-tanks of the new right (such as the Adam Smith Institute, the Institute for Economic Affairs and the Centre for Policy Studies) is both stark and telling. If the latter were characterised in the 1970s by their attempts to prepare the groundwork for the Thatcherite crusade and to contribute to a sea change in the 'climate of opinion', the think-tanks of the self-styled 'radical centre' in the 1990s have consigned their creativity to the parameters of a free-market liberalism whose ascendancy they refuse to challenge. The result has been a welter of detailed policy prescription and very little else.

The futility of such an exercise was clearly revealed by Labour's obvious reluctance to declare its economic (or for that matter political) colours in the run-up to the 1997 election, choosing instead to make a political virtue of its anonymity on economic policy whilst hinting strongly at fiscal rectitude and macro-economic conservatism. The experience of 1987 and 1992 certainly made Labour wary of macro-economic hostages to fortune in the pre-election period. Yet there is another (and more positive) way to make a political virtue out of this reluctance to divulge detailed policy proposals in advance of an election. This is to follow the strategy of the Conservatives in 1979 and to engage not in a debate about economic policy detail, but about the need for a new economic paradigm which might inform substantive policy initiatives at a later stage. As the experience of the Thatcher governments since 1979 makes clear, institutional changes do not occur overnight. The only means to effect a decisive break with the institutional compromises of the past is to retain office whilst formulating and reformulating policy within a consistent economic and political paradigm. It was the existence of precisely such a paradigm that allowed a series of disaggregated and iterative policy changes to cohere over time into a process of cumulative structural transformation from 1979 to the present day. If Labour in office is to impose a new trajectory upon the institutions, processes and practices of the British economy and polity, then it must first win the battle to define and project a new economic paradigm – a battle for hearts and minds.

So what might this paradigm consist of? Economically, it is imperative that New Labour identifies the conditions of existence of a renewed growth dynamic, the conditions for the restoration of an *investment-led* growth dynamic to the British economy. Indeed, this is perhaps the one thing that Labour's 1997 election manifesto needed to establish – and one thing it certainly did not. The conditions of national economic growth might here be conceived of not in terms of 'blunt', economy-wide instruments of macro-economic demand-management, but rather in terms of 'sharp', local and regional interventions (principally on the supply side) that are sensitive to institutional and cultural specificities and both adaptive to evolving regional trajectories of economic growth and responsive to changing external circumstances and conditions of competitiveness (national, European and global). Such a vision might thus project *regional structures of innovation* and *regional institutions of investment.* These would promote complementary, yet potentially highly differentiated, regional growth dynamics that, although centrally co-ordinated, would be *regionally sustained* through specific, adaptive and flexible regional institutions embodying the principle of *regional 'stakeholding'.*

Behind this vision lies the basic premise that British industrial capital has to be encouraged to think long term if its competitiveness is to be restored through modernisation, diversification and strategic investment in new technologies, 'human capital' and new management techniques.[18] This requires a fundamental change in the mind set of British industrialists *and* a transformation of the institutional contexts within which such a mind set has arisen and become entrenched. This is a clear example of how a change in the perceptions of (domestic industrial) capital must go hand in hand with a programme of financial reform, (regional) institutional design and constitutional redesign. The vision is one of regional infrastructures of investment facilitating distinct, independent and indigenous regional growth trajectories. The role of the centre within this schema is to promote co-operation between regional economies, to militate against (and in certain instances outlaw) mutually destructive regional competitive strategies (such as regulatory undercutting to attract inward investment) and to facilitate the access of the British regions to European funds and to an emergent 'third tier' of trans-regional governance within Europe (Jeffery 1996).

In seeking to flesh out this alternative economic project, Labour need not return to an empty blackboard. For, though clearly underdeveloped, aspects of its former regional industrial policy might provide the basis for an alternative accumulation strategy. Labour's Industry Forum, particularly in its 1994 industrial policy manifesto *Winning for Britain*, developed an (albeit implicit) challenge to the ascendancy of macro-economic conservatism and neo-liberal economics more generally, emphasising: (i) industrial strategy; (ii) supply-side dirigisme; (iii) the need to establish and sustain indigenous regional growth profiles; and, above all, (iv) the subordination of the interests of finance capital to those of industrial capital and fiscal policy to an industrial modern-isation strategy (Labour Party Industry Forum 1994; see also Regional Policy Commission 1996).

The contradictions between such supply-side dirigisme and the fiscal fortitude so prominently expounded by the shadow Treasury team under Gordon Brown were not to go unnoticed – and they have since been resolved in favour of the latter. Since 1994, Labour's emphasis upon industrial strategy has gradually been diluted and its policy proposals first softened and then removed one by one as the supremacy of the Treasury team has been reasserted in the face of this challenge from within, and the shadow DTI team consigned once again to the margins.[19]

Yet even if Labour were to return to its earlier flirtations with regionally differentiated industrial regeneration strategies in seeking to project and develop an alternative growth dynamic, it would have to give far greater attention to the institutional architecture of regions as discrete, dynamic and competitive economies. A number of points might here be made.

First, Labour must seek to construct a nexus of regional agencies, institutions and organisations. This must be sufficiently flexible to formulate, monitor and reformulate complementary economic develop-ment strategies at the local, sub-regional and regional levels, whilst guaranteeing a dedicated supply of long-term financial capital for regional infrastructural and industrial investment. The resulting *re-gional structures of innovation* must be sensitive to the specificity of distinct regional economies, carving out for them competitive niches within the European and global market. To promote maximum produc-tive investment within the regional economy, a reform of pension fund legislation is also in order. This might involve two distinct but related components designed to promote new regional pension funds, on the one hand, and to encourage a 'regionalisation' of the investment portfolios of existing pension funds (the largest institutional investors operating in Britain today), on the other. The institutional details of such a regional reform package are discussed in more detail in the next chapter.

This nexus of regional agencies might be complemented at the central government level by a national fund for investment and infrastructure, administered by a national investment bank. This would provide large-scale and long-term funding, on the basis of competitive bidding, for substantial regional and trans-regional infrastructural projects (such as the Channel Tunnel rail link, the second Severn bridge, or the electrification of the west coast rail line).

This leaves the question of the role for national economic policy. If regional development agencies are to be involved in the *governance* of regional economic development (managing and seeking to achieve complementarity between local, sub-regional and regional initiatives), then the central role of the national state must be to perform a *meta-governance* function (managing and seeking to achieve compatibility between various regional growth strategies and providing macro-economic conditions conducive to a diversity of regionally differentiated accumulation strategies). The national state must serve to protect regional economies from mutually destructive competitive strategies, to facilitate and co-ordinate European resource procurement and, where appropriate, to provide matching funds.

Conclusion: getting from 'here' to 'there'

This brings us to perhaps the most important issue of all: the strategy to effect the transition from A to B. In fact, a process and mechanism of change are implicit in the above discussion, yet it bears repetition. There is much that the British left today can learn from the success of the new right in the late 1970s in providing a voice to narrate the contradictions (perceived and experiential) of the post-war state regime, enlisting such contradictions as symptoms in a resonant crisis diagnosis.

Though the institutions, practices and processes of the post-war settlement were by no means dismantled overnight, Thatcher's accession to power did serve to define and symbolise a discursive and paradigmatic shift with a past to which there could no longer be a return. The mobilisation of a sense of crisis and transition out of popular experiences of the late 1970s and the projection of an alternative economic and political paradigm would redefine the parameters within which economic policy would be formulated, assessed and reformulated. This would, in turn, facilitate a cumulative though iterative evolution of policy, mapping out a broad (if uneven) trajectory of change.

It is precisely such a sea change in ideas that Labour must seek to orchestrate if its 'renewal' is not to see it sacrifice social democracy for short-term political expediency. Yet, as I have sought to demonstrate, to effect this transition in government is no small task. It is, nonetheless, imperative if Labour is not to tie itself in office (as it threatens to do) to the management of a set of state institutions and practices that are deeply contradictory, have already proved themselves beyond the capacity of Majorite managerialism and whose contradictions are likely to be exacerbated by New Labour's residual social democratic sensitivities. The contemporary context, like that of the late 1970s, is one of profound and protracted state failure, social dislocation and economic contradiction. This presents New Labour with a clear choice: does it seek to project itself as the party of fiscal rectitude and managerial competence – the natural heir to the legacy of Thatcherism – or does it seek to diagnose and narrate the crisis of the British state, arguing the case for a decisive break with the structures, practices and ideologies of a decaying state regime?

The evidence of recent experience would suggest that, in so far as it has recognised the choice, it has chosen the former option. The cost may indeed prove to be British social democracy itself.

Postscript

The first version of this chapter was written some time before the 1997 general election. In the proceeding pages, I have sought to update, expand and develop that earlier analysis in the light of subsequent developments. Yet the broad structure of the argument has remained essentially intact. It is perhaps, then, appropriate that I should consider and respond directly to Mark Wickham-Jones' rejoinder (1997b) to the earlier article (Hay 1997b), which raises a number of crucial issues concerning the status of the modified structural dependence thesis.

That the British Labour Party won the 1997 general election is surely testament to the success of its internalisation of a form of modified structural dependence theory similar to that advanced by

Mark Wickham-Jones. Yet the sheer scale of its majority may present certain difficulties for a party in government that did much to diminish expectations and aspirations for itself whilst in opposition. For although the party continued to proclaim its advocacy of 'national renewal', arguably there was precious little in its manifesto to indicate how such renewal might be achieved (Panitch and Leys 1997: 259–60). This suggests something of a paradox. For if moderation and capital appeasement would appear, both for Przeworski and Wallerstein as for the Labour Party, the condition of electoral success for social democratic parties, arguably such strategies restrict the space within which these parties in power can instigate the institutional reform that an electoral catharsis such as that of May 1997 might lead the electorate to expect. It is in the context of such a strategic paradox that Wickham-Jones' important response should be situated. It is concerned with two central issues: (i) the relationship between analytical, normative and empirical claims; and (ii) the status of the modified structural dependence thesis.

Wickham-Jones' principal charge is that in my initial response to his article (Hay 1997b; Wickham-Jones 1997b) I confused, and perhaps even conflated, normative, analytical and indeed empirical questions, letting my desire for a more genuinely social democratic alternative to the neo-liberal orthodoxy of the times get in the way of a more dispassionate assessment both of what was indeed happening and the parameters of what was possible.

Though my argument appealed to both analytical and normative issues, I had certainly hoped to bracket the analytical from the normative, the normative from the analytical. Given such confusion, however, it is perhaps appropriate that I attempt to clarify my position by spelling out the normative and analytical issues submerged in the above analysis. The purpose of my original response to Wickham-Jones, and my critique of the modified structural dependence thesis more generally, was to argue that the analytical premise upon which it was founded is false. That premise – *that since the state is structurally dependent upon capital it must internalise the preferences of the latter and hence engage in preference-accommodation or capital appeasement* – I rejected and continue to reject. This is an analytical statement (whether it is held to be valid or not). If it is accepted, it suggests a further proposition – *that there are alternatives for social democratic parties within the contours of contemporary capitalism to capital appeasement and preference-accommodation*. This, too, is an analytical proposition. If it, too, is accepted (an interpretative as opposed to an empirical matter) along with two further propositions – that the British economy is currently characterised by deeply entrenched structural weaknesses (an analytical claim) and that capital currently resists reform measures designed to address such structural weaknesses (an empirical claim) – then it follows logically that the *general* case for the politics of preference-shaping can be made and defended on its own.

Up to this point, the argument hinges purely on analytical and empirical claims. Indeed, it is only if one accepts these analytical claims that the normative issues become significant. For if the state's dependence on capital does indeed dictate that social democratic parties must accommodate the *existing* preferences of capital, New Labour's nascent neo-liberalism is perhaps the best that can be expected. Whether one likes it or not is irrelevant; this is simply the end of the story. It is thus *only* if one accepts that there are a range of feasible alternatives to preference-accommodation that the irreducibly *normative question* of which strategic alternative is to be preferred acquires any relevance. This is precisely why I sought to keep the issue of the space within which social democratic parties must operate separate from the question of what might fill that space.

This raises a second, and equally significant, issue. In his original article, the status of the modified structural dependence thesis was somewhat ambiguous. In his reply, Wickham-Jones seems to distance himself quite considerably from Przeworski and Wallerstein (and, indeed, from the position of his earlier article), explicitly acknowledging and accepting many of the criticisms levelled against the modified structural dependence thesis by myself and others.[20] Moreover, he now suggests that the usefulness of the thesis resides not so much in the theory of the *constraints placed upon social democratic parties and governments* that it offers, but in the *model of the way in which such parties behave* that it provides. This latter interpretation is entirely consistent with the argument of this chapter.

This seems like a significant concession and a significant modification of his earlier position. For it is one thing to suggest that Labour behaves in its dealings with capital *as though* the modified structural dependence theory were accurate (a view with which I concur); it is quite another to argue that a social democratic party seeking election *must behave in this manner* since the modified structural dependence theory accurately identifies the constraints within which it must operate (a view I reject). Wickham-Jones would appear to have moved from the latter position in his original article (arguing, for instance, that to prevent capital flight in government Labour had to moderate its programme of economic reform in opposition) to the former position in his reply (arguing merely that Labour behaved as if this were so).[21] Yet whether this represents a modification of his existing position or not, it is clear that he now subscribes to the view that the modified structural dependence thesis of Przeworski and Wallerstein provides, at best, a useful heuristic model of the way Labour has behaved (empirically) in opposition.

This strikes me as a very unusual and, indeed, a somewhat dangerous use of theory. For if Wickham-Jones' argument all along was that Labour exhibited behaviour consistent with the modified structural dependence thesis *and* he also believed (i) that alternatives to preference-accommodation and capital appeasement did indeed exist for Labour and were feasible (a view to which he now claims to subscribe)[22] and (ii) that the British economy does indeed suffer from persistent structural weaknesses to which capital is largely oblivious (a view he now also claims to hold),[23] then it is somewhat surprising that he did not feel the need to reject the 'logic of no alternative' to which the structural dependence thesis inexorably leads. The danger is that Wickham-Jones might be seen as providing evidence supportive of a theory whose basic conclusion (the lack of an alternative) he in fact rejects and which in turn might be taken as justifying (as the only option available) behaviour that is in fact damaging to Labour's prospects of restoring an indigenous investment and growth dynamic to the British economy.[24] Wickham-Jones' likely response – that his intention was not to judge but to describe in dispassionate fashion Labour's strategic deliberations – cannot entirely absolve him of responsibility for an argument that seems to suggest (and is certainly likely to be taken as suggesting) that there was no alternative for Labour other than simple accommodation to the preferences of capital.

The comment, reiterated in his reply, that 'the British case, between 1989 and 1992, confirmed much of the pessimism of Przeworski and Wallerstein' only indicates the full extent of the confusion (1997b: 258). A number of points might here be made:

1 It is difficult to see how the British case (or, indeed, any single case) could provide confirmation of such a theory – particularly when it is recalled that Wickham-Jones rejects many of its basic assumptions, together with its generality, and apparently chose it in

the first place because the British Labour Party at this time seemed
to exhibit behaviour consistent with its predictions.

2 It is unclear whether the pessimism of which Wickham-Jones
   speaks is a pessimism born of the understanding that capital appeasement is inevitable or that social democratic parties will act *as
   though* it is inevitable.

3 If, as the passage would seem to indicate, Labour's recent history is
   to be interpreted as confirming a pessimism born of the understanding that there *is no alternative* to preference-accommodation, then
   such a comment stands in marked contrast to much of what
   Wickham-Jones argues in the rest of his reply.

4 If Labour's chosen path to power does make Wickham-Jones pessimistic about the prospects for social democracy (as well it might)
   and, as he later suggests (1997b: 260), there were alternative
   strategies, is this pessimism not at least in part a consequence of our
   own failure and/or reluctance to engage in the normative enterprise
   of presenting alternatives on which social democratic parties might
   have drawn?

This brings us full circle. For if social democratic parties are to offer
alternatives to the pervasive neo-liberal orthodoxies of the times –
orthodoxies now internalised by financial and industrial capitals alike
across Europe, North America and the antipodes – the left must find
once again the voice to convince capital and labour alike of the
pathologies of neo-liberalism for employment, investment and sustained economic growth. This requires both analytical rigour and
normative inventiveness. The left must provide a clear mapping of the
contours of contemporary capitalism, assessing the extent to which the
parameters of the politically and economically possible have indeed
been circumscribed by financial liberalisation, heightened capital mobility, currency speculation and economic globalisation. It must also
turn its attention from what is feasible and pragmatic to what is
desirable, from the analytical to the normative. If contemporary political practice is so often about suppressing the electorate's expectations
of what is considered possible and feasible such that they conform to a
neo-liberal conception of the political 'good', it is perhaps only by
considering once again what is politically and economically desirable
that we can begin to raise expectations of what is possible and feasible.
In this much, at any rate, the analytical and the normative are
inextricably linked. It is to such issues that we turn in the final chapter.

Notes

1 This, of course, assumes that the natural rate of profit in a more regulated economy will be no greater than that in a deregulated, free-market economy. Given extant patterns of investment in the global economy, there may be very good reasons for questioning such a (simplifying) assumption (see, *inter alia*, Dicken 1998; Frankel 1997; Hirst and Thompson 1996).

2 It is, of course, not exclusively one of perceptions in the sense that invested capital may become embedded in a locality in the form, say, of physical plant. Accordingly, disinvestment, as we shall see, may be difficult and/or costly whatever the potential projected gains.

3 'Systematic luck' notwithstanding. See Dowding (1996).

4 On the state as a custodian of the general interest of capital see Hay (1999d). On the state as an 'ideal collective capitalist' see Altvater (1973); Engels (1878: 338); Offe (1974: 40).

5 For current purposes (and current purposes alone), I will here follow William Connolly's suggestion that 'policy x is more in A's [*real*] interest than policy y, if A were he [*sic*] to experience the results of both x and y, would choose x' (Connolly 1972: 472).

6 It should, perhaps, be noted at this point that the imposition of penalties by markets for the pursuit of traditionally social democratic measures is by no means an exclusively contemporary phenomenon. Labour and, indeed, Conservative governments have been periodically plagued by currency crises throughout the post-war period. The qualitative novelty of such developments should, then, not be overemphasised (for more detail see Watson 1998).

7 If only in the sense that it has thus far acted in a manner entirely consistent with the modified structural dependence thesis.

8 For evidence of this macro-economic policy convergence between the parties, see Brown (1994, 1995b); see also the *Economist*, 6 April 1996 (p. 15); Heffernan (1996); Sanders (1996).

9 Given the seemingly propitious economic condition at the time of Labour's election victory (Sanders 1998), this may seem like a rather strange and catastrophist image to present. Nonetheless, as noted in chapter 2, the stage in the economic cycle may well have served to hide temporarily the long-term and accelerating secular deterioration of the British economy. This has been exacerbated – and can only be exacerbated further – by a pervasive (now bipartisan) anti-statism which conceives of the free play of the market as the (only) means by which structural competitiveness might be restored. 'If it's broken, don't fix it' would seem to express rather well the spirit of the times. At the time of writing, with Britain hovering on the brink of recession, the degree of

'brokenness' of the economy may soon be cruelly exposed (see also Buxton *et al.* 1998; Cox *et al.* 1997; Kitson and Michie 1996; Watson 1997).

10 The spectre of the Winter of Discontent continued to haunt the party in the period up the 1997 election, acting as the symbolic epitome of all that must be expurgated were Labour to exorcise the demons of the past. This is tellingly revealed in Peter Mandelson and Richard Liddle's (grossly inaccurate, yet telling) comment that 'Old Labour couldn't even bury the dead' (1996; for a somewhat different account see Hay 1996a).

11 This assumes, of course, that such a governing economic and political paradigm can be identified. Whilst this may not always be the case, in the specific context under consideration that economic and political para-digm is neo-liberalism. On paradigm shifts see Hall (1993).

12 This threefold conception of the requirements of a coherent (state) project is adapted from John Dunn's similar attempt to outline 'the demands which it is reasonable to make of a political theory' (1984: 1–2; see also Hay 1996b: 157 n. 16, 174–6).

13 For a powerful statement of this position see Wood (1995).

14 There is precious little evidence of foreign direct investors relocating plant in pursuit of the benefits of low-taxation environments, far less of exit in immediate response to, or anticipation of, the election of a social democratic government. Garrett, for instance, finds significant positive correlations between left-labour power in the advanced capitalist econo-mies and both net foreign direct investment for 1991–4 (inflows minus outflows) and changes in foreign direct investment over the same period (1998: 142, table 6.5). Social democratic corporatist economies, he suggests, 'remained attractive to asset holders with (or contemplating) lasting stakes in them' (1998: 141), even after the removal of restrictions on capital flows. Such evidence would suggest that the modified struc-tural dependence thesis, however plausible or intuitive theoretically, is simply wrong empirically.

15 Even this threat, however, has tended to be exaggerated – as has its qualitative novelty. As a number of authors have noted, a statistically significant correlation remains between the rate of domestic saving, on the one hand, and the rate of domestic investment, on the other (Feldstein and Horioka 1980; Frankel 1993; Obstfeld 1995). This is in marked contrast to the predictions of the financial globalisation thesis. It is only on the currency markets, characterised, as they increasingly are, by intense short-term speculative activity that financial globalisation is genuinely well advanced.

16 For an interesting attempt from the left to defend the thesis that there is no alternative within contemporary capitalism to neo-liberalism see Wood (1995). For powerful rebuttals of the arguments advanced by the right to defend such a view see Boyer and Drache (1996); Hirst and Thompson (1996).

17 For a singularly inappropriate attempt to compare the draft Labour manifesto for the 1997 election with that of the Conservatives in 1979, see Halpern and Wood (1996).

18 Investment in human capital, however, is no substitute for investment in productive capacity. Indeed, arguably, without the latter the former is likely to prove of precious little benefit to the economy. See Michie and Smith (1996).

19 Robin Cook's 'promotion' to the position of shadow Foreign Secretary is clearly not unrelated. It had the effect, despite Blair's claim to the contrary at the time, of weakening significantly his influence over Labour's economic policy. Margaret Beckett's similar replacement (by Peter Mandelson in the first Cabinet reshuffle of Labour's period in government) threatens to have a similar effect when it comes to implementing the more discretionary aspects of the *Fairness at Work* white paper (Department of Trade and Industry 1998). I am indebted to conversations with Chris Howell on this latter point (see Howell 1998).

20 Indeed, the only aspects of my criticism of the modified structural dependence theory with which he takes issue are: (i) that 'capital *must* act directly against its own best interests'; (ii) that it is possible for a state to act in the best interest of capital; and (iii) that 'it is possible for a state to promote economic growth, if it is prepared to disregard the demands made upon it by business' (Wickham-Jones 1997b: 259). As it happens, none of these are central to the critique of the modified structural dependence theory that I present and each is misrepresented by Wickham-Jones in his summary. As it is not crucial to what follows, I will not labour the point. However, my argument is not that capital *must* act contrary to its own best interests, but that, given its fractured nature, its pervasive short-termism and its collective action problems (all acknowledged by Wickham-Jones), it is difficult to see how it is capable of defining its own best interests in the first place or, for that matter, what those interests might be. The state is blessed with no more privileged vantage point from which to assess such interests, but *is* better placed to consider the longer-term consequences for capital of particular courses of action and is also capable of providing a co-ordination function which individual capitals on their own will consistently fail to provide. Finally, if the state is to promote economic growth through strategic reform and restructuring, as I suggest in the British case it should, it is imperative that it takes very seriously, and indeed seeks to mould, the perceived interests of business.

21 Thus, as he suggests, 'regardless of the criticisms made of both structural dependence theory and its modified version, leading Labour politicians continue to act in accordance with the parameters laid out by Przeworski and Wallerstein'. Frustratingly absent from his analysis, however, is any discussion of whether they need do so (Wickham-Jones 1997b: 262).

22 As for instance when he argues: 'I do not doubt that other feasible options were available to the party before 1992.... My article was concerned not with what they should have done, but rather how their anxiety about markets came to shape their strategic choices' (Wickham-Jones 1997b: 260).

23 See his comments on British economic decline (Wickham-Jones 1997b: 264, n. 5).

24 Such prospects, as I have argued consistently, require Labour either to reject or, better still, to educate the perceived interest of (sections of) British industrial capital.

6 Labouring Under False Pretences? Dedication, industrial capacity and indigenous investment

Tony Blair's landslide electoral victory presents the party in power with a rare, perhaps even unprecedented, opportunity to revitalise and modernise Britain's ailing and antiquated manufacturing economy. If it is to do so, it must remain true to its long-standing (indeed, historic) commitment to restore an indigenous investment ethic to British capitalism. In this final chapter, I argue that this, in turn, requires the party to reject the very neo-liberal orthodoxies which it offered to the electorate as evidence of its competence, moderation and 'modernisation', which it has internalised and which it apparently now views as circumscribing the parameters of the politically and economically possible in an era of globalisation (on which see also Hay and Watson 1998).

In this context, New Labour enjoys an almost unique advantage: a mandate for change, reflected in its (initial) 179-seat overall majority, more fundamental than that it sought. Yet such a situation does present certain difficulties for a party whose manifesto and supporting policy documents contained, at best, a submerged radicalism couched within the rhetoric of competence, consensus and conciliation. The position, then, is one of opportunity and threat. Judged purely on the scale of its defeat and the recriminatory ructions that currently engulf the party, the Conservatives would appear consigned to the electoral margins for at least two terms. This provides Labour with a rare (and much-needed) opportunity to think long term. Yet, despite its best intentions, the situation is also that in which expectations of reform – and rapid reform at that – exceed both Labour's declared ambition and, in all likelihood, the capacity of even a more resolutely radical government (with a clearly reforming manifesto and a mandate) to deliver. More-over, despite the much-vaunted vibrancy of the British economy, difficult decisions face the newly incumbent administration. In particular, these concern: (i) Europe and the relative costs (economic *and* political) of membership or exclusion from a European single currency early in the millennium; (ii) the relative wage–skill profile of the British labour market and hence the nature of the competitive position and mode of insertion of the national economy within European and global economic dynamics; and, perhaps more acutely still, (iii) Britain's distinctive lack of manufacturing investment, the paucity of its capital stock, the obsolescence of much of its beleaguered manufacturing capacity and its characteristic shortfall of 'dedicated' capital. The most long-standing and ultimately the most fundamental of these concerns is the third.[1] Accordingly, it is this that provides the principal focus of attention in this chapter.

In sum, propitious and/or contingent circumstances present New Labour in power with a rare, perhaps even unprecedented, opportunity (at least since 1945). That is, to make a decisive, if initially incremental and cumulatively radicalising, break with a decaying neo-liberal economic and political paradigm comprehensively rejected (at least in its governing form) at the polls. It is *only* by making a break with neo-liberal orthodoxy that New Labour in government can deliver the economic competence it so avidly espoused in opposition. With the dark clouds of economic recession looming ominously on the not so distant horizon, this can only become ever more pressing. Yet, at this point, it is perhaps only appropriate to note once again that it is certainly easier to make the case for the obsolescence of the old paradigm and the need for a decisive break with the nostrums of the past (as the Conservatives did between 1975 and 1979) *in opposition*. Suffice to say, however, that even in the absence of a pervasive sense of the crisis of neo-liberal economics, the perception that Blair's accession to power heralds a new beginning in British politics may still provide New Labour with the space in which to project an alternative and to impose a new trajectory upon the structures of the British state and economy.

The central contention in what is to follow is that if New Labour is to demonstrate the *economic* competence of its electoral convictions, it must first rediscover the *political* courage of its former policy convictions, challenging (and ultimately rejecting) the terms by which that competence has come to be understood. Indeed, more broadly, it must transcend the pervasive neo-liberal paradigm that has come to circumscribe the parameters of what is considered politically and economically feasible, possible and desirable in Britain as elsewhere. Though sacrificed or, on a more favourable reading, *relegated* to the

Downsian electoral imperative that seemingly came to dominate the revision of policy in the pre-election period, traces of precisely such an alternative economic and political vision can still be identified (though ever more faintly) in the party's (heavily diluted) proposals on industrial, regional and financial reform.[2] Originating in the Policy Review itself, they were associated in particular with the shadow DTI under the tutelage of first Bryan Gould and, subsequently, Robin Cook. Yet the contradictions evident at the time between this dirigiste conception of a supply-side 'developmental state' and the developing fiscal fortitude of the shadow Treasury team have clearly been resolved, for the time being, in favour of the latter.[3] In this chapter, my aim is to return to the former, to reclaim the potentially radical and, within the context of neo-liberal economics, *heretical* core of New Labour's erstwhile industrial and regional strategy and to review critically the political and economic alternatives available to New Labour once the shackles of the neo-liberal paradigm have been cast off.

Such reflections are unapologetically speculative, experimental and prognostic. Although, as noted in the previous chapter, Labour has been served by a band of diligent and dedicated think-tanks producing a profusion of policy proposals, such think-tanks have been characterised by their considerable caution. Straying only infrequently from the bounds of (neo-liberal) convention, they have failed to learn the lessons of the more innovative think-tanks of the new right, which identified for themselves a clear role in changing, in the terms of the Centre for Policy Studies, the 'climate of opinion'. In so doing, they created new space for subsequent policy design and eventual implementation, thereby contributing to a broad trajectory of change rather than tinkering on the margins of the existing paradigm by immersing themselves in the minutiae of policy. It is only by engaging in self-consciously speculative and experimental thought – beyond the boundaries of an ascendant neo-liberal orthodoxy which equates and conflates competence with macro-economic conservatism, fiscal fortitude and managed welfare retrenchment – that the left might rediscover the space and the vision to animate an alternative programme of reform.[4]

To illustrate the point, globalisation and the 'logic of no alternative' that it seems to imply have often been deployed in recent years as the rhetorical device by which the aspirations of the left and, indeed, the electorate more generally have been disciplined and downsized (in

Britain as in western Europe, the antipodes and North America).[5] Yet once we consider that it is only within the context of the restrictive neo-liberal – indeed, *monetarist* – world view that financial liberalisation significantly erodes the autonomy of the national state to engage in macro-economic management, this 'logic of no alternative' is exposed for the construct of neo-liberalism that it surely is. For, as John Grieve Smith notes:

> it is ironic that the monetarist approach should have become fashionable, with its almost exclusive reliance on interest rates as the instrument for macroeconomic control, when interest rate policy has become increasingly sensitive to international capital flows and exchange-rate considerations leaving individual countries increasingly less room for manoeuvre. (1996: 13)

The result, as noted elsewhere, is macro-economic inflexibility and labour-market flexibility as the burden of 'competitiveness' is placed on labour rather than capital (Hay and Watson 1998). If we are then to repoliticise the economic and to reclaim local, regional and national economic spaces, as indeed welfare states, from the deregulatory ravages of a liberalising global political economy, we must retain and renew our capacity to think outside the parameters of those who would tell us that there is no alternative. This concluding chapter constitutes a modest attempt to do precisely that.

In what follows, I consider the problem (for problem it is) of productive investment. I concentrate in particular on policy priorities for the expansion of manufacturing capacity and the rejuvenation of the productive economy through the restoration of an indigenous investment ethic to British capitalism. Yet before considering the space for alternatives, it is first important to consider the broader diagnosis of the affliction to which such reforms must constitute a response and the distinctiveness and intractability of this British condition.

Lacking dedication: the pathologies of British capitalism

The argument that British capitalism is distinctive, exceptional even, has a long and distinguished pedigree amongst critics of the left, for whom its characteristic pathologies can be traced to the peculiar dislocation of financial and industrial capital and the persistent ascendancy of the former. It is associated in particular with the so-called

'Anderson–Nairn theses', published in a series of instalments in *New Left Review* from the early 1960s (Anderson 1992; Nairn 1976, 1994). In recent years, the argument has received something of a revival, being dusted off and repackaged in the form of Will Hutton's blistering polemic, *The State We're In*, and its somewhat more conciliatory sequel, *The State to Come* (1996, 1997).[6] The argument is elegant in its simplicity. Britain's distinctive pathologies can be traced ultimately to the incomplete nature of its bourgeois revolution. Lacking the creative destruction of a genuinely revolutionary upheaval, Britain's precocious capitalism inherited much of its institutional architecture and cultural distinctiveness from the feudal era. A fossilised traditionalism, the trappings of an aristocratic elite and the superstructures of the *ancien régime* survived the transition to capitalism by and large intact. These peculiarities of primacy were to become what they remain today – fetters on continued economic development and capital accumulation.

An antiquated and semi-autocratic system of government and an unwritten constitution providing no formal democratic rules served, as it serves, to protect the exclusive, self-serving and subterranean networks of a pervasive and elitist Oxbridge-educated English Establishment and the traditions of 'gentlemanly capitalism'. The result is an imperious (and once imperial) financial system which is risk averse, short term in its calculations and notorious for its unwillingness to support investment and innovation.

In the current context, these generic tendencies of British capitalism are reflected in a body of company law which discourages long-term strategic investment, a macro-economic policy-making process that institutionalises the interests of financial over industrial capital and a banking system in which capital is rarely available to industry in the long term on a competitive basis. The result is an economy emphasising finance over manufacturing and overseas over domestic investment. It is characterised by pervasive under-employment, low wages, a massive skills deficit, a consistent lack of industrial capacity and a vicious circle of low productivity growth, low investment and lack of innovation.

It is easy to see how such a diagnosis of the British affliction might inform proposals for institutional – particularly financial – reform. Yet it is important to note that advocates of systematic attempts to address Britain's distinctive manufacturing investment shortfall have not relied exclusively on such a formulation. The so-called Cambridge School have, in particular, drawn upon the work of comparative political economists who identify clear clusterings in the institutional arrangements of otherwise distinct 'national capitalisms' in making their own case for institutional reform.[7] Thus, prominent in discussions of industrial performance and under-investment in Britain (and perhaps increasingly so) has been the comparison drawn between the 'Anglo-US model' of capitalism, on the one hand, and the 'German–Japanese' or 'Nippo-Rhenish model', on the other (Albert 1993; Cerny 1993; Gerschenkron 1962; Zysman 1983; Zysman and Tyson 1983).[8]

Despite their obvious similarities, there are important differences between these two approaches. The theorists of British exceptionalism have developed a general analysis of what they take to be the specificity of British capitalism. This allows them, for instance, to trace the arcane and anachronistic character of British democracy (as reflected in an unwritten constitution and an unelected second chamber) to the same institutional legacy (that of an incomplete bourgeois revolution) that is also taken to account for Britain's peculiar dislocation of financial and industrial capital. The same is not true of the comparative political economists. Taking their lead from Gerschenkron's pioneering analysis, they conceive of finance as 'the conduit for all economic activity in market economies' and concentrate accordingly upon the distinctiveness of *financial–industrial relations* (Pollin 1995: 28). These they see as underpinning the specificity of distinct national capitalisms. In so doing, they identify clear differences between financial systems and hence clear differences in the institutional relationships which pertain between industrial and financial capital in different national contexts. Yet their analysis, unlike that of Anderson and Nairn, emphasises institutional similarities and clusterings of national capitalisms, which are seen as displaying common characteristics by virtue of the type of financial system they exhibit. Thus the distinctiveness of British capitalism, which Anderson and Nairn attribute to British exceptionalism, the comparative political economists attribute to the specificity of a financial system based on capital markets that Britain shares with the USA.[9] What in one account is seen as a product of singularity, peculiarity and specificity is, in the other, seen as closely approximating one-half of the ideal–typical dualism between whose poles the financial systems of the advanced capitalist economies can be organised.

In fact, much of the literature on comparative capitalisms is centrally structured around the distinction between what, in Gerschenkron's (1962) original analysis, were the different developmental trajectories of British and German capitalism, respectively, and what, in more recent work, has resolved itself into the distinction between the 'capital market-based' systems of the Anglo-US model and the 'bank-based' systems of the German–Japanese model.[10] The latter is characterised by a relatively cheap supply of 'dedicated' capital, long-term investment and correspondingly high levels of manufacturing growth, a committed and 'tutelary' (or guardianship) relationship between manufacturers as investors of capital and banks (in the German case, *Hausbanken*) as suppliers of capital and an active role for the state in the allocation of credit to private firms. In marked contrast, the former exhibits an arm's-length relationship between finance and industry and a limited role for government. It is characterised in turn by short-termism, 'fluid' as opposed to 'dedicated' capital, high target rates of return, the constant threat of hostile take-overs, a lack of committed and long-term investment and correspondingly low levels of manufacturing investment, capacity and growth (see table 6.1).

If, in Albert Hirschmann's terms, the bank-based financial systems of Germany and Japan are more dialogic and are governed by *voice* (a *sotto voce* relationship between manufacturers and financiers perhaps),

Table 6.1 Standardised levels (rank on Maddison's scale) of savings, investment and growth

	Savings, 1960–87	Fixed investment, 1960–87	Annual rate of growth, 1950–89
UK	6	7	6
Canada	5	5	5
France	4	4	4
Germany	2	3	3
Japan	1	1	1
Korea	3	2	2
USA	7	6	7

The figures in this table are derived from Maddison's values for total gross savings as a percentage of GDP at current market prices, gross fixed domestic investment as a percentage of GDP at current market prices and rate of growth of GDP per capital (average annual compound growth rate).

Source: Watson and Hay (1998, table A.1.1), calculated from Maddison (1995: 171–80).

then the capital market-based system of the Anglophone model is characterised in contrast by a distinct lack of dialogue and communication, by *raised* voices and ultimately by *exit*.[11] Such a depiction of the contours of contemporary capitalism leads its proponents – most of them British or American, it should be noted – to conclude with Pollin that 'the bank-based systems achieve superior performance in three crucial areas: promoting longer time horizons, encouraging financial stability, and providing a framework for the successful implementation of government policy' (1995: 35).

In fact, the diagnosis of the *Anglo-US* affliction offered by such an analysis is, in many respects, little different from that of the *British* affliction presented by the likes of Anderson and Nairn and certainly by Hutton. It points to four distinctive pathologies of a capital market-based financial system for manufacturing capacity, investment and growth: short-termism; risk aversion; a propensity to acquisitions, mergers and asset-stripping as opposed to rescue strategies where companies fall into difficulties; and a series of adverse consequences for the economy's more general ability to respond to recession. Though closely related, it is worth considering each separately and in turn.

Short-termism

Short-termism, widely identified and widely acknowledged as an almost 'natural' quality of a capital market-based financial system, is generally regarded as having the most adverse consequences for the rest of the economy. The allocation of finance on the basis of prices established in competitive capital markets dominated by the desire for liquidity (Watson 1999c), together with the overarching concern of institutional investors (such as pension funds) for rapid returns (in line with quarterly assessments of their performance), have conspired to lock the financial system into a mind set dominated by immediate concerns at the expense of longer-term time horizons (Buckle and Thompson 1995: 308–14). This pervasive short-term ethos is exported to industry in two ways. First, those firms either too small or too new to be able to raise finance by other means become directly dependent upon financial institutions and are thus forced to internalise the temporally parochial paradigm of their sponsors. As Simon Lee observes:

> UK financial institutions have made capital available to industry only
> at such a prohibitively high cost and for repayment over such a

punitively short period of time that industrial companies have been
confronted with one of the highest costs of capital in the world.
(1996b: 113)

Yet even those more established and substantial concerns capable of
raising equity on the stock market are not immune from the infectious
short-termism of the financial institutions. For in an active market for
corporate control in which hostile take-overs, mergers and acquisitions
abound (and for which capital is more readily available), corporate
managers simply cannot afford the luxury of long-term considerations
and must concentrate instead on the short-term performance criteria
necessary to stave off predators (Cowling 1990).

Risk aversion
If financial institutions within a capital market-based system display a
pathological short-termism, they are at least equally risk averse, exhibiting a marked preference for *guaranteed* returns on investment that
are, preferably, almost instantaneous. Again, this reflects a desire for
liquidity and the remarkably short time frame over which investments
are expected to pay for themselves (Bond and Jenkinson 1996; Confederation of British Industry 1994). Since riskier investments, almost
by definition, require a more dedicated supply of capital, potentially
locking in otherwise fluid assets, financial institutions in a capital
market-based system are reluctant to commit capital to such projects.
For as John Zysman notes:

> long-term loans must be repaid from future profits and therefore, as a
> minimum, the bank must make an assessment [a potentially risky
> projection] of the company's competitive future ... short-term loans
> can simply be secured against existing company assets. (1983: 195)

Short-termism and risk aversion are thus inextricably interwoven.
Moreover, in a climate dominated by the time horizons of the capital
markets, risk aversion is (like short-termism itself) similarly internalised by industry. If small and/or new firms are forced to abandon
potentially risky capital investment projects since a supply of venture
capital is simply unavailable to them on competitive terms (from
financial institutions interested above all in liquidity and immediate
profitability), it might be thought that larger firms would be better
placed to make more speculative investments. Sadly, this is rarely the
case. For although such firms are, indeed, in a position to raise equity,

in a highly developed stock market in which the performance of fund managers is judged on a quarterly (even monthly) basis, the raising of equity to fund risky projects is itself a risky venture, exposing the company to the close attentions of predators. In this way, the 'discipline' of the capital markets imposes itself on the entire domestic economy, radically condensing time horizons and militating against risk-taking.

Acquisitions, mergers and asset-stripping

In bank-based financial systems in which the industrial–financial relation is characterised by dedication, reciprocity, mutuality and commitment on both sides, banks tend to respond to management problems within firms by launching often highly intrusive and interventionist rescue strategies.[12] In capital market-based systems, by contrast, corporate difficulties tend instead to precipitate a wholly different set of processes as the vultures gather overhead. Here, the lack of dedication of financial institutions and the absence of what Stephen Woolcock (1996) terms 'relationship banking' becomes cruelly apparent – to the considerable detriment of the company experiencing difficulties.

In such situations, pressure mounts on institutional investors (such as pension funds, which may often have a majority stake in the company concerned) to sell their share-holding to predator holding companies. Indeed, where a potential bidder seeks control of the company, the share price will tend to rise (by the so-called 'bidding premium'). This reflects anticipated future profit arising either from projected efficiency gains or, more likely, asset-stripping. Should the take-over bid prove unsuccessful, it is extremely unlikely that the share price will remain at its inflated level. This then provides a powerful, and in most cases a *sufficient*, incentive for institutional investors to accept take-over offers (if not actively to court them) that can only boost their quarterly performance (Buckle and Thompson 1995: 309–10; Franks and Mayer 1990; Kester 1992; Woolcock 1996).

Yet were this enticement not in itself sufficient, three further factors exacerbate the tendency of institutional investors to abandon their stake in companies experiencing difficulties to the vultures of the market in corporate control – to 'the so-called triple alliance of corporate raiders, junk bond dealers (merchant banks selling-off high yielding bonds created to finance take-overs) and arbitrageurs (people taking positions in companies they predict will be targets for corporate raiders)' (Cowling 1990: 14). First, bankruptcy laws in Britain, as in the USA, severely penalise relationship banking. For direct intervention on the part of a bank in the affairs of an ailing company is likely to result in the bank losing seniority in any subsequent debt claims. This, as Woolcock notes, provides 'a fairly powerful disincentive to active intervention' (1996: 137). Second, strict insider-trading legislation in Britain and the USA also militates against an active role for institutional shareholders. Thus, intervention in the affairs of a customer in difficulty is simply not an option for institutional investors (who may, in all likelihood, lack expertise in corporate affairs) if they are to remain within the bounds of the law (Blake 1995: 486–98; see also Blake 1992; Gourevitch 1996: 243). Finally, deregulation has led to intense competition amongst banks and other financial institutions in Britain in recent years. As Woolcock again observes:

> this has tended to undermine any relationship banking that existed. Faced with strong competition, banks have tried to 'poach' new customers, and companies have found an advantage in maintaining links with competing institutions in order to get the best conditions. As a result close relationships, based on trust, between companies and banks have become harder rather than easier to maintain. (1996: 187)

In such a context, rescue strategies are rarely contemplated, confirming a tendency in capital market-based financial systems for acquisitions, mergers and asset-stripping as a response to corporate failure.

Responses to recession
In capital market-based systems, the expectation on manufacturers during a recession is for a large-scale shedding of under-utilised capacity and a laying-off of workers – an expectation which companies may choose to disappoint but only at a likely cost to their share price. Thus, as John Grieve Smith notes of the UK:

> the roles of the suppliers of risk capital and the members of the company (its work-force) have become reversed. If profits are hit, dividends are maintained and employees sacked ... employees bear a much greater risk than the suppliers of capital. (1996: 19; see also 1997: 217)

In bank-based financial systems such as Germany and Japan, by contrast, dedicated investors will seek to preserve jobs and capacity at a short-term cost to themselves of dividends on their investment.

The consequences for the relative ability of capital market-based economies to respond to recession are severe. They are characteristically slower to recover, since their beleaguered capital stock places them in a poor position to respond to any upturn in demand. Moreover, the loss of sector-specific skills and specialist capital equipment may be difficult to replace, because of both the existence of significant sunk costs and the lack of a dedicated supply of venture capital (Dixit 1992; Kitson and Michie 1997). Given this shortfall of manufacturing capacity, a recovery in the domestic economy is likely to result in a significant influx of imports from bank-based economies less hasty to shed capacity during recession and hence better placed to respond to rising demand after the recession. The result, almost inevitably, is a growing trade imbalance and pressure on the currency. Historically, British governments anxious to preserve sterling's role as a reserve currency have responded to such a set of circumstances through deflationary strategies (rather than devaluation), further compounding the problems for manufacturers by weakening international competitiveness and hence sacrificing profits and future investment (Gamble 1994; Newton and Porter 1988; Zysman 1983: 172–80). Accordingly, the largely self-fulfilling expectation on the part of capital markets that, in recession, manufacturers will shed workers and industrial capacity has profoundly adverse consequences for both the ability of the economy to cope with recession and the level of employment over the entire economic cycle.

Putting the 'political' back into comparative political economy

As the above analysis would perhaps suggest, both the extensive literature on comparative capitalisms and the exceptionalism thesis serve to highlight in clear and unambiguous fashion a series of *common* institutional and/or more broadly structural weaknesses of the British economy. Whether these are attributed to the incomplete character of Britain's bourgeois revolution and the developmental pathologies of a precocious capitalism, or to a capital market-based financial system that it shares with the USA, a stark and remarkably consistent diagnosis of the British affliction is presented. Both accounts provide an important indication of the challenge that confronts New Labour in power if it is to remain true to successive manifesto commitments to restore an indigenous investment ethic to British capitalism[13] and, arguably, to succeed where the more professedly reformist Attlee and Wilson administrations failed.[14]

Nonetheless, if such accounts provide an indication of the magnitude of the task facing Blair's government and a detailed mapping of the institutional contours of a financial–industrial system in profound need of systematic reform (and hence an important checklist against which a range of policy options can be assessed), then the theoretical basis for the shared diagnosis they offer is not altogether unproblematic. Before considering what might be done to alleviate the obdurate structural weaknesses of the British economy, then, it is first important to sound a number of notes of theoretical caution which apply in equal measure to the exceptionalism thesis and the broader literature on comparative capitalisms.

First, the structure of both accounts is institutionalist and, indeed, economistic – the former broadly Marxist or at least Marxisant, the latter (in the North American tradition of statism and neo-institutionalism) Weberian or neo-Weberian. It is, perhaps, unremarkable then that both tend to exhibit the distinctive pathologies of institutionalist analysis (old and new, Marxist and Weberian alike), namely an overarching concern with institutional formation (a strong 'creational bias') and, thereafter, with institutional constraint, inertia and stasis or at best an incremental evolution. The danger is that a certain 'logic of historical and institutional inevitability' is conjured, as the specificity, whether of Britain's precocious capitalism or of the Anglo-US model, is seen as the institutionally guaranteed, trans-historical and immutable consequence of an initial moment of creational catharsis. Thus Barry Eichengreen, in an analysis that is by no means unrepresentative argues:

> Britain ... acquired a very different set of institutions [to Germany] as a legacy of her early industrialisation. The capital requirements of early industrialisation having been modest, she inherited a banking system that specialised in the provision of trade credit, rather than industrial finance. Early industrial technology having offered limited economies of scale and scope, she inherited an industrial structure dominated by atomistic, single-plant firms.

Bringing the analysis rapidly up to date, and following David Soskice, he continues:

> It was in no-one's interest to deviate from the institutional norm unless others did so simultaneously ... there was no mechanism for coordinating a shift from one equilibrium to the other ... there was no exceptional post-war window for change.... Britain's relatively poor growth performance is not blamed on anyone's lack of acuity. There were no unexploited opportunities for industrialists, bankers or unionists in the absence of a solution to the coordination problem created by the historical inheritance. (1996: 216–1; Soskice 1989).

In other words, the institutional pathologies of British capitalism in the post-war period and today can be traced to Britain's early industrialisation and the character of its bourgeois revolution (incomplete or otherwise). The distinctive nature of its institutions has remained essentially unchallenged, unchanged and intact. To be fair to Eichengreen, his account (and that of Soskice, on whom he draws) – unlike those of many comparative political economists – does posit a mechanism by which the institutional rigidities of a financial system born of early industrialisation became entrenched. Nonetheless, a clear creational bias is displayed and a logic of historical inevitability conjured. The absence of political actors from such a narrative is surely telling. It indicates once again a residual economism.

The danger of such a formulation is that the structure of the analysis itself serves to absolve political actors of all responsibility for the reproduction of what may appear, with the benefit of hindsight, a seamless web of institutional continuity, yet which the historiographic evidence would suggest is in fact the product of highly contingent political and economic strategies and struggles.

Two forms of such absolution are perhaps particularly significant. First, economistic institutionalism of this sort may serve to absolve and exonerate (whatever its intentions) those governments, most notably those of Attlee and Wilson, which identified structural weaknesses in the British economy relating to an investment shortfall and the need for industrial modernisation but which failed, despite their (stated) aims, to bring about significant and lasting reform (in this area). While apportioning blame for such policy failures may not in itself be terribly informative or edifying, such moments of thwarted institutional reform surely warrant far closer scrutiny than they have thus far been accorded by authors within this tradition. Recent historiographic research would certainly suggest that the opportunity for reform (in 1945 and 1964 at any rate) was indeed far greater than that acknowledged by institutional political economists, while also identifying key sources of resistance to institutional reform. The latter point is particularly crucial. For whereas comparative political economists and theorists of British exceptionalism might dismiss the perception of an opportunity (if not the need) for institutional reform as simple misinformation on the part of the Attlee or Wilson administrations, historiographers can point to the often highly contingent factors and interests which thwarted the reform strategies of both governments, giving potentially vital clues to future policy makers.[15]

Second, and perhaps of even greater significance, is the tendency for the *logic* and *structure* (if not the spirit) of such accounts to absolve governments (such as those of Thatcher and Major) which might otherwise be seen as exacerbating the persistent pathologies of Britain's 'precocious capitalism'. Such a tension is perhaps particularly acute in Hutton's account of *The State We're In*.[16] For despite developing a passionate and vitriolic critique of Thatcherite free-market fervour and a detailed charge sheet, the structure of the analysis – that of a trajectory of decline established over the course of three centuries – leaves little room for the havoc that Hutton wishes to attribute to the Thatcher governments. Given his central argument that the British state has been 'handed down virtually intact from the settlement of 1688' (1996: 4), it would seem frankly disingenuous to apportion too much responsibility to contemporary political figures for a seemingly inexorable spiral of precipitous decay established hundreds of years before Thatcher drew first breath.[17]

If this should make us exceedingly wary of the residual structuralist tendencies of such institutionalist accounts, which, at worst, reduce political actors to mere bearers of institutional logics (associated in turn with distinct and immutable 'national capitalisms'), then we should perhaps be equally wary of the converse tendency – that of voluntarism. This is often evidenced in accounts which advocate more or less direct institutional transfers from one national model to another. The concomitant assumption – that all that is required to resolve the problems of specific national capitalisms is sufficient will on the part of a political elite to borrow, copy or adapt institutional logics which may prove functional elsewhere – clearly flies in the face of institutionalism's more characteristic emphasis upon institutional specificity, path dependence and inertia.[18] Thus, as argued elsewhere:

> it is one thing to trace and chart the institutional connections of specific national capitalisms and their functional effects at particular

stages in their historical development; it is quite another to imply that such 'institutional fixes' are transferable and will work equally well within the very different circumstances pertaining in other economies. (Hay 1997d: 100)

The above comments perhaps indicate the need for a certain caution in the deployment of stylised, if parsimonious, institutional models of national capitalisms and their trajectories in guiding discussions of policy options. They also suggest the need to consider more systematically the extent to which the parameters of the politically and economically possible are indeed circumscribed by institutional factors (and, it is worth emphasising, *perceptions* of institutional factors) and the processes by which those parameters are themselves altered over time. Yet if this suggests the need for a greater sensitivity *in considerations of political strategy and policy alternatives* to *political* factors in general, and the political mechanisms of economic and institutional reform in particular, then this should not be seen as compromising the overall strength of the literature on comparative capitalisms and the persuasive and parsimonious diagnoses of the British affliction that it offers. It does, however, point to the need to recognise that such accounts are partial, relatively abstract, deliberately stylised and hence insufficiently complex to grasp the specificity and contingency of processes of institutional change and reform.

Such cautionary remarks, however, do not entail an indiscriminate rejection of this form of institutional enquiry. An analysis based on the specific institutional pathologies of the capital market-based financial system in Britain is necessary if we are to assess the extent of the challenge that Labour faces in any attempt to secure a consistent and competitive supply of dedicated capital. In the sections that follow we turn our attentions to industrial and institutional priorities suggestive of a modernising alternative to the pervasive neo-liberal orthodoxy of the times.

Instilling an indigenous investment ethic amongst institutional investors

necessity is the mother of invention.

British-based investors constitute the largest purchasers of portfolio assets in the world. If Labour is to reinstil within the British economy an indigenous investment ethic, it is above all imperative that it considers systematic reform of the institutional, legal and, indeed, more broadly perceptual environment in which portfolio investors (such as pension funds and insurance companies) operate. Consider pension funds. These represent the largest institutional investors in Britain and contribute significantly to the speculative and short-term bias of the capital markets. Recent figures indicate that UK pension funds accounted for some 70 per cent of gross national product in 1993, holding some 52 per cent of shares in quoted companies (HM Treasury 1996; see also HM Treasury 1993; Bond *et al.* 1996). Moreover, as David Blake notes, if we include insurance companies as well, then:

> institutional investors' ownership of UK companies' equity has increased from less than 30 per cent in the early 1960s to more than 60 per cent in the early 1990s. It has been estimated that about fifty top fund managers have effective control (51 per cent) of UK industry. (1995: 485)

It might be thought that, given the long-term nature of pension fund activity and the relatively stable and predictable character of both their inflows (in the form of employers' and employees' contributions) and their outflows (in the form of actual pension payments), pension funds might be exemplary dedicated long-term investors in domestic manufacturing industry. Sadly, nothing could be further from the truth. As Randy Barber and Teresa Ghilarducci observe in a perceptive discussion of the pathologies of portfolio investment in the USA that is equally applicable to Britain:

> these massive pools of capital are uniquely suited to fund long-term investments because their liabilities are stable, predictable and extended over many decades. However, over the past two decades, pension funds often invested very differently in capital markets as their mostly futile pursuit of above-average returns contributed heavily to 'short-termism' and speculation in the economy as a whole ... arguably, their behaviour was one of the main detriments to prospects for long-term economic growth, employment creation, and increases in real income. (1993: 288)[19]

Despite predictable and long-term liabilities, then, pension funds on both sides of the Atlantic display a marked preference for highly liquid assets that they often retain for less than two years.

Table 6.2   Asset allocation of UK pension funds in 1979 and 1989

	Asset allocation 1979 (%)	Asset allocation 1989 (%)
UK equity	44	52
Overseas equity	6	14
UK bonds	23	13
Overseas bonds	0	1
Index-linked bonds	0	3
UK property	22	10
Overseas property	0	1
Other	6	8

Source: Blake (1992: 20).

Table 6.3   Overseas holdings of UK pension funds, 1993

	Share of total investment
Canada	9
France	5
Germany	3
Japan	14
UK	27
USA	4

Source: HM Treasury (1996, table A.2.10).

As well as this pathological aversion to dedicated investment, institutional investors in recent years have channelled vast and growing quantities of capital overseas. This tendency has accelerated significantly since financial deregulation, in particular the abolition of exchange controls on overseas investment on 24 October 1979 (see tables 6.2 and 6.3).

Once the almost complete absence of regulatory restrictions on the investment activities of portfolio investors and their highly privileged tax status are considered,[20] the case for reform becomes overwhelming, particularly when it is realised that a significant proportion of current pension fund assets represent accumulated effective tax concessions on the part of the Exchequer.

Yet if pension fund reform can be justified purely on the basis of the contribution of such institutional investors to the pervasive short-term, risk-averse and speculative character of investment activity in Britain, it can also be justified more narrowly in terms of the consequences of current practice for the employment opportunities of those whose pension contributions such funds manage. Under the 1961 Trustee Investments Act, the trustees of pension funds are limited in the extent to which they can influence, steer or restrict the investment choices of fund managers. Appropriately enough, trustees have a statutory 'fiduciary responsibility' to act in the 'best interests' of those for whom the fund has either a current or future liability. Though singularly ambiguous and open to multiple and mutually incompatible interpretations, 'best interests' have, following the 1983 Megarry judgement, come to be interpreted in narrowly financial terms.

In 1982, half of the trustees of the mineworkers' pension fund – those representing the National Union of Mineworkers (NUM) – refused to endorse the investment proposals submitted for approval by the fund manager on the grounds that the proposed investment of mineworkers' capital in overseas securities and competing energy sources (in particular investment in oil companies) did not reflect the 'best interests' of current, former or, indeed, future miners. Ironically perhaps, the National Coal Board (NCB) (whose representatives constituted the other five trustees of the pension fund) took the NUM to court, arguing that in refusing to endorse the fund manager's proposed investment portfolio for 1982, the NUM trustees were 'risking the investment performance of the fund and hence damaging the financial interests of the fund's beneficiaries' (Blake 1992: 33). Interestingly, they chose not to dispute the NUM's claim that the proposed investment portfolio was indeed deleterious to any broader conception of the mineworkers' 'best interests' and the interests of the British coal industry more generally. It is acutely ironic that they should effectively take the NUM to court for placing the interests of the industry (and hence, presumably, those of the NCB) above their own members' more parochial financial interest.

In a staggering and momentous decision, Sir Robert Megarry found in favour of the NCB, in the following terms:

> When the purpose of the trust is to provide financial benefits for the beneficiaries, as is usually the case, the best interests of the beneficiaries are normally their best financial interests. In the case of a power of

investment, as in the present case, the power must be exercised so as to yield the best return for the beneficiaries, judged in relation to the risks of the investment in question. (Megarry 1983)

Having defined 'best interests' in such a narrow and restrictive manner, he went on to suggest that 'the current pensioners had *no financial interest in the success of the coal industry, and neither would future pensioners once they had retired*' (Blake 1995: 322, emphasis added). The Megarry judgement established an important precedent. Arguably, it outlawed (and effectively continues to outlaw) strategies of *socially responsible investment* (SRI) or *economically targeted investment* (ETI). SRI and ETI have become increasingly popular in the USA. Both seek to avoid certain types of investment on ethical, political or religious grounds, whilst concentrating investment activity in projects considered to be of social value to the community.[21]

The above analysis presents a significant, unanswered and, I would contend, largely unanswerable case for institutional reform. Though a variety of proposals and reform strategies to maximise the potential benefits of pension funds' investments to the productive economy might be considered, I here present merely a basic outline of one such reform strategy.

In so doing, my aim is not to produce a series of detailed policy proposals designed to address the persistent shortfall of dedicated productive investment in the domestic economy. Rather, in what follows, I hope to suggest how an alternative conception of the parameters of the politically and economically possible, liberated from the shackles of a restrictive neo-liberal economic imagery, might inform a more developmental and modernising strategy for the domestic economy. Though such an alternative paradigm might equally inform policy at spatial scales above the national, I restrict myself to domestic considerations (though see Hay and Watson 1998). In so doing, my intention is to demonstrate that heightened capital mobility in an era of financial liberalisation need not entail a withering of the political autonomy of the nation(al) state.

Conditional exemption from capital gains tax
Perhaps the simplest, certainly the most obvious, and arguably the crudest, reform that would significantly alter the investment environment in which pension funds operate would be to remove their status as gross funds and hence their exemption from capital gains tax and income tax (Crotty and Goldstein 1993). Enticing though such a

measure might at first appear, however, there are at least two likely
adverse consequences of such a reform. Whether these outweigh its
potential benefits is, nonetheless, still arguable. Removal of exemption
from capital gains tax, particularly if it were linked to the introduction
of a two-tier capital gains tax designed to penalise short-term investment activity,[22] would provide a powerful incentive for pension funds
to reconsider their investment portfolios, increasing their share of
longer-term and hence more dedicated forms of investment. In the
debit column, the introduction of such a measure would be likely, at
least in the short term, to precipitate an exodus of pension funds from
the British capital market as they relocated offshore. Second, even if
this could be avoided, it is likely that the extension of capital gains tax
would merely be passed directly on to pension policy holders in the
form of lower dividends from which to fund personal pensions.

This suggests the need to consider more subtle and slightly more
complex measures. These would have to be capable of providing
significant incentives for pension funds to modify their characteristically short-term and risk-averse investment behaviour, but without
penalising those that did (as would a blanket withdrawal of all
exemptions from capital gains tax). Two such measures warrant consideration. In the first, exemption from capital gains tax for gross
funds would be retained but rendered *conditional*. In order to remain
eligible, funds would have to demonstrate a balanced investment
portfolio in which a certain percentage of total investments were held
long term (say, over five years). This proportion could be gradually
increased (either as part of the legislation itself, or, preferably, in
successive budget statements) to a target level, allowing flexible and
incremental yet cumulatively significant change. *Such a reform would
not alter the privileged tax status of all but the most entrenched and
recalcitrant of institutional investors.* Further conditions could also be
set. Thus, in an attempt to reverse the haemorrhaging of potentially
productive investment capital overseas, continued exemption from
capital gains tax could be made conditional upon the investment of a
certain proportion of fund holdings in British assets (equity, bonds or
property).

Failure to meet such conditional criteria could be penalised in more
or less stringent ways. Most preferable, perhaps, at least in the short
term, would be for a relatively lenient policing of the exemption
criteria, exposing only that share of a fund's short-term or overseas
investments in excess of the exemption proportion to capital gains tax,

with no further penalty. Were this judged (on the basis of experience) to provide an insufficient incentive, penalties for a failure to meet the criteria could be introduced, or, in the harshest scenario, *all* gains on short-term or overseas investments (or possibly even all investment gains) could be exposed to capital gains tax for funds falling foul of the exemption criteria. Clearly, such a reform (or series of reforms) could be introduced with or without proposals for a two-tier capital gains tax more generally.

The advantages of *conditional exemption from capital gains tax* over a simple extension of capital gains tax to all institutional investors are clear – investors satisfying the stipulated exemption criteria would suffer no penalty and reform could be introduced incrementally, slowly yet cumulatively transforming the investment ethos of fund managers. Nonetheless, the introduction of such measures poses certain logistical difficulties. Exemption conditional on long-term investment relies on a system of refundable tax credits in which tax assessments can be calculated only retrospectively. This is likely to prove costly and complicated to introduce and implement, though not necessarily pro-hibitively so.

Administratively simpler, though somewhat less flexible, would be to introduce capital gains tax on short-term gains (and, potentially, on returns on overseas investments), to be compensated for by credits on tax-deductible long-term gains. Credits could also be accumulated for SRIs, ETIs and special bond issues designed to promote productive investment in the local and regional economy (see below). Given the comparative simplicity of implementing such a scheme, of the three considered this strategy is perhaps to be preferred. Nonetheless, the logistics of conditional exemption from capital gains tax warrant further consideration.

The obligations of trustees

If the argument for reform of the privileged tax status of gross funds is overwhelming, that for reform of the law governing the obligations and composition of boards of trustees is no less so. Here it is surely tempting to propose a simple amendment to the 1961 Trustee In-vestments Act that would serve to redefine the notion of the 'best interests' of pension fund beneficiaries (current and future) in more inclusive terms. In an attempt to overturn the precedent set by the Megarry judgement, trustees would be obliged to consider not only 'the best financial interests' of their beneficiaries, but the consequences of potential investments for the industry and the community.[23] Trustees would be required to provide a statement of the criteria by which investment decisions were made and would be expected to be answerable to those criteria in justifying particular investments. The amendment to the Act would also mandate the representation of beneficiaries on the board of trustees, a measure that would have considerably more force were it linked in this way to a revision of the concept of 'best interests'.[24] As well as a necessary step in the democratisation of pension funds, such a reform of the law governing trustees is a condition of providing tax credits for SRI and ERI (as proposed above).

Regional development, regional investment

Those ideas that Labour developed in opposition which sought to redress the persistent shortfall of dedicated investment in the productive economy and the need for industrial modernisation tended to focus on the need for differentiated, but nonetheless complementary, regional industrial development and investment strategies (Gould 1990; Labour Industry Forum 1994; Regional Policy Commission 1996). Consistent supply-side intervention might here make a virtue of spatially uneven development by promoting managed yet differentiated regional development strategies (cf. Pierre 1995). In keeping with such a reform agenda which emphasises the need for industrial strategy, supply-side dirigisme, indigenous and differentiated regional growth profiles, and the subordination of the interests of finance to industrial capital, a series of specifically regional institutional reforms designed to promote investment in the regional economy might be proposed. In the following section I return to, build upon and develop further the analysis of the previous chapter, considering, respectively, regional pension funds, regional investment portfolios and bonds and a broader nexus of regional institutions.

Regional pension funds and the regionalisation of institutional investment

Again, perhaps the simplest, the most obvious and the crudest means to increase investment in the regional economy would appear to be the introduction of a network of specifically regional pension funds. It is worth considering what such institutions might look like. These new and initially small public schemes would operate much like existing private pension funds. They would take the form of what Fred Block terms 'quasi-public financial institutions' (1992: 291). Though initially capitalised with public funds, they would, thereafter, be expected to produce profits from their investment activities without further reliance on public resources. In the first instance, however, they would receive significant tax advantages from the centre (which might eventually be whittled away as they became more commercially competitive).[25] In order to qualify for such favourable tax concessions and credits, they would have to invest a significant proportion of their assets in regionally based institutions and projects and on a medium- to long-term basis. The same tax credits would also be made available to private pension funds satisfying similar investment criteria.

The boards of such regional pension funds would be composed in equal measure of beneficiaries and representatives of the regional community (if linked to the creation of regional tiers of government, democratically elected regional officials); their statement of investment criteria would embody the principles of dedicated long-term investment, regional commitment, expansion of regional industrial capacity, job creation and social responsibility. They would effectively act as a second source of investment capital for regional industry.

Yet alluring though such a prospect might seem, there are considerable logistical difficulties with such a scheme. Its benefits are clear – gross investment gains in the productive economy, an increased supply of dedicated capital and potential distributional gains. Yet to allow workers to participate in the regional pension fund corresponding to the region in which they work (as opposed to that in which the corporate and financial headquarters of their employer is located) would result in a substantial increase in the complexity and cost of administering in-payments.[26] Given this consideration, it is likely that regional pension funds would prove a feasible alternative to private pension schemes only for the self-employed, leaving them relatively small in scale and hence relatively insignificant in terms of their contribution to productive regional investment. This suggests that strategies for enticing existing (private) pension funds into a greater regionalisation of their investment activities may ultimately prove more fruitful, though by no means incompatible, with the introduction of small regional pension funds.

Such a strategy would be based on tax credits. In addition to credits on long-term investment, the regional development agencies (RDAs) proposed in Labour's 1997 election manifesto would be encouraged to package regional investment portfolios in the form of *regional bonds*, to be traded amongst institutional investors such as pension funds. RDAs would here act as investment brokers, intermediating between regional industry on the one hand and institutional investors on the other, providing information about long-term investment prospects. Inclusion of a company's stock within the regional investment portfolio might, at the discretion of the specific RDA, be made conditional upon a democratisation of corporate governance or compatibility with a broader strategy of regional economic development.

The institutionalisation of regional innovation: towards regional structures of innovation

The above proposals in turn suggest the need for a nexus of regional institutions dedicated to the supply of investment capital on competitive terms to regional industry. It should be the goal of the government to ensure that each regional economy has access to a financial sector dedicated to the provision of capital over the long term for projects regarded as contributing to the overall competitiveness of the regional economy. One such nexus of regional institutions might comprise the following.

1 *Regional and metropolitan development agencies (RDAs and MDAs)*. Each region should have an RDA with a principal responsibility for the promotion of economic development in the region.[27] Each RDA would be directly accountable to a democratically elected regional chamber, but would retain a substantial degree of operational independence, acting, as the Regional Policy Commission suggests, as the 'executive arm' of the regional government in the area of economic development (1996: vii, 33–6). The board of each RDA would be appointed by the regional government but should include the representation of trade unions, local authorities and both industrial and financial capital. The RDA would be mandated to draw up a regional development strategy, to be approved within the regional chamber and by the Secretary of State, on the basis of wide consultation within the region. The implementation, monitoring and (subject to approval within the regional chamber) adaptation of the regional development strategy to changing internal and external circumstances would be the primary responsibility of the RDA on a day-to-day basis.[28]

2 *Regional investment banks (RIBs)*. Each regional economy should
   have access to a financial sector dedicated to the provision of
   industrial finance over the long term. Institutional reform at the
   regional level would thus see the creation of a series of non-profit-
   making investment and commercial banks, which might channel
   savings and institutional investments to the productive economy.
   Such dedicated regional financial institutions would be able to
   provide capital on a long-term and competitive basis to fund
   regional industrial investment and capital projects that were seen as
   contributing to the overall competitiveness of the regional economy
   and were considered compatible with the regional development
   strategy.[29] As Paul Hirst suggests, such funds 'would be greatly
   favoured by national legislation giving a privileged tax position for
   investors and for the institutions' (1994: 87). Such tax advantages
   for productive investment might eventually be made dependent
   upon a democratisation of corporate governance, to embody a wider
   conception of stakeholding (thus rewarding companies that gave
   representation to workers, consumers and the local community on
   their boards). RIBs, in co-operation with RDAs, might also be given
   the autonomy to bundle together regional investment portfolios that
   could be traded (to institutional investors and individuals alike) in
   the form of long-term regional bonds and which would be eligible
   for favourable tax concessions.
3 *Regional training agencies (RTAs)*. These would be mandated to act
   strategically to provide long-term training, skilling and reskilling
   programmes that were flexible and responsive to the rapidly
   changing competitive requirements of a dynamic regional economy.
   They would, effectively, provide the human capital to operation-
   alise the enhanced physical capital arising from higher levels of
   regional productive investment. RTAs would be responsible for co-
   ordinating the involvement of further- and higher-education
   institutions and apprenticeship schemes in the provision of an
   appropriately and highly skilled local labour force, in line with the
   regional development strategy and with other key regional institutions.
4 *Regional economic fora*. These would provide a public legitimation
   function for regional economic development strategies, in which
   RDAs, RIBs and RTAs would be required to defend publicly their
   performance and contribution to a regional development strategy to
   an assembly comprising representatives of the local and regional

business communities, the local and regional trade unions and local and regional authorities.

Such a nexus of dedicated regional financial institutions would promote distinct regional structures of innovation (cf. Freeman and Soete 1997), serving to provide capital on a long-term and competitive basis to fund regional industrial investment and capital projects seen as contributing to the overall growth dynamic of the regional economy.

Conclusion

These reflections constitute a modest attempt to outline some of the measures that an incumbent Labour administration might consider in seeking to restore an indigenous investment ethic to British capitalism. It must be reiterated that it has not been, nor is it, my intention to offer detailed policy outlines in the form of an 'alternative industrial policy manifesto' for Labour in power. The above proposals are speculative and experimental and should be judged accordingly. My concern has been to stimulate and open up discussion of the nature of the British affliction and the extent of the measures required to address it in the light of the contribution of comparative political economists and contemporary theorists of British exceptionalism.

Labour's 1997 manifesto contained a commitment to combat Britain's significant and enduring problem of under-investment. It is a moot point whether that commitment represents a merely rhetorical reaffirmation of a pledge that it no longer intends to prioritise, or a restatement of an underlying and consistent diagnosis of the principal structural weakness of the British economy which the party in government is dedicated to addressing. The jury, to give New Labour the benefit of the doubt, is still out. Either way, I suggest, some attempt must be made to restore to British capitalism an ethos of dedication and long-term investment and, hence, to close the capital stock gap with the other major industrialised economies. Otherwise, to quote Michael Kitson and Jonathan Michie:

> the alternative is to accept that … [Britain] cannot compete with these countries and that its comparable competitors are the newly industrial-ised countries, with all that this entails for domestic living standards and employment opportunities. (1997: 46)

Yet, as I have been at pains to demonstrate, to restore such an investment ethic to British capitalism is no easy accomplishment and cannot be achieved in the space of a few years. It requires significant and cumulatively radical institutional reform and a yet more fundamental transformation of the very conceptual and ideational environment within which economic policy and investment decisions are made. These, I have suggested, are necessary, but not in themselves sufficient, conditions to establish in Britain a reinvigorated growth dynamic.

If any aspect of the above diagnosis is correct, then, for New Labour and a renewed and revitalised left, it is time to find out whether necessity is indeed 'the mother of invention'. If it is not, then, sadly, New Labour's modernisation may have come at the ultimate price of Britain's modernisation. If my remaining optimism is misplaced, then New Labour may indeed be labouring under false pretences....

Notes

1 If only in the sense that it has the most direct consequences for the others.
2 Indeed, though Labour retains a fairly nominal commitment to regional institutions (in the form of regional development agencies) there is now precious little substance to its rhetoric of industrial reform and renewal and neither rhetoric nor substance with respect to financial reform.
3 For a brief genealogy of Labour's conception of industrial strategy and the financial reform required to support it see Lee (1996b: 136–8); see also Gamble (1992); Wickham-Jones (undated).
4 That the think-tanks of the self-styled 'radical centre', whatever else their strengths, failed to provide Labour in opposition with a consistent alternative to the neo-liberal orthodoxy should not be taken as implying a broader silence on the left. In the context of the present discussion, the work of authors like Keith Cowling, Roger Sugden, Jonathan Michie and John Grieve Smith, on whom I draw extensively, has provided a consistent corrective to the emerging consensus and a series of rigorously analytical, visionary and often highly detailed alternative policy proposals. The influence of Cowling, in particular, on the Policy Review process has already been noted. In the USA, the work of Robert Pollin, Gary A. Dymski and Gerald Epstein, amongst others, has performed a similar role.
5 For a much fuller elaboration of this argument see Hay and Watson (1998). On the 'logic of no alternative' see Hay (1998c); Watson (1999b, 1999c).

6 Hutton, presumably out of some concern for the broader reception of his ideas, does not publicly acknowledge his debt to Anderson and Nairn's brand of new left Marxism, though at certain points in the text the lineage of the argument is unmistakable. See Barrett-Brown (1995); Hay (1997d: especially 89–92); Leys (1995: especially 4–5).

7 In an indication of the basic compatibility of these apparently rather divergent accounts, Hutton himself relies quite extensively on discussions of the comparative strengths of the German–Japanese 'model'. Pollin, too, makes explicit reference to affinities between the writings of Nairn and comparative political economists such as Gerschenkron (1995: 30, n. 8).

8 For applications to the problems of British under-investment see in particular Eichengreen (1996); Lee (1996b); Pollin (1995).

9 Given Hutton's reliance at various points in his argument on both the exceptionalism thesis and the comparative political economy of Albert in particular, it is perhaps unsurprising that on this he seems to equivocate.

10 The distinction between 'bank-based' and 'capital market-based' financial systems is in fact Pollin's. As well as the works already cited see Gourevitch (1996); Kester (1996); Orrù (1993); Porter (1996); Woolcock (1996).

11 Hirschmann defines his terms in the following way: 'by exit, I mean withdrawal from a relationship with a person or organisation.... The direct and more informative way of alerting management is to alert it: this is voice' (1986: 78–9, see also Hirschmann 1970).

12 Thus, as Dimitri Vittas notes, the banks 'have an active part in arranging mergers and take-overs and have occasionally used their strength to prevent the purchase of stakes in German companies by "undesirable" elements ... the banks have supervised the rescue of a number of companies, saving jobs and gaining considerable goodwill in the process' (1978: 80). In a similar vein, John Zysman points to the intervention of the banks in the early 1980s to 'restructure the troubled Telefunken company and the Deutsche Bank's refusal to allow Mercedes Benz to fall under foreign control' as reinforcing the impression that 'the banks patrol the borders of German industry ... mak[ing] possible a more directed process of market-led adjustment' (1983: 265).

13 See, in particular, Labour Party (1997: 10–13); see also Labour Party (1995: especially chapter 5); Labour Party Industry Forum (1994: 12–16); Labour Party (1993); Brown (1995c, 1996).

14 There is a voluminous literature on both the Attlee and Wilson governments' ultimately abortive attempts at institutional and industrial modernisation. On the Attlee government see in particular Johnmann (1991); Mercer (1991); Pollard (1992); Tiratsoo and Tomlinson (1993); Tomlinson (1994). For a brief review see Hay (1996b: 34–5). On Wilson see Grant (1982); Lee (1996a); Longstreth (1979); Shanks (1977); Young and Lowe (1974); Zysman (1983: 212–20).

15 See in particular the work of Johnmann, Mercer, Tiratsoo and Tomlinson cited above.

16 That this tension should be particularly transparent in Hutton's work is, in many respects, a reflection of his (laudable) efforts to reject an institutionalism which tends to depoliticise and downplay the extent and significance of institutional change and, hence, of his attempt to restore the 'political' to comparative political economy. Nonetheless, this same tension between a desire to apportion responsibility for economic and political failure, on the one hand, and an account which implies a certain institutional logic of inevitability independent of the actions of political agents, on the other, is considerably more widespread. Indeed, it tends to plague all institutionalist accounts of national capitalisms which emphasise a moment (or moments) of institutional genesis and subsequent inertia and continuity (see Hay and Wincott 1998; Hay 1998b).

17 For a much more sustained discussion of these issues see Hay (1997d).

18 Geoffrey Garrett's implicit and casual suggestion that Britain under Labour might simply choose a set of encompassing labour-market institutions to facilitate a social democratic corporatist road to competitiveness in a global era is a case in point. That this comes at the end of an otherwise impressive analysis of the constraints and opportunities associated with globalisation should not lead us to underestimate the voluntarism it implies. See Garrett (1998: chapter 6).

19 For a similar interpretation of pension fund activity in Britain see Cosh *et al.* (1990).

20 As gross funds, pension funds are exempt from capital gains tax and enjoy relief from income tax on investments in the UK (and, where mutual tax agreements exist, on overseas investments). The so-called 'switching costs' for such institutional investors are thus significantly lower than for all other investors. See Blake (1995: 322).

21 On SRI and ETI see Barber and Ghilarducci (1993: 298–305); Bruyn (1987).

22 Such a tax was tentatively proposed by Labour, after lengthy consultation and an indication of broad support from the CBI, in 1996. However, following the departure of Howard Davies as director-general in September 1996, the CBI distanced itself from such measures, whilst, predictably enough, the National Association of Pension Funds, fearing the likely extension of the measure to all investors (institutional and otherwise), dismissed the proposal as unworkable. A senior Labour official then indicated that although a two-tier capital gains tax would be considered, the party was not committed to such a measure. It remains, like many other fallen policy commitments, officially 'under consideration'. As David Wighton in the *Financial Times* commented at the time, 'if Labour were to drop the idea it would be left with few concrete proposals [arguably none] for tackling what it sees as a central weakness of the economy' (1996).

23 For similar proposals for the USA see D'Arista and Schlesinger (1993); Pollin (1995: 51).

24 For similar proposals see Barber and Ghilarducci (1993); Block (1992: 277–303); Hutton (1995); Porter (1996).

25 If administered successfully, this need only be a short- to medium-term tax concession. Given the herding instincts of fund managers, once expectations have changed, behaviour is unlikely to revert rapidly to past practices.

26 Yet to insist that employees could contribute only to the regional pension fund corresponding to the location of their employer's corporate headquarters would defeat entirely the purpose of the exercise, further concentrating investment funds in the south-east of England and weakening the employee's sense of contribution to a strategy of regional development. I am indebted to Matthew Watson for this observation.

27 The RDAs are, of course, the sole remaining aspect of Labour's regional industrial strategy. Needless to say, the role projected for them by the government is rather more modest than that presented in earlier policy statements (see Labour Party Industry Forum 1994; Regional Policy Commission 1996). This is, in turn, rather more modest than that envisaged here.

28 It should be noted that the promotion of RDAs and MDAs and, indeed, regional tiers of government would greatly facilitate the procurement of the European Union's Structural Funds, which are often dependent upon regional submissions. Such submissions are, in the context of metropolitan and regional fragmentation and inter-local rivalries, often difficult to formulate (see Hay and Jessop 1995; Martin and Pearce 1993; for a more general discussion see Stoker *et al.* 1996).

29 On the reform of regional financial institutions see Block (1992, 1996); Campen (1993); Hirst (1994: 122–47).

Bibliography

Aaronovitch, S. (1981) *The Road From Thatcherism: The Alternative Economic Strategy*. London: Lawrence and Wishart.

Abrams, M., Rose, R. and Hinden, R. (1960) *Must Labour Lose?* Harmondsworth: Penguin.

Addison, P. (1975) *The Road to 1945: British Politics and the Second World War*. London: Cape.

Akyüz, Y. and Cornford, A. (1995) 'International Capital Movements: Some Prospects for Reform', in J. Michie and J. G. Smith (eds), *Managing the Global Economy*. Oxford: Oxford University Press.

Albert, M. (1993) *Capitalism Against Capitalism*. London: Whurr.

Albo, G. (1997) 'A World Market of Opportunities? Capitalist Obstacles and Left Economic Policy', in L. Panitch (ed.), *Ruthless Criticism of All That Exists: Socialist Register 1997*. London: Merlin.

Alcock, P. (1992) 'The Labour Party and the Welfare State', in M. J. Smith and J. Spear (eds), *The Changing Labour Party*. London: Routledge.

Aldrich, J. H. (1997) 'When is it Rational to Vote?', in D. C. Mueller (ed.), *Perspectives on Public Choice: A Handbook*. Cambridge: Cambridge University Press.

Altvater, E. (1973) 'Notes on Some Problems of State Interventionism', *Kapitalistate*, 1, 97–108 and 2, 76–83.

Amin, A. (1994) 'Post-Fordism: Models, Fantasies and Phantoms of Transition', in A. Amin (ed.), *Post-Fordism: A Reader*. Oxford: Blackwell.

Amin, A. and Robins, K. (1990) 'The Re-emergence of Regional Economies? The Mythical Geography of Flexible Accumulation', *Environment and Planning D: Society and Space*, 8, 7–34.

Amin, A. and Thrift, N. (1992) 'Neo-Marshallian Nodes in Global Networks', *International Journal of Urban and Regional Research*, 16, 571–87.

Anderson, P. (1992) *English Questions*. London: Verso.

Andrews, D. M. (1994) 'Capital Mobility and State Autonomy: Towards a Structural Theory of International Monetary Relations', *International Studies Quarterly*, 38, 193–218.

Arrow, K. J. (1951) *Social Choice and Individual Values*. New York: John Wiley.

Ashton, D., Green, F. and Hopkins, M. (1989) 'The Training System of British Capitalism', in F. Green (ed.), *The Restructuring of the UK Economy*. Hemel Hempstead: Harvester Wheatsheaf.

Bale, T. (1996) 'The Death of the Past: Symbolic Politics and the Changing of Clause IV', in D. Farrell *et al.* (eds), *British Elections and Parties Yearbook, Vol. 6*. London: Frank Cass.

Barber, R. and Ghilarducci, T. (1993) 'Pension Funds, Capital Markets, and the Economic Future', in G. A. Dymski, G. Epstein and R. Pollin (eds), *Transforming the US Financial System*. Armonk, NY: M. E. Sharpe.

Barnet, R. J. and Cavanagh, J. (1994) *Global Dreams: Imperial Corporations and the New World Order*. New York: Simon and Schuster.

Barrett-Brown, M. (1995) 'The New Orthodoxy', in M. Barrett-Brown and H. Radice, *Democracy Versus Capitalism*, Socialist Renewal Pamphlet No. 4, London: European Labour Forum.

Bates, R. H. and Lein, D-H. D. (1985) 'A Note on Taxation, Development and Representative Government', *Politics and Society*, 14, 53–70.

Becker, G. S. (1983) 'A Theory of Competition Among Interest Groups for Political Influence', *Quarterly Journal of Economics*, 48, 371–400.

Bell, D. S. and Shaw, E. D. (eds) (1994) *Conflict and Cohesion in West European Social Democratic Parties*. London: Pinter.

Berger, S. and Dore, R. (eds) (1996) *National Diversity and Global Capitalism*. Ithaca, NY: Cornell University Press.

Berman, S. (1998) *The Social Democratic Moment*. Cambridge, MA: Harvard University Press.

Best, M. (1990) *The New Competition: Institutions of Industrial Restructuring*. Cambridge, MA: Harvard University Press.

Bishop, M. and Kay, J. (1988) *Does Privatisation Work? Lessons from the UK*. London: London Business School.

Blackburn, R. (1997) 'Reflections on Blair's Velvet Revolution', *New Left Review*, 223, 3–16.

Blair, T. (1994) *Socialism*. London: Fabian Society.

—— (1995) *Let Us Face the Future: The 1945 Anniversary Lecture*. London: Fabian Society.

—— (1996) *New Britain: My Vision of a Young Country*. London: Harper Collins.

Blake, D. (1992) *Issues in Pension Funding*. London: Routledge.

—— (1995) *Pension Schemes and Pension Funds in the United Kingdom*. Oxford: Clarendon Press.

Block, F. (1987a) 'The Ruling Class Does Not Rule: Notes on the Marxist Theory of the State', in *Revising State Theory*. Philadelphia, PA: Temple University Press.

—— (1987b) 'Beyond Relative Autonomy: State Managers as Historical Subjects', in *Revising State Theory*. Philadelphia, PA: Temple University Press.

—— (1992) 'Capitalism without Class Power', *Politics and Society*, 20, 277–303.

—— (1996) 'A Second Paradox of Thrift: Investment Strategies and the Future', in N. R. Goodwin (ed.), *As If The Future Mattered: Translating Social and Economic Theory into Human Behaviour*. Ann Arbor, MI: University of Michigan Press.

Blyth, M. M. (1997a) '"Any More Bright Ideas?": The Ideational Turn of Comparative Political Economy', *Comparative Politics*, 29, 229–50.

—— (1997b) 'Moving the Political Middle: Redefining the Boundaries of State Action', *Political Quarterly*, 68, 231–40.

—— (1998a) 'Why Do Conservatives Build Welfare States While Social Democrats Dismantle Them? Towards an Evolutionary Understanding of State Transformation', paper presented to the European Consortium for Political Research, University of Warwick, 23–28 March.

—— (1998b) 'From Ideas and Institutions to Ideas and Interests: Beyond the "Usual Suspects?"', paper presented at the Eleventh Conference of Europeanists, Baltimore, MD, 26–28 February.

—— (1999) 'Globalisation or Disembedded Liberalism? Institutions, Ideas, and the Double Movement', in C. Hay and D. Marsh (eds), *Globalization, Welfare Retrenchment and the State*. London: Macmillan, forthcoming.

Bond, S. R., Devereuz, M. P. and Gammie, M. J. (1996) 'Tax Reform to Promote Investment', *Oxford Review of Economic Policy*, 12 (2), 109–17.

—— and Jenkinson, T. (1996) 'The Assessment: Investment Performance and Policy', *Oxford Review of Economic Policy*, 12 (2), 1–29.

Boyer, R. and Drache, D. (eds) (1996) *States Against Markets: The Limits of Globalisation*. London: Routledge.

Brenner, R. (1998) *The Economics of Global Turbulence: A Special Report on the World Economy, 1950–98*. Special issue of *New Left Review*, 229.

Brivati, B. (1996) *Hugh Gaitskell: A Biography*. London: Richard Cohen Books.

—— (1997) 'Earthquake or Watershed? Conclusions on New Labour in Power', in B. Brivati and T. Bale (eds), *New Labour in Power: Precedents and Prospects*. London: Routledge.

—— and Bale, T. (eds) (1997) *New Labour in Power: Precedents and Prospects*. London: Routledge.

Brown, G. (1994) *How Can We Conquer Unemployment?* London: Labour Party.

—— (1995a) *A Budget for Britain: Labour's Strategy for Investment*. London: Labour Party Industry Forum, 1 November.

—— (1995b) Speech to Labour Party Conference. London: Labour Party.

—— (1995c) Labour's Macroeconomic Framework. Speech to the Labour Finance and Industry Group. London: Labour Party.

—— (1996) Speech to CBI Annual Conference, 11 November. London: Labour Party.

Bruyn, S. (1987) *The Field of Social Investing*. Cambridge: Cambridge University Press.

Buckle, M. and Thompson, J. (1995) *The UK Financial System* (2nd edn). Manchester: Manchester University Press.

Burk, K. and Cairncross, A. (1992) *'Goodbye, Great Britain': The IMF Crisis*. New Haven, CT: Yale University Press.

Butler, D. and Kavanagh, D. (1992) *The British General Election of 1992*. London: Macmillan.

—— and —— (1997) *The British General Election of 1997*. London: Macmillan.

Buxton, T. (1998) 'The Foundations of Competitiveness: Investment and Innovation', in T. Buxton, P. Chapman and P. Temple (eds), *Britain's Economic Performance* (2nd edn). London: Routledge.

——, Chapman, P. and Temple, P. (eds) (1998) *Britain's Economic Performance* (2nd edn). London: Routledge.

Campbell, J. L. (1998) 'Institutional Analysis and the Role of Ideas in Political Economy', *Theory and Society*, 27, 377–409.

Campbell, M. (1998) 'Pensions: Redressing the Balance', *Political Quarterly*, 69, 14–22.

Campen, J. (1993) 'Banks, Communities and Public Policy', in G. A. Dymski, G. Epstein and R. Pollin (eds.) *Transforming the US Financial System*. Armonk, NY: M. E. Sharpe.

Cerny, P. G. (1990) *The Changing Architecture of Politics*. London: Sage.

—— (1993) 'The Deregulation and Re-regulation of Financial Markets in a More Open World', in P. G. Cerny (ed.), *Finance and World Politics: Markets, Regimes and States in the Post-hegemonic Era*. Aldershot: Edward Elgar.

—— (1995) 'Globalisation and the Changing Logic of Collective Action', *International Organisation*, 49, 595–625.

—— (1997) 'Paradoxes of the Competition State: The Dynamics of Political Globalisation', *Government and Opposition*, 32, 251–74.

Chapman, P. (1998) 'Human Capital Issues', in T. Buxton, P. Chapman, and P. Temple (eds), *Britain's Economic Performance* (2nd edn). London: Routledge.

Coates, D. (1994) *The Question of UK Decline: The Economy, State and Society*. London: Harvester Wheatsheaf.

—— (1996) 'Labour Governments: Old Constraints and New Parameters', *New Left Review*, 219, 62–77.

—— (1999) 'Why Growth Rates Differ', in C. Hay and D. Marsh (eds), *Putting the 'P' Back into IPE*, special issue of *New Political Economy*, 4 (1), forthcoming.

Cohen, B. J. (1998) *The Geography of Money*. Ithaca, NY: Cornell University Press.

Commission on Public Policy and British Business (1997) *Promoting Prosperity: A Business Agenda for Britain*. London: Vintage.

Confederation of British Industry (1994) *Realistic Returns: How Do Manufacturers Assess New Investment?* London: Confederation of British
Industry.

Connolly, W. E. (1972) 'On "Interests" in Politics', *Politics and Society*, 2,
459–77.

—— (1993) *The Terms of Political Discourse* (3rd edn). Oxford: Blackwell.

Cook, R. (1996) 'A Radical Agenda for a New Millennium', *Renewal*, 5, 9–
16.

Coopey, R., Fileding, S. and Tiratsoo, N. (eds) (1993) *The Wilson Governments, 1964–1970*. London: Pinter Press.

Cosh, A., Hughes, A. and Singh, A. (1990) 'Take-overs and Short-termism:
Analytical and Policy Issues in the UK', in *Take-overs and Short-termism
in the UK*, Industrial Policy Paper No. 3. London: Institute for Public
Policy Research.

Cowling, K. (1990) 'The Strategic Approach to Economic and Industrial
Policy', in K. Cowling and R. Sugden (eds), *A New Economic Policy for
Britain: Essays on the Development of Industry*. Manchester: Manchester
University Press.

—— and Sugden, R. (eds) (1990) *A New Economic Policy for Britain: Essays
on the Development of Industry*. Manchester: Manchester University
Press.

—— and —— (1994) 'Industrial Strategy: Guiding Principles and the
European Context', in P. Bianchi, K. Cowling and R. Sugden (eds),
*Europe's Economic Challenge: Analyses of Industrial Strategy. An
Agenda for the 1990s*. London: Routledge.

Cox, A., Lee, S. and Sanderson, J. (1997) *The Political Economy of Modern
Britain*. London: Edward Elgar.

Crewe, I. (1986) 'On the Death and Resurrection of Class Voting: Some
Comments on *How Britain Votes*', *Political Studies*, 35, 620–38.

—— (1988) 'Has the Electorate Become Thatcherite?', in R. Skidelsky (ed.),
Thatcherism. London: Chatto and Windus.

—— (1992) 'Changing Votes and Unchanging Voters', *Electoral Studies*, 11,
335–45.

—— (1993) 'The Thatcher Legacy', in A. King, I. Crewe, D. Denver, K. Newton,
P. Norton, D. Sanders and P. Seyd, *Britain at the Polls 1992*. Chatham,
NJ: Chatham House.

Crosland, A. (1956) *The Future of Socialism*. London: Jonathan Cape (1985
reprint).

Crossman, R. (1985) *The Crossman Diaries: Selections of the Diaries of a
Cabinet Minister, 1964–70*. London: Methuen.

Crotty, J. R. and Goldstein, D. (1993) 'Do US Financial Markets Allocate
Credit Efficiently? The Case of Corporate Restructuring in the 1980s', in
G. A. Dymski, G. Epstein and R. Pollin (eds), *Transforming the US
Financial System*. Armonk, NY: M. E. Sharpe.

Crouch, C. (1997) 'The Terms of the Neo-Liberal Consensus', *Political Quarterly*, 68, 352–60.

Crozier, M., Huntingdon, S. and Watanuki, J. (1975) *The Crisis of Democracy*. New York: New York University Press.

Curtice, J. (1997) 'Plenary Address', Political Studies Association annual conference, University of Ulster, Jordanstown.

D'Arista, J. W. and Schlesinger, T. (1993) 'The Parallel Banking System', in G. A. Dymski, G. Epstein and R. Pollin (eds), *Transforming the US Financial System*. Armonk, NY: M. E. Sharpe.

Denver, D. (1997) 'The Results: How Britain Voted', in A. Geddes and J. Tonge (eds), *Labour's Landslide: The British General Election of 1997*. Manchester: Manchester University Press.

—— (1998) 'The British Electorate in the 1980s', *West European Politics*, 21, 197–217.

—— and Hands, G. (1997) 'Turnout', in P. Norris and N. T. Gavin (eds), *Britain Votes 1997*. Oxford: Oxford University Press.

Department of Trade and Industry (1998) *Fairness at Work*. London: HMSO.

Dicken, P. (1998) *Global Shift: Transforming the World Economy* (3rd edn). New York: Guilford Press.

Dixit, A. (1992) 'Investment and Hysteresis', *Journal of Economic Perspectives*, 6, 107–32.

Dolowitz, D. (1998) *Learning From America: Policy Transfer and the Development of the British Workfare State*. Brighton: Sussex Academic Press.

——, McAnulla, S., Marsh, D. and Richards, R. (1996) 'Thatcherism and the Three "R"'s: Radicalism, Realism and Rhetoric in the Third Term of the Thatcher Government', *Parliamentary Affairs*, 49, 455–70.

Dorey, P. (1995) *The Conservative Party and the Trade Unions*. London: Routledge.

Dowding, K. (1996) *Power*. Buckingham: Open University Press.

Downs, A. (1957) *An Economic Theory of Democracy*. London: Harper Collins.

Drache, D. (1996) 'From Keynes to K-Mart: Competitiveness in a Corporate Age', in R. Boyer and D. Drache (eds), *States Against Markets: The Limits of Globalisation*. London: Routledge.

Driver, C. (1996) 'Tightening the Reins: The Capacity Stance of UK Manufacturing Firms, 1976–95', in J. Michie and J. G. Smith (eds), *Creating Industrial Capacity: Towards Full Employment*. Oxford: Oxford University Press.

—— (1998) 'The Case of Fixed Investment', in T. Buxton, P. Chapman and P. Temple (eds), *Britain's Economic Performance* (2nd edn). London: Routledge.

Dunleavy, P. (1991) *Democracy, Bureaucracy and Public Choice*. Hemel Hempstead: Harvester Wheatsheaf.

—— and O'Leary, B. (1984) *Theories of the State: The Politics of Liberal Democracy*. London: Macmillan.

—— and Ward, H. (1991) 'Party Competition – The Preference Shaping Model', in P. Dunleavy, *Democracy, Bureaucracy and Public Choice*. Hemel Hempstead: Harvester Wheatsheaf.

Dunn, J. (1984) *The Politics of Socialism: An Essay in Political Theory*. Cambridge: Cambridge University Press.

Eatwell, J. (1992) 'The Development of Labour Policy, 1987–92', in J. Michie (ed.), *The Economic Legacy 1987–92*. London: Academic Press.

—— (1996) 'Unemployment on a World Scale', in J. Eatwell (ed.), *Global Unemployment: Loss of Jobs in the '90s*. New York: M. E. Sharpe.

Edgell, S. and Duke, V. (1991) *A Measure of Thatcherism: A Sociology of Britain*. London: Harper Collins.

Eichengreen, B. (1996) 'Explaining Britain's Economic Performance: A Critical Note', *Economic Journal*, 106, 213–18.

——, Tobin, J. and Wyplosz, C. (1995) 'Two Cases for Sand in the Wheels of International Finance', *Economic Journal*, 105, 162–72.

Elliott, G. (1993) *Labourism and the English Genius: The Strange Death of Labour England?* London: Verso.

Elliott, L. (1997) 'Brown Puts Faith in George', *Guardian*, 7 May.

Ellison, N. (1997) 'From Welfare State to Post-welfare Society? Labour's Social Policy in Historical and Contemporary Perspective', in B. Brivati and T. Bale (eds), *New Labour in Power: Precedents and Prospects*. London: Routledge.

Engels, F. (1878) *Anti-Dühring*. Moscow: Progress Publishers (1947 reprint).

Epstein, L. (1980) *Political Parties in Western Democracies*. London: Transaction Publishers.

Esping-Andersen (ed.) (1996) *Welfare States in Transition: National Adaptations in Global Economies*. London: Sage.

Evans, P. (1997) 'The Eclipse of the State? Reflections on Stateness in an Era of Globalisation', *World Politics*, 50, 62–87.

Feldstein, M. and Horioka, C. (1980) 'Domestic Saving and International Capital Flows', *Economic Journal*, 90, 314–29.

Fielding, S. (1997) 'Labour's Path to Power', in A. Geddes and J. Tonge (eds), *Labour's Landslide*. Manchester: Manchester University Press.

Finegold, D. and Skocpol, T. (1995) *State and Party in America's New Deal*. Madison, WI: University of Wisconsin Press.

—— and Soskice, D. (1988) 'The Failure of Training in Britain: Analysis and Prescription', *Oxford Review of Economic Policy*, 4 (3), 21–53.

Fiorina, M. P. (1997) 'Voting Behaviour', in D. C. Mueller (ed.), *Perspectives on Public Choice: A Handbook*. Cambridge: Cambridge University Press.

Foreman-Peck, J. and Manning, D. (1988) 'How Well is BT Performing? An International Comparison of Telecommunications Total Factor Productivity', *Fiscal Studies*, 9, 54–67.

Frankel, J. A. (1993) 'Quantifying International Capital Mobility in the 1980s', in *On Exchange Rates*. Cambridge, MA: MIT Press.

—— (1997) *Regional Trading Blocs in the World Economic System*. Washington, DC: Institute for International Economics.

Franklin, M. (1985) *The Decline of Class Voting*. Oxford: Clarendon Press.

Franks, J. and Mayer, C. (1990) 'Corporate Ownership and Corporate Control: A Study of France, Germany and the United Kingdom', *Economic Policy*, 10, 189–231.

Freeman, C. and Soete, L. (1997) *The Economics of Industrial Innovation* (3rd edn). Cambridge, MA: MIT Press.

Gallie, W. B. (1956) 'Essentially Contested Concepts', *Proceedings of the Aristotelian Society*, 56, 167–98.

Gamble, A. (1992) 'The Labour Party and Economic Management', in M. J. Smith and J. Spear (eds), *The Changing Labour Party*. London: Routledge.

—— (1994) *Britain in Decline: Economic Policy, Political Strategy and the State* (4th edn). London: Macmillan.

—— and Kelly, G. (1996) 'Stakeholder Capitalism and One Nation Socialism', *Renewal*, 4 (1), 23–32.

——, Payne, A., Hoogvelt, A., Dietrich, M. and Kenny, M. (1996) 'Editorial: New Political Economy', *New Political Economy*, 1 (1), 5–11.

Garrett, G. (1998) *Partisan Politics in the Global Economy*. Cambridge: Cambridge University Press.

Gavin, N. T. and Sanders, D. (1997) 'The Economy and Voting', in P. Norris and N. T. Gavin (eds), *Britain Votes 1997*. Oxford: Oxford University Press.

George, S. and Haythorne, D. (1996) 'The British Labour Party', in J. Gaffney (ed.), *Political Parties and the European Union*. London: Routledge.

Gerschenkron, H. (1962) *Economic Backwardness in Historical Perspective*. Cambridge, MA: Harvard University Press.

Giddens, A. (1984) *The Constitution of Society*. Cambridge: Polity Press.

Gillespie, R. and W. E. Paterson (eds) (1993) *Rethinking Social Democracy in Western Europe*. London: Frank Cass.

Glyn, A. (1989) 'The Macro-anatomy of the Thatcher Years', in F. Green (ed.), *The Restructuring of the UK Economy*. Hemel Hempstead: Harvester Wheatsheaf.

—— (ed.) (1998) *Economic Policy and Social Democracy*. Special issue of *Oxford Review of Economic Policy*, 14 (1).

Gould, B. (1990) 'Introduction', in K. Cowling and R. Sudgen (eds), *A New Economic Policy for Britain*. Manchester: Manchester University Press.

Gourevitch, P. A. (1996) 'The Macroeconomics of Microinstitutional Differences in the Analysis of Comparative Capitalism', in S. Berger and R. Dore (eds), *National Diversity and Global Capitalism*. Ithaca, NY: Cornell University Press.

Gramsci, A. (1971) *Selections from Prison Notebooks*. London: Lawrence and Wishart.

Grant, W. (1982) *The Political Economy of Industrial Policy*. London: Butterworth.

Habermas, J. (1975) *Legitimation Crisis*. London: Heinemann.

Hall, P. A. (1993) 'Policy Paradigms, Social Learning and the State: The Case of Economic Policy-Making in Britain', *Comparative Politics*, 25, 175–96.

Hall, S. (1979) 'The Great Moving Right Show', *Marxism Today*, reprinted in S. Hall and M. Jacques (eds) (1983), *The Politics of Thatcherism*. London: Lawrence and Wishart.

—— (1995) 'Son of Margaret', *New Statesman and Society*, 6 October.

——, Critcher, C., Jefferson, T., Clarke, J. and Roberts, B. (1978) *Policing the Crisis: Mugging, the State and Law and Order*. London: Macmillan.

—— and Jacques, M. (eds) (1983) *The Politics of Thatcherism*. London: Lawrence and Wishart.

—— and —— (eds) (1989) *New Times*. London: Lawrence and Wishart.

—— and Jessop, B. (1985) 'Authoritarian Populism: A Reply', *New Left Review*, 151, 115–24.

Halpern, D. and Wood, S. (1996) 'Comparable Revolutions? Thatcherism '79 and Labour's "Road to the Manifesto"', *Renewal*, 4 (1), 10–18.

Hantrais, L. (1995) *Social Policy in the European Union*. New York: St Martin's Press.

Haq, M., ul, Kaul, I. and Grunberg, I. (eds) (1996) *The Tobin Tax: Coping with Financial Volatility*. Oxford: Oxford University Press.

—— and Temple, P. (1998) 'Economic Policy and the Changing International Division of Labour', in T. Buxton, P. Chapman, and P. Temple (eds), *Britain's Economic Performance* (2nd edn). London: Routledge.

Harrop, M. (1997) 'The Pendulum Swings: The British General Election of 1997', *Government and Opposition*, 32, 305–19.

Hart, J. A. (1992) *Rival Capitalists: International Competitiveness in the United States, Japan and Western Europe*. Ithaca, NY: Cornell University Press.

Haseler, S. (1969) *The Gaitskellites: Revisionism in the British Labour Party*. London: Macmillan.

Hassan, G. and Shaw, E. (1996) 'From Old Labour to New Labour: An Interview with Eric Shaw', *Renewal*, 4 (3), 51–9.

Hay, C. (1993) 'The Dangerous Mythology of New Times', *Common Sense*, 13, 63–7.

—— (1994) 'Labour's Thatcherite Revisionism: Playing the "Politics of Catch-Up"', *Political Studies*, 42 (4), 700–7.

—— (1995) 'Structure and Agency', in D. Marsh and G. Stoker (eds), *Theory and Methods in Political Science*. London: Macmillan.

—— (1996a) 'Narrating Crisis: The Discursive Construction of the "Winter of Discontent"', *Sociology*, 30, 253–77.

—— (1996b) *Re-stating Social and Political Change*. Buckingham: Open University Press.

—— (1997a) 'Blaijorism: Towards a One-Vision Polity?', *Political Quarterly*, 68, 372–9.

—— (1997b) 'Anticipating Accommodations, Accommodating Anticipations: The Appeasement of Capital in the "Modernisation" of the British Labour Party, 1987–1992', *Politics and Society*, 25, 234–56.

—— (1997c) 'Divided By a Common Language: Political Theory and the Concept of Power', *Politics*, 17, 45–52.

—— (1997d) 'A Sorry State? Diagnosing the British Affliction', *Socialism and Democracy*, 11, 87–104.

—— (1998a) 'Political Time and the Temporality of Crisis: On Institutional Change as Punctuated Evolution', paper presented at the European Consortium of Political Research, Warwick University, April.

—— (1998b) 'That Was Then, This is Now: The Revision of Policy in the "Modernisation" of the British Labour Party, 1992–97', *New Political Science*, 20 (1), 7–32.

—— (1998c) 'Globalisation, Welfare Retrenchment and the "Logic of No Alternative": Why Second-Best Won't Do', *Journal of Social Policy*, 27 (4), 525–32.

—— (1998d) 'The "Crisis" of Keynesianism and the Rise of Neoliberalism in Britain: A Dialectical Institutionalist Approach', paper presented at the conference Comparative Institutional Analysis: The Rise and Development of Neoliberalism in the 1980s and 1990s, Dartmouth College, New Hampshire, USA.

—— (1999a) 'Continuity and Discontinuity in British Political Development', in D. Marsh, J. Buller, C. Hay, J. Johnston, P. Kerr, S. McAnulla and M. Watson, *Postwar British Politics in Perspective*. Cambridge: Polity Press.

—— (1999b) *Political Analysis: Key Themes and Contemporary Controversies*. London: Macmillan.

—— (1999c) 'Crisis and British Political Development', in D. Marsh, J. Buller, C. Hay, J. Johnston, P. Kerr, S. McAnulla and M. Watson, *Postwar British Politics in Perspective*. Cambridge: Polity Press.

—— (1999d) 'Marxism and the State: Flogging a Dead Horse?', in A. Gamble, D. Marsh and T. Tant (eds), *Marxism and Social Science*. London: Macmillan.

—— and Jessop, B. (1995) 'The Governance of Local Economic Development and the Development of Local Economic Development', paper presented at the American Political Studies Association annual conference, Chicago, August.

—— and Marsh, D. (1999a) 'Demystifying Globalisation', in C. Hay and D. Marsh (eds), *Demystifying Globalisation*. London: Macmillan.

—— and —— (1999b) 'Conclusion: Analysing and Explaining Postwar British Political Development', in D. Marsh, J. Buller, C. Hay, J. Johnston, P. Kerr, S. McAnulla and M. Watson, *Postwar British Politics in Perspective*. Cambridge: Polity Press.

—— and —— (eds) (1999c) 'Putting the "P" Back into IPE: Towards a New International Political Economy?', in C. Hay and D. Marsh (eds), special issue of *New Political Economy*, 4 (1), forthcoming.

—— and Watson, M. (1998) *Rendering the Contingent Necessary: New Labour's Neo-Liberal Conversion and the Discourse of Globalisation.* Center for European Studies' Program for the Study of Germany and Europe, Working Paper No. 8.4. Cambridge, MA: Harvard University.

—— and —— (1999) 'Labour's Economic Policy: Studiously Courting Competence', in G. R. Taylor (ed.), *The Impact of New Labour*. London: Macmillan.

—— and Wincott, D. (1998) 'Structure, Agency and Historical Institutionalism', *Political Studies*, 46 (5), 951–7.

Heath, A. and Jowell, R. (1994) 'Labour's Policy Review', in A. Heath, R. Jowell and J. Curtice, with B. Taylor, *Labour's Last Chance? The 1992 Election and Beyond*. Aldershot: Dartmouth.

——, —— and Curtice, J. (1985) *How Britain Votes*. Oxford: Pergamon.

——, —— and —— (1987) 'Trendless Fluctuation: A Reply to Crewe', *Political Studies*, 35, 256–77.

——, ——, ——, Evans, G., Field, J. and Witherspoon, S. (1991) *Understanding Political Change: The British Voter 1964–87*. Oxford: Pergamon.

——, —— and ——, with Taylor, B. (1994) *Labour's Last Chance? The 1992 Election and Beyond*. Aldershot: Dartmouth.

—— and Paulson, B. (1992) 'Issues and the Economy', *Political Quarterly*, 63, 431–47.

Heffernan, R. (1996) 'Accounting for New Labour: The Impact of Thatcherism, 1979–1995', in I. Hampsher-Monk and J. Stanyer (eds), *Contemporary Political Studies 1996*. Oxford: Blackwell/Political Studies Association.

—— and Marquesee, M. (1992) *Defeat from the Jaws of Victory: Inside Kinnock's Labour Party*. London: Routledge.

Helleiner, E. (1994) *States and the Reemergence of Global Finance*. Ithaca, NY: Cornell University Press.

—— (1995) 'Explaining the Globalisation of Financial Markets: Bringing States Back In', *Review of International Political Economy*, 2, 315–41.

—— (1996) 'Post-globalisation: Is the Financial Liberalisation Trend Ever Likely to be Reversed?', in R. Boyer and D. Drache (eds), *States Against Markets: The Limits of Globalisation*. London: Routledge.

Hewitt, P. and Mandelson, P. (1989) 'The Labour Campaign', in I. Crewe and M. Harrop (eds), *Political Communications: The General Election of 1987*. Cambridge: Cambridge University Press.

Hills, J. (ed.) (1996) *New Inequalities: The Changing Distribution of Income and Wealth in the United Kingdom*. Cambridge: Cambridge University Press.

Hinich, M. J. and Munger, M. C. (1997) *Analytical Politics*. Cambridge: Cambridge University Press.

Hirschmann, A. O. (1970) *Exit, Voice and Loyalty*. Cambridge, MA: Harvard University Press.
—— (1986) 'Exit and Voice: An Expanding Sphere of Influence', in *Rival Views of Market Society*. Cambridge, MA: Harvard University Press.
Hirst, P. (1989) 'The Politics of Industrial Policy', in P. Hirst and J. Zeitlin (eds), *Reversing Industrial Decline? Industrial Structure and Policy in Britain and Her Competitors*. Oxford: Berg.
—— (1994) *Associative Democracy: New Forms of Economic and Social Governance*. Cambridge: Polity Press.
—— and Thompson, G. (1994) 'Globalisation, Foreign Direct Investment and International Governance', *Organisation*, 1, 277–303.
—— and —— (1995) 'Globalisation and the Future of the Nation State', *Economy and Society*, 24, 408–42.
—— and —— (1996) *Globalisation in Question*. Cambridge: Polity Press.
HM Treasury (1993) *Share Ownership: The Share Register Survey Report*. London: HMSO.
—— (1996) *Overseas Investment and the UK: Explanations, Policy Implications, Facts and Figures*. London: HMSO.
Hotelling, H. (1929) 'Stability in Competition', *Economic Journal*, 39, 41–57.
Howell, C. (1995/6) 'Turning to the State: Thatcherism and Trade Unionism', *New Political Science*, 33/4, 13–50.
—— (1998) 'From New Labour to No Labour? The Blair Government in Britain', paper presented to the American Political Science Association annual conference, Boston, 3–6 September.
Howell, D. (1980) *British Social Democracy: A Study in Development and Decay* (2nd edn). New York: St Martin's Press.
Huber, E. and Stephens, J. D. (1998) 'Internationalisation and the Social Democratic Model: Crisis and Future Prospects', *Comparative Political Studies*, 31, 353–97.
Hughes, C. and Wintour, P. (1990) *Labour Rebuilt: The New Model Party*. London: Fourth Estate.
Hutton, W. (1995) 'Failings of the British Financial System', in S. Milner (ed.), *Could Finance Do More for British Business?* London: Institute for Public Policy Research.
—— (1996) *The State We're In* (revised edn). London: Viking.
—— (1997) *The State to Come*. London: Viking.
Ingham, G. (1984) *Capitalism Divided? The City and Industry in British Social Development*. London: Macmillan.
International Social Security Association (1995) *Trends in Social Security, No. 8*. Geneva: International Social Security Association.
Jacques, M. (1979) 'Breaking Out of the Impasse', *Marxism Today*, reprinted in S. Hall and M. Jacques (eds) (1983), *The Politics of Thatcherism*. London: Lawrence and Wishart.

Jeffery, C. (1996) 'Towards a "Third Level" in Europe? The German *Länder* in the European Union', *Political Studies*, 44, 253–66.

Jenkins, P. (1987) *Mrs Thatcher's Revolution: The Ending of the Socialist Era*. Cambridge, MA: Harvard University Press.

Jessop, B. (1980) 'The Transformation of the State in Post-war Britain', in R. Scase (ed.), *The State in Western Europe*. New York: St Martin's Press.

—— (1990) *State Theory: Putting Capitalist States in Their Place*. Cambridge: Polity Press.

—— (1992) 'From Social Democracy to Thatcherism: Twenty-Five Years of British Politics', in N. Abercrombie and A. Warde (eds), *Social Change in Contemporary Britain*. Cambridge: Polity Press.

—— (1993) 'Towards a Schumpeterian Workfare State? Preliminary Remarks on Post-Fordist Political Economy', *Studies in Political Economy*, 40, 7–40.

—— (1994) 'Post-Fordism and the State', in A. Amin (ed.), *Post-Fordism: A Reader*. Oxford: Blackwell.

—— (1995) 'Towards a Schumpeterian Workfare Regime in Britain? Reflections on Regulation, Governance and the Welfare State', *Environment and Planning A*, 27, 1613–26.

—— (1997) 'Interpretative Sociology and the Dialetic of Structure and Agency', *Theory, Culture and Society*, 13, 119–28.

——, Bonnett, K. and Bromley, S. (1990) 'Farewell to Thatcherism? Neo-Liberalism and New Times', *New Left Review*, 179, 81–102.

——, ——, —— and Ling, T. (1984) 'Authoritarian Populism, "Two Nations" and Thatcherism', *New Left Review*, 147, 32–60.

——, ——, —— and —— (1985) 'Thatcherism and the Politics of Thatcherism: A Reply to Hall', *New Left Review*, 153, 87–101.

——, ——, —— and —— (1987) 'Popular Capitalism, Flexible Accumulation and Left Strategy', *New Left Review*, 165.

——, ——, —— and —— (1988) *Thatcherism: A Tale of Two Nations*. Cambridge: Polity Press.

—— and Stones, R. (1992) 'Old City and New Times', in L. Budd and S. Whimster (eds), *Global Finance and Urban Living*. London: Routledge.

Johnmann, L. (1991) 'Labour and Private Industry, 1945–51', in N. Tiratsoo (ed.), *The Attlee Years*. London: Pinter.

Jones, T. (1996) *Remaking the Labour Party: From Gaitskell to Blair*. London: Routledge.

Kavanagh, D. (1987) *Thatcherism and British Politics: The End of Consensus?* Oxford: Oxford University Press.

—— (1992) 'The Postwar Consensus', *Twentieth Century British History*, 3, 175–90.

—— (1997) *The Reordering of British Politics*. Oxford: Oxford University Press.

—— and Morris P. (1994) *Consensus Politics: From Attlee to Major* (2nd edn). Oxford: Blackwell.

Kenny, M. and Smith, M. J. (1997a) 'Discourses of Modernisation: Gaitskell, Blair and the Reform of Clause IV', in C. Pattie, D. Denver, J. Fisher and S. Ludlam (eds), *British Election and Parties, Vol. 7*. London: Frank Cass.

—— and —— (1997b) '(Mis)Understanding Blair', *Political Quarterly*, 68, 220–30.

Kerr, P. (1999) 'The Postwar Consensus: A Woozle that Wasn't', in D. Marsh, J. Buller, C. Hay, J. Johnston, P. Kerr, S. McAnulla and M. Watson, *Postwar British Politics in Perspective*. Cambridge: Polity Press.

—— and Marsh, D. (1996) 'False Dichotomies and Failed Assumptions: Revising and Revisiting the Consensus Debate', in I. Hampsher-Monk and J. Stanyer (eds), *Contemporary Political Studies 1996*. Oxford: Blackwell/Political Studies Association.

—— and —— (1999) 'Explaining Thatcherism: Towards a Multi-dimensional Approach', in D. Marsh, J. Buller, C. Hay, J. Johnston, P. Kerr, S. McAnulla and M. Watson, *Postwar British Politics in Perspective*. Cambridge: Polity Press, forthcoming.

——, McAnulla, S. and Marsh, D. (1997) 'Charting Late-Thatcherism: British Politics Under Major', in S. Lancaster (ed.), *Developments in Politics*. Ormskirk: Causeway.

Kester, W. C. (1992) 'Industrial Groups as Systems of Contractual Governance', *Oxford Review of Economic Policy*, 83, 24–44.

—— (1996) 'American and Japanese Corporate Governance: Convergence to Best Practice?', in S. Berger and R. Dore (eds), *National Diversity and Global Capitalism*. Ithaca, NY: Cornell University Press.

King, A. (1975) 'Overload: Problems of Governing in the 1970s', *Political Studies*, 23, 284–96.

—— (1993) 'The Implications of One-Party Government', in A. King, I. Crewe, D. Denver, K. Newton, P. Norton, D. Sanders and P. Seyd, *Britain at the Polls 1992*. Chatham, NJ: Chatham House.

—— (1998) 'Why Labour Won – At Last', in A. King, D. Denver, I. McLean, P. Norton, D. Sanders and P. Seyd, *New Labour Triumphs: Britain at the Polls 1997*. Chatham, NJ: Chatham House.

King, D. S. and Wickham-Jones, M. (1995) 'Social Democracy and Rational Choice Marxism', in T. Carver and P. Thomas (eds), *Rational Choice Marxism*. London: Macmillan.

Kingdom, J. (1992) *No Such Thing as Society? Individualism and Community*. Buckingham: Open University Press.

Kirscheimer, O. (1966) 'The Transformation of the Western European Party System', in J. La Palombara and M. Weiner (eds), *Political Parties and Political Development*. Princeton, NJ: Princeton University Press.

Kitschelt, H. (1994) *The Transformation of European Social Democracy*. Cambridge: Cambridge University Press.

——, Lange, P., Marks, G. and Stephens, J. D. (eds) (1999) *Continuity and*

Change in Contemporary Capitalism. Cambridge: Cambridge University Press.

Kitson, M. and Michie, J. (1996) 'Britain's Industrial Performance Since 1960: Underinvestment and Relative Decline', *Economic Journal*, 106, 196–212.

—— and —— (1997) 'Manufacturing Capacity, Investment and Employment', in J. Michie and J. G. Smith (eds), *Employment and Economic Performance*. Oxford: Oxford University Press.

Krieger, J. (1991) 'Class Consumption and Collectivism: Perspectives on the Labour Party and Electoral Competition in Britain', in F. F. Piven (ed.), *Labour Parties in Post-industrial Societies*. Cambridge: Polity Press.

Krugman, P. (1996) 'Competitiveness: A Dangerous Obsession', in *Pop Internationalism*. Cambridge, MA: MIT Press.

Kuhn, T. S. (1962) *The Structure of Scientific Revolutions*. Chicago, IL: University of Chicago Press.

Kurzer, P. (1993) *Business and Banking*. Ithaca, NY: Cornell University Press.

Labour Party (1990) *Looking to the Future*. London: Labour Party.

—— (1992) *It's Time to Get Britain Working Again. Election Manifesto*. London: Labour Party.

—— (1993) *Labour's Economic Approach*. London: Labour Party.

—— (1995) *A New Economic Future for Britain*. London: Labour Party.

—— (1996a) *Building Prosperity: Flexibility, Efficiency and Fairness at Work. Road to the Manifesto Document*. London: Labour Party.

—— (1996b) *New Opportunities for Business*. London: Labour Party (Policy and Information Briefing Taskforce).

—— (1996c) *Visions for Growth: A New Industrial Strategy for Britain*. London: Labour Party.

—— (1997) *New Labour: Because Britain Deserves Better. Election Manifesto*. London: Labour Party.

Labour Party Industry Forum (1994) *Winning for Britain: Labour's Strategy for Industrial Success*. London: Labour Party.

Larner, W. (1997) '"A Means to an End": Neoliberalism and State Processes in New Zealand', *Studies in Political Economy*, 52, 7–38.

Layard, R. (1997) *What Labour Can Do?* London: Warner Books.

Lee, S. (1996a) 'Manufacturing', in D. Coates (ed.), *Industrial Policy in Britain*. London: Macmillan.

—— (1996b) 'Finance for Industry', in J. Michie and J. G. Smith (eds), *Creating Industrial Capacity: Towards Full Employment*. Oxford: Oxford University Press.

Leibfried, S. and Pierson, P. (eds) (1995) *European Social Policy: Between Fragmentation and Integration*. Washington, DC: Brookings Institute.

Lent, A. and Sowemimo, M. (1996) 'Remaking the Opposition?', in S. Ludlam and M. J. Smith (eds), *Contemporary British Conservatism*. London: Macmillan.

Letwin, S. (1992) *The Anatomy of Thatcherism*. London: Fontana.

Levitt, T. (1983) 'The Globalisation of Markets', *Harvard Business Review*, May–June, 92–102.

Leys, C. (1986) 'The Formation of British Capital', *New Left Review*, 160, 114–20.

—— (1990) 'Still a Question of Hegemony', *New Left Review*, 181, 119–28.

—— (1995) 'A Radical Agenda for Britain', *New Left Review*, 212, 3–13.

—— (1997) 'The British Labour Party Since 1989', in D. Sassoon (ed.), *Looking Left: European Socialism After the Cold War*. London: I. B. Tauris.

—— and Panitch, L. (1997) 'Beyond the Soundbites: The General Election in Britain', *Radical Philosophy*, 84, 2–5.

Lindblom, C. E. (1977) *Politics and Markets*. New York: Basic Books.

—— (1988) 'Democracy and the Economy', in *Democracy and the Market System*. Oslo: Norwegian University Press.

Longstreth, F. (1979) 'The City, Industry and the State', in C. Crouch (ed.), *State and Economy in Contemporary Capitalism*. London: Macmillan.

Lowe, R. (1990) 'The Second World War, Consensus and the Foundation of the Welfare State', *Twentieth Century British History*, 1, 152–82.

Lukes, S. (1974) *Power: A Radical View*. London: Macmillan.

Maddison, A. (1995) *Explaining the Economic Performance of Nations: Essays in Time and Space*. Aldershot: Edward Elgar.

Mandelson, P. and Liddle, R. (1996) *The Blair Revolution: Can New Labour Deliver?* London: Fontana.

Margetts, H. and Smyth, G. (eds) (1994) *Turning Japanese: Britain With a Permanent Party of Government*. London: Routledge.

Marlow, J. D. (1996) *Questioning the Post-war Consensus Thesis: Towards an Alternative Account*. Aldershot: Dartmouth.

Marquesee, M. (1997) 'New Labour and its Discontents', *New Left Review*, 224, 127–42.

Marsh, D. (1992) *The New Politics of British Trade Unionism: Union Power and the Thatcher Legacy*. London: Macmillan.

—— (1996) 'Explaining "Thatcherite" Policies: Beyond Uni-dimensional Explanation', *Political Studies*, 43, 595–613.

—— (1999) 'Introduction: Explaining Change in the Postwar Period', in D. Marsh, J. Buller, C. Hay, J. Johnston, P. Kerr, S. McAnulla and M. Watson, *Postwar British Politics in Perspective*. Cambridge: Polity Press, forthcoming.

——, Buller, J., Hay, C., Johnston, J., Kerr, P., McAnulla, S. and Watson, M. (1999) *Postwar British Politics in Perspective*. Cambridge: Polity Press, forthcoming.

—— and Rhodes, R. A. W. (eds) (1992a) *Implementing Thatcherite Policies*. Buckingham: Open University Press

—— and —— (1992b) 'Implementing Thatcherism: Policy Change in the 1980s', *Parliamentary Affairs*, 45, 33–51.

—— and —— (1995) 'Evaluating Thatcherism: Over the Moon or Sick as a Parrot', *Politics*, 15, 49–54.

Marshall, G., Rose, D., Newby, H. and Vogler, C. (1988) *Social Class in Modern Britain*. London: Hutchinson.

Martin, S. J. and Pearce, G. R. (1993) 'European Regional Development Strategies: Strengthening Meso-government in the UK?', *Regional Studies*, 27, 681–6.

McAnulla, S. (1999) 'The Post-Thatcher Era', in D. Marsh, J. Buller, C. Hay, J. Johnston, P. Kerr, S. McAnulla and M. Watson, *Postwar British Politics in Perspective*. Cambridge: Polity Press.

McNamara, K. R. (1998) *The Currency of Ideas: Monetary Politics in the European Union*. Ithaca, NY: Cornell University Press.

McSmith, A. (1996) *Faces of Labour: The Inside Story*. London: Verso.

Megarry, Sir R. (1983) *Judgement in the Matter of the Trusts of the Mineworkers' Pension Scheme*, CH 1983, M No. 5498 (reprinted 1994).

Mercer, H. (1991) 'The Labour Governments of 1945–51 and Private Industry', in N. Tiratsoo (ed.), *The Attlee Years*. London: Pinter.

Michie, J. (ed.) (1992) *The Economic Legacy 1987–92*. London: Academic Press.

—— and Smith, J. G. (eds) (1996) *Creating Industrial Capacity: Towards Full Employment*. Oxford: Oxford University Press.

Miliband, R. (1970) *Parliamentary Socialism* (2nd edn). London: Merlin.

Milne, S. and Thomas, R. (1997) 'Welfare to Work Sets Tough Terms', *Guardian*, 4 July.

Moene, O-K. and Wallerstein, M. (1995) 'How Social Democracy Worked', *Politics and Society*, 23, 185–211.

Mommen, A. (1999) 'Transnational Neoliberalisation', in A. Mommen (ed.), *Transnational Neoliberalisation*. London: Routledge.

Morgan, K. O. (1984) *Labour in Power, 1945–51*. Oxford: Oxford University Press.

Moon, J. (1993) *Innovative Leadership in Democracy: Policy Change Under Thatcher*. Aldershot: Dartmouth.

—— (1994) 'Evaluating Thatcherism: Sceptical Versus Synthetic Approaches', *Politics*, 14, 43–9.

—— (1995) 'Evaluating Thatcher: Did the Cow Jump Over? A Reply to Marsh and Rhodes', *Politics*, 15, 113–17.

Moses, J. W. (1994) 'Abdication from National Policy Autonomy: What's Left to Leave?', *Politics and Society*, 22, 125–48.

Nairn, T. (1976) 'The Twilight of the British State', *New Left Review*, 101/2, 3–61.

—— (1994) 'The Sole Survivor', *New Left Review*, 200, 41–8.

—— (1997) 'Sovereignty After the Election', *New Left Review*, 224, 3–18.

National Institute of Economic and Social Research (1990) 'Policy Options Under a Labour Government', *National Institute Economic Review*, November.

Newton, K. (1993) 'Caring and Competence: The Long, Long Campaign', in A. King, I. Crewe, D. Denver, K. Newton, P. Norton, D. Sanders and P. Seyd, *Britain at the Polls 1992*. Chatham, NJ: Chatham House.

Newton, S. and Porter, D. (1988) *Modernisation Frustrated: The Politics of Industrial Decline in Britain Since 1900*. London: Unwin Hyman.

Norris, P. (1997) 'Anatomy of a Labour Landslide', in P. Norris and N. T. Gavin (eds), *Britain Votes 1997*. Oxford: Oxford University Press.

North, D. C. (1990) *Institutions, Institutional Change and Economic Performance*. Cambridge: Cambridge University Press.

Norton, P. (1998) 'The Conservative Party: "In Office But Not in Power"', in A. King, D. Denver, I. McLean, P. Norton, D. Sanders and P. Seyd, *New Labour Triumphs: Britain at the Polls 1997*. Chatham, NJ: Chatham House.

Notermans, T. (1997) 'Social Democracy and External Constraints', in R. W. Cox (ed.), *Spaces of Globalisation*. New York: Guilford.

Obstfeld, M. (1995) 'International Capital Mobility in the 1990s', in P. Kenen (ed.), *Understanding Interdependence: The Macroeconomics of the Open Economy*. Princeton, NJ: Princeton University Press.

Offe, C. (1974) 'Structural Problems of the Capitalist State', in K. von Beyme (ed.), *German Political Studies*. Beverley Hills, CA: Sage.

—— (1975) 'The Theory of the Capitalist State and the Problem of Policy Formation', in L. N. Lindberg, R. Alford, C. Crouch and C. Offe, *Stress and Contradiction in Modern Capitalism*. Lexington, MA: D. H. Heath.

—— (1984) *The Contradictions of the Welfare State*. Cambridge, MA: MIT Press.

—— and Ronge, V. (1975) 'Theses on the Theory of the State', *New German Critique*, 6, 137–47.

Ohmae, K. (1990) *The Borderless World: Power and Strategy in the Interlinked Economy*. London: Collins.

—— (1996) *The End of the Nation State: The Rise of Regional Economies*. New York: Free Press.

Oppenheim, C. (1993) *Poverty: The Facts*. London: Child Poverty Action Group.

Ordeshook, P. C. (1997) 'The Spatial Analysis of Elections and Committees: Four Decades of Research', in D. C. Mueller (ed.), *Perspectives on Public Choice: A Handbook*. Cambridge: Cambridge University Press.

Organisation for Economic Cooperation and Development (1996) *Economic Outlook 59*. Paris: OECD.

Ormerod, P. (1996) 'National Competitiveness and State Interventionism', *New Political Economy*, 1, 119–28.

Orrù, M. (1993) 'Institutional Cooperation in Japanese and German Capitalism', in S. Sjöstrand (ed.), *Institutional Change: Theory and Empirical Findings*. Armonk, NY: M. E. Sharpe.

O'Shea, A. (1984) *Formations of Nations and People*. London: Routledge.

Padgett, S. and Paterson, W. E. (1991) *A History of Social Democracy in Postwar Europe*. London: Longman.

Panitch, L. (1976) *Social Democracy and Industrial Militancy: The Labour Party, the Trade Unions and Incomes Policy, 1945–1974*. Cambridge: Cambridge University Press.

—— and Leys, C. (1997) *The End of Parliamentary Socialism: From New Left to New Labour*. London: Verso.

Parker, D. (1995) *Measuring Efficiency Gains from Privatisation*, Occasional Papers in Industrial Strategy No. 36, University of Birmingham.

Pashukanis, E. V. (1978) *A General Theory of Law and Marxism*. London: Ink Links.

Paterson, W. E. (1993) 'Reprogramming Democratic Socialism', *West European Politics*, 16, 1–4.

—— and Thomas, A. H. (eds) (1986) *The Future of Social Democracy*. Oxford: Clarendon Press.

Peffley, M. (1984) 'The Voter as Juror: Attributing Responsibility for Economic Conditions', *Political Behaviour*, 6, 275–94, reprinted in M. Lewis-Beck and H. Eulau (eds) (1985) *Economic Conditions and Electoral Outcomes*. New York: Agathon.

——, Feldman, S. and Sigelman, L. (1987) 'Economic Conditions and Party Competence: Process of Belief Revision', *Journal of Politics*, 49, 100–21.

Peltzmann, S. (1976) 'Toward a More General Theory of Regulation', *Journal of Law and Economics*, 19, 211–40.

Perryman, P. (ed.) (1996) *The Blair Agenda*. London: Lawrence and Wishart.

Petty, R. E. and Cacioppo, J. T. (1986) *Communication and Persuasion*. New York: Springer Verlag.

Pierre, J. (1995) 'Policy Diffused, Policy Confused? The Politics of Regional Industrial Development in Sweden', *Regional and Federal Studies*, 5, 173–97.

Pierson, P. (1994) *Dismantling the Welfare State? Reagan, Thatcher and the Politics of Retrenchment*. Cambridge: Cambridge University Press.

—— (1996) 'The New Politics of the Welfare State', *World Politics*, 48, 143–79.

Pimlott, B. (1988) 'The Myth of Consensus', in L. M. Smith (ed.), *The Making of Britain: Echoes of Greatness*. London: Macmillan.

—— (1989) 'Is the Postwar Consensus a Myth?', *Contemporary Record*, 2 (6), 12–14.

Piven, F. F. (ed.) (1991) *Labour Parties in Postindustrial Societies*. Cambridge: Polity Press.

—— (1997) 'Is it Global Economics or Neo-Laissez-Faire?', *New Left Review*, 213, 107–14.

Pollard, S. (1980) *The Wasting of the British Economy*. London: Croom Helm.

—— (1992) *The Development of the British Economy* (2nd edn). Aldershot: Edward Arnold.

Pollin, R. (1995) 'Financial Structures and Egalitarian Economic Policy', *New Left Review*, 214, 26–61.

—— (ed.) (1997) *The Macroeconomics of Saving, Finance and Investment*. Ann Arbor, MI: University of Michigan Press.

Ponting, C. (1990) *Breach of Promise: Labour in Power, 1964–1970*. Harmondsworth: Penguin.

Pontusson, J. (1992) *The Limits of Social Democracy: Investment Politics in Sweden*. Ithaca, NY: Cornell University Press.

Porter, M. E. (1996) 'Capital Choices: National Systems of Investment', in N. R. Goodwin (ed.), *As If the Future Mattered: Translating Social and Economic Theory into Human Behaviour*. Ann Arbor, MI: University of Michigan Press.

Przeworski, A. (1985) *Capitalism and Social Democracy*. Cambridge: Cambridge University Press.

—— (1990) *The State and the Economy Under Capitalism*. New York: Harwood Academic.

—— and Sprague, J. (1986) *Paper Stones: A History of Electoral Socialism*. Chicago, IL: University of Chicago Press.

—— and Wallerstein, M. (1988) 'Structural Dependence of the State on Capital', *American Political Science Review*, 82, 11–30.

Rapkin, D. P. and Strand, J. R. (1995) 'Competitiveness: Useful Concept, Political Slogan, or Dangerous Obsession?', in D. P. Rapkin and W. P. Avery (eds), *National Competitiveness in a Global Economy*. London: Lynne Reinner.

Regional Policy Commission (1996) *Renewing the Regions: Strategies for Regional Economic Development*. Sheffield: PAVIC Publications.

Reich, R. (1992) *The Work of Nations*. New York: Vintage Books.

—— (1997) 'The Dangers of Moving to the Mushy Middle', *Observer*, 27 April.

Reynolds, P. and Coates, D. (1996) 'Conclusion', in D. Coates (ed.), *Industrial Policy in Britain*. London: Macmillan.

Riddell, P. (1983) *The Thatcher Government*. Oxford: Martin Robertson.

—— (1991) *The Thatcher Era and its Legacy*. Oxford: Blackwell.

Rieger, E. and Leibfried, S. (1998) 'Welfare State Limits to Globalisation', *Politics and Society*, 26, 363–90.

Rosamond, B. (1992) 'The Labour Party, Trade Unions and Industrial Relations', in M. J. Smith and J. Spear (eds), *The Changing Labour Party*. London: Routledge.

Rose, N. (1996) 'The Death of the Social? Re-figuring the Territory of Government', *Economy and Society*, 25, 327–56.

Rose, R. (1997) 'The New Labour Government: On the Crest of a Wave', in P. Norris and N. T. Gavin (eds), *Britain Votes 1997*. Oxford: Oxford University Press.

Rothstein, B. (1996) *The Swedish Model and the Bureaucratic Problem of Social Reforms*. Pittsburgh, PA: University of Pittsburgh Press.

Rowthorn, B. (1989) 'The Thatcher Revolution', in F. Green (ed.), *The Restructuring of the UK Economy*. Hemel Hempstead: Harvester Wheatsheaf.

Rubery, J. (1989) 'Labour Market Flexibility in Britain', in F. Green (ed.), *The Restructuring of the UK Economy*. Hemel Hempstead: Harvester Wheatsheaf.

Russell, C. (1996) 'New Labour: Old Tory Writ Large?', *New Left Review*, 219, 78–88.

Rustin, M. (1989) 'The Politics of Post-Fordism, or the Trouble with New Times', *New Left Review*, 174, 54–78.

Sabel, C. F. (1994) 'Flexible Specialisation and the Re-emergence of Regional Economies', in A. Amin (ed.), *Post-Fordism: A Reader*. Oxford: Blackwell.

Sachs, J. D. and Warner, A. (1995) 'Economic Reform and the Process of Global Integration', *Brookings Papers on Economic Activity*, 1, 1–118.

Sanders, D. (1993) 'Why the Conservative Party Won – Again', in A. King, I. Crewe, D. Denver, K. Newton, P. Norton, D. Sanders and P. Seyd, *Britain at the Polls 1992*. Chatham, NJ: Chatham House.

—— (1996) 'Economic Performance, Management Competence and the Outcome of the Next General Election', *Political Studies*, 44, 203–31.

—— (1998) 'The New Electoral Battlefield', in A. King, D. Denver, I. McLean, P. Norton, D. Sanders and P. Seyd, *New Labour Triumphs: Britain at the Polls 1997*. Chatham, NJ: Chatham House.

Särlvik, B. and Crewe, I. (1983) *Decade of Dealignment*. Cambridge: Cambridge University Press.

Sassoon, D. (1996) *One Hundred Years of Socialism*. London: I. B. Tauris.

—— (ed.) (1997) *Looking Left: European Socialism After the Cold War*. London: I. B. Tauris.

Savage, S. P., Atkinson, R. and Robins, L. (1994) *Public Policy in Britain*. London: Macmillan.

Scharpf, F. (1991) *Crisis and Choice in European Social Democracy*. Ithaca, NY: Cornell University Press.

Scherman, K. G. (1995) 'Major Changes in Sweden's Pension System', *Ageing International*, June, 27–31.

Schmidt, V. (1995) 'The New World Order Inc.: The Rise of Business and the Decline of the Nation-State', *Daedalus*, 124, 75–106.

Schumpeter, J. (1950) *Capitalism, Socialism and Democracy*. New York: Harper and Brothers.

Seldon, A. (1994) 'Consensus: A Debate too Long?', *Parliamentary Affairs*, 47, 501–14.

Self, P. (1993) *Government by the Market? The Politics of Public Choice*. London: Macmillan.

Seyd, P. (1993) 'Labour: The Great Transformation', in A. King, I. Crewe, D.

Denver, K. Newton, P. Norton, D. Sanders and P. Seyd, *Britain at the Polls 1992*. Chatham, NJ: Chatham House.

—— (1998) 'Tony Blair and New Labour', in A. King, D. Denver, I. McLean, P. Norton, D. Sanders and P. Seyd, *New Labour Triumphs: Britain at the Polls 1997*. Chatham, NJ: Chatham House.

—— and Whiteley, P. (1992) 'Labour's Renewal Strategy', in M. J. Smith and J. Spear (eds), *The Changing Labour Party*. London: Routledge.

Shanks, M. (1977) *Planning and Politics: The British Experience, 1960–74*. London: Allen and Unwin.

Shaw, E. (1988) *Discipline and Discord in the Labour Party*. London: Routledge.

—— (1993) 'Towards Renewal? The British Labour Party's Policy Review', *West European Politics*, 16, 112–32.

—— (1994) *The Labour Party Since 1979: Crisis and Transformation*. London: Routledge.

—— (1997) 'The Trajectory of New Labour: Some Preliminary Thoughts', paper presented to the American Political Science Association, Washington, DC, 28–31 August.

Shonfield, A. (1965) *Modern Capitalism: The Changing Balance of Public and Private Power*. Oxford: Oxford University Press/RIIA.

Smith, J. G. (1996) 'Rebuilding Industrial Capacity', in J. Michie and J. G. Smith (eds), *Creating Industrial Capacity: Towards Full Employment*. Oxford: Oxford University Press.

—— (1997) 'Devising a Strategy for Pay', in J. Michie and J. G. Smith (eds), *Employment and Economic Performance: Jobs, Inflation and Growth*. Oxford: Oxford University Press.

Smith, M. J. (1992a) 'A Return to Revisionism? The Labour Party's Policy Review', in M. J. Smith and J. Spear (eds), *The Changing Labour Party*. London: Routledge.

—— (1992b) 'The Labour Party in Opposition', in M. J. Smith and J. Spear (eds), *The Changing Labour Party*. London: Routledge.

—— (1994) 'Understanding the "Politics of Catch-Up": The Modernisation of the Labour Party', *Political Studies*, 42, 708–15.

—— and Spear, J. (1992) *The Changing Labour Party*. London: Routledge.

Smith, P. (1997) 'Britain: The Longest Decade', in *Millennial Dreams: Contemporary Culture and Capital in the North*. London: Routledge.

Smithies, A. (1941) 'Optimum Location in Spatial Competition', *Journal of Political Economy*, 49, 429–39.

Soskice, D. (1989) 'Wage Determination: The Changing Role of Institutions in the Advanced Industrial Economies', *Oxford Review of Economic Policy*, 6, 36–61.

Stephens, J. D. (1997) 'The Scandinavian Welfare States: Achievements, Crisis and Prospects', in G. Esping-Andersen (ed.), *Welfare States in Transition*. London: Sage.

Stephenson, H. (1980) *Mrs Thatcher's First Year*. London: Jill Norman.

Stoker, G., Hogwood, B. and Bullman, U. (1996) 'Do We Need Regional Government?', *Talking Politics*, 9, 191–5.

Stokes, D. (1963) 'Spatial Models of Party Competition', *American Political Science Review*, 57, 368–77.

Swank, D. (1992) 'Politics and the Structural Dependence of the State in Democratic Capitalist Nations', *American Political Science Review*, 86, 11–30.

Taylor, C. (1960) 'What's Wrong with Capitalism?', *New Left Review*, 2, 5–11.

Taylor, G. R. (1997) *Labour's Renewal*. London: Macmillan.

Taylor-Gooby, P. (1996) 'In Defence of Second-Best Theory: State, Class and Capital in Social Policy', *Journal of Social Policy*, 26, 171–92.

Terry, L. (1997) 'Travelling the Hard Road to Renewal: A Continuing Conversation with Stuart Hall', *Arena Journal*, 8, 39–58.

Thompson, N. (1996) 'Supply Side Socialism: The Political Economy of New Labour', *New Left Review*, 216, 37–54.

Tiratsoo, N. (ed.) (1991) *The Attlee Years*. London: Pinter.

—— and Tomlinson, J. (1993) *Industrial Efficiency and State Intervention: Labour 1939–51*. London: Routledge.

Tomlinson, J. (1993) 'Mr Attlee's Supply-Side Socialism', *Economic History Review*, 46, 1–22.

—— (1994) *Government and the Enterprise Since 1900*. Oxford: Clarendon Press.

—— (1997) 'Economic Policy: Lessons from Past Labour Governments', in B. Brivati and T. Bale (eds), *New Labour in Power: Precedents and Prospects*. London: Routledge.

Toulouse, C. and Worcester, K. (1995/6) 'Introduction: After Thatcher', *New Political Science*, 33/4, 1–12.

Vickers, J. and Yarrow, G. (1995) *Privatisation: An Economic Analysis*. Cambridge, MA: MIT Press.

Vittas, D. (1978) *Banking Systems Abroad*. London: Inter-Bank Research Organisation.

von Weizsacker, C. C. (1971) 'Notes on Endogenous Changes of Tastes', *Economic Theory*, 3, 345–72.

Wade, R. (1996) 'Globalisation and its Limits: Reports of the Death of the National Economy are Greatly Exaggerated', in S. Berger and R. Dore (eds), *National Diversity and Global Capitalism*. Ithaca, NY: Cornell University Press.

Walker, A. (ed.) (1996) *The New Generational Contract*. London: University College London Press.

—— and Maltby, T. (1997) *Ageing Europe*. Buckingham: Open University Press.

—— and Walker, C. (1987) *The Growing Divide: A Social Audit, 1979–87*. London: Child Poverty Action Group.

Ward, H. (1995) 'Rational Choice Theory', in D. Marsh and G. Stoker (eds), *Theory and Methods in Political Science*. London: Macmillan.

Watson, M. (1997) 'New Labour, But the Same Old Monetarism Accentuating the Same Old Capacity Constraints', University of Birmingham, mimeo.

—— (1998) 'Beyond Economistic Accounts of the State, Beyond Economistic Accounts of Globalisation', unpublished manuscript, University of Birmingham.

—— (1999a) 'Globalisation and British Political Development', in D. Marsh, J. Buller, C. Hay, J. Johnston, P. Kerr, S. McAnulla and M. Watson, *Postwar British Politics in Perspective*. Cambridge: Polity Press, forthcoming.

—— (1999b) 'The New Malthusian Economics: Globalisation, Inward Investment and the Discursive Construction of the Competitive Imperative', in C. Hay and D. Marsh (eds), *Globalisation, Welfare Retrenchment and the State*. London: Macmillan, forthcoming.

—— (1999c) 'Rethinking Capital Mobility, Reregulating Financial Markets', in C. Hay and D. Marsh (eds), *Putting the 'P' Back into IPE*, special issue of *New Political Economy*, 4 (1), 55–75.

—— and Hay, C. (1998) 'In the Dedicated Pursuit of Dedicated Capital: Restoring an Indigenous Investment Ethic to British Capitalism', *New Political Economy*, 3 (3), 407–26.

Webb, S., Kemp, M. and Millar, J. (1996) 'The Changing Face of Low Pay in Britain', *Policy Studies*, 17, 255–71.

Weiss, L. (1997) 'Globalisation and the Myth of the Powerless State', *New Left Review*, 225, 84–114.

Wickham-Jones, M. (1995a) 'Recasting Social Democracy: A Note on Hay and Smith', *Political Studies*, 43, 698–702.

—— (1995b) 'Anticipating Social Democracy, Preempting Anticipations: Economic Policy-Making in the British Labour Party, 1987–1992', *Politics and Society*, 23, 465–94.

—— (1996) *Economic Strategy and the Labour Party: Politics and Policy-Making, 1970–83*. London: Macmillan.

—— (1997a) 'How the Conservatives Lost the Economic Argument', in A. Geddes and J. Tonge (eds), *Labour's Landslide*. Manchester: Manchester University Press.

—— (1997b) 'Social Democracy and Structural Dependence: The British Case. A Note on Hay', *Politics and Society*, 25, 257–65.

—— (undated) 'The Ties That Bind: Blair's Search for Business Credibility', University of Bristol, unpublished manuscript.

Wighton, D. (1996) 'CBI opposes Labour's Reform Plan', *Financial Times*, 23 September.

Wolfe, J. (1991) 'State Power and Ideology in Britain: Mrs Thatcher's Privatisation Programme', *Political Studies*, 39, 237–52.

Wood, E. M. (1995) *Democracy Against Capitalism: Renewing Historical Materialism*. Cambridge: Cambridge University Press.

Woolcock, S. (1996) 'Competition Among Forms of Corporate Governance in the European Community: The Case of Britain', in S. Berger and R. Dore (eds), *National Diversity and Global Capitalism*. Ithaca, NY: Cornell University Press.

Yarrow, G. (1986) 'Privatisation in Theory and Practice', *Economic Policy*, 2, 323–78.

—— (1989) 'Privatisation and Economic Performance in Britain', *Carnegie-Rochester Conference Series on Public Policy*, 31, 303–44.

Young, S. and Lowe, A. (1974) *Intervention in the Mixed Economy*. London: Croom Helm.

Zysman, J. (1983) *Government, Markets and Growth*. Ithaca, NY: Cornell University Press.

—— and Tyson, L. (eds) (1983) *American Industry in International Competition: Government Policies and Corporate Strategies*. Ithaca, NY: Cornell University Press.

Index

Note: 'n.' after a page reference indicates a note on that page and is followed by the note number.

Aaronovitch, Sam 65
Abrams, Mark 23
acquisitions *see* mergers
Adam Smith Institute 168
Addison, Paul 21
advertising, political 33
agency *see* structure and agency
Akyüz, Y. 37
Albert, Michel 27, 29, 165, 186, 209n.9
Albo, Greg 26
Alcock, Peter 117
Aldrich, J. H. 82
Alternative Economic Strategy 65
Altvater, Elmar 177n.4
Amin, Ash 29, 114
Anderson, Perry 42, 63, 165, 185, 186, 188, 209n.6
Andrews, David 156
Ashton, David 69, 70
asset-stripping *see* mergers
Assisted Places Scheme 115
Attlee, Clement 5, 7, 8, 15, 21
Attlee government 7, 39n.6, 155, 193–5, 209n.14
Australian Labor Party 39n.8, 136

balance of payments 75n.24
Bale, Tim 5, 18, 141n.1
Bank of England 74n.14, 137–8, 143n.26
Barber, Randy 197, 210n.21, 211n.24
Barnet, R. J. 30
Barrett-Brown, Michael 209n.6
Bates, R. H. 149
Becker, Gary S. 149
Beckett, Margaret 132, 144n.29, 179n.19
Bell, D. S. 26
Benefits Agency, medical service 139
Berger, Suzanne 27, 28, 136, 142n.18
Berman, Sheri 34
Best, Michael 114
bipartisan convergence 20, 21, 28, 73n.13, 75n.24, 77, 90, 92, 105–41, 160
    in constitutional reform 108
    in education and training policy 108, 114–17
    in labour-market policy 108–14
    in social policy 108
Bishop, M. 69
'Black Wednesday' 72n.11, 75n.26, 102, 134
Blackburn, Robin 130, 134, 141n.1
Blair, Tony 1, 2, 3, 5, 7, 10, 15, 16, 17, 18, 33, 39n.5, 40n.12, 53, 105, 106, 110, 113, 117, 130, 132, 133, 141n.5, 142n.11, 142n.15, 143n.27, 161, 162, 181

Blair revolution 3, 5
Blake, David 191, 197, 198, 199, 200, 210n.20
Block, Fred 147, 152, 153, 204, 211n.24, 211n.29
Blyth, Mark 27, 57, 64, 76
Bond, Simon R. 27, 189, 197
Boyer, Robert 136, 142n.18, 178n.16
Brenner, Robert 27
British Rail 139
British Telecom 132
Brivati, Brian 18, 22, 40.n11, 141n.1
Brown, Gordon 137–8, 143n.24, 143n.26, 156, 170, 177n.8, 209n.13
Bruyn, S. 210n.21
Buckle, M. 188, 190
Burk, K. 58
Butler, David 60, 140
Buxton, Tony 59, 64, 74n.14, 178n.9

Cacioppo, J. T. 60
Cairncross, Sir Alec 58
Callaghan, Jim
Callaghan government 3, 5
Campaign Strategy Committee 95
Campbell, John L. 34
Campbell, M. 25, 26
Campen, J. 211n.28
capacity constraints 73–4n.14, 74n.21
capital flight 106, 136, 140, 148, 156, 163
capital flows, liberalisation 30, 37, 120, 136
capital gains tax 143n.25, 200–2, 210n.20
    conditional exemption 200–2
capital
    dedicated 165, 187, 198, 201, 207
    financial 8, 155, 185
    human 169, 179n.18
    industrial 8, 169, 180n.23, 185
    preferences of 149, 151–3, 162, 163, 173, 175
capitalism
    Anglo-US model 27, 186–92, 193
    distinctiveness of British 27, 184–92, 194
    German model 27, 186–7, 191
    Japanese model 27, 186–7, 191
    models of national 27
    Scandinavian model 27
capitalist convergence 30
Castle, Dame Barbara 143n.21
catastrophic equilibrium 71
'catch-all party' 23, 24, 40n.19, 77
Cavanagh, J. 30
Centre for Policy Studies 168, 183
Cerny, Philip G. 28, 29, 155, 186

237

Chapman, Paul 69
child benefit 119, 120
City of London 75n.24, 150
City–Bank–Treasury nexus 165
class dealignment, 24–5, 35–6, 40n.19
class voting 24, 35–6
    absolute 24, 35–6
    relative 24, 35–6, 40n.17
Clause IV 5, 17
Clinton, Bill 6
Coates, David 21, 27, 141n.1, 150, 160
Cohen, Benjamin J. 155
Commission on Public Policy and British Business 22
Communist Party 11
communitarianism 160
competition
    state 29
    international 30
Competition and Consumer Standards Office 133
competitiveness 33, 63, 64, 69, 74n.20, 75n.22, 120, 124, 136, 140, 151, 153, 159, 169, 184, 192, 210n.18
Confederation of British Industry (CBI) 143n.25, 150, 189, 210n.22
Connolly, William E. 30, 177n.5
consensus
    concept of 20–1, 73n.12
    post-Thatcher 22, 73n.12, 106, 127
    post-war 21, 40n.15, 73n.12, 106, 127, 166
Conservative Party 9, 67, 97
convergence, *see* bipartisan convergence, capitalist convergence
Cook, Robin 126, 144n.32–3, 179n.19, 183
Coopey, Richard 6
Cornford, A. 37
corporatism 8, 11, 24, 28, 72n.9, 165
Cosh, A. 210n.19
council tax 51
Cowling, Keith 27, 70, 165, 189, 190, 208n.4
Cox, Andrew 22, 178n.9
Crewe, Ivor 18, 23, 34, 59, 68, 141n.2
crisis 9, 21, 26, 28, 43, 64, 66, 68, 71, 161, 166, 167, 171, 172
Crosland, Anthony 16–17, 39–40n.10, 53
Crossman, Richard 6, 39n.4
Crotty, James 200
Crouch, Colin 40n.14, 59
Crozier, Michel 147
Curtice, John 24, 99

D'Arista, J. W. 211n.23
Daily Mail 38
Davies, Howard 210n.22
decline, British economic 22, 70, 166, 180n.23
demand-side intervention 140
Democratic Party (US) 6
demographic pressure 25–6
Demos 11, 168
Denver, David 23, 98–9
Department of Trade and Industry (DTI) 123, 125, 126, 159, 183
developmental state 183
devolution, Scottish 130
Dicken, Peter 177n.1
district health authorities (DHAs) 121, 122
divergence, bipartisan 132–3
Dixit, Avinash 192

Dobson, Frank 138
Dolowitz, David 43, 47, 72n.5, 143n.22
Dore, Ronald 27, 28, 136, 142n.18
Dorey, Peter 108
Dorrell, Stephen 138
Dowding, Keith 177n.3
Downs, Anthony 76–103
Drache, Daniel 136, 142n.18, 163, 178n.16
Driver, Kieran 74n.14
Dunleavy, Patrick 60, 76, 80, 82, 84–5, 103 n.4
Dunn, John 178n.12
Dymski, Gary, A. 208n.4

Eatwell, John 19, 155–6
economically targeted investment (ERI) 200, 202, 203, 210n.21
economics, neo-classical 61, 78–9
economism 37, 38
Eichengreen, Barry 22, 37, 59, 193–4, 209 n.8
election manifesto, Labour
    1992 111
    1997 108
electoral turnout 98–9
Elliott, Gregory 4, 6, 17, 20, 22, 39n.10, 40n.14, 54
Elliott, Larry 137
Ellison, Nick 18
Engels, Friedrich 177n.4
Epstein, Gerald 208n.4
Epstein, L. 60, 67, 95
Esping-Andersen, Gosta 27
European Union Structural Funds 211n.28
Evans, Peter 37
Exchange Rate Mechanism 70, 72n.10
Export Credit Guarantee Departments 133
Export Intelligence Service 133

Fabian Society 7, 15
Feldstein, M. 178n.15
Fielding, Steven 141n.1
financial markets, deregulation 30, 37, 156
financial systems 186–92
    'bank-based' 27, 187–92, 209n.10
    'capital market-based' 27, 165, 187–92, 209 n.10
Financial Times 138
Finegold, David 69, 153
Fiorina, M. P. 76
flexibility, labour market 69
flying pickets 141n.4
focus groups 96, 103n.8
Foot, Michael 5, 40n.13
Fordism 28, 29, 62
Foreman-Peck, J. 69
Frankel, Jeffrey A. 177n.1, 178n.15
Franklin, Mark 23, 34
Franks, J. 190
Freeman, Christopher 207

Gaitskell, Hugh 17
Gallie, W. B. 30
Gamble, Andrew 1, 22, 99–100, 166, 192, 208n.3
'gang of four' 44
Garrett, Geoffrey 25, 27, 28, 54–5, 72n.9, 136, 163, 178n.14, 210n.18
Gavin, Neil T. 72n.11, 76

general election
 1979 167
 1983 96
 1987 106, 150, 159
 1992 67, 105, 108, 117, 150, 153, 159
 1997 39, 54, 75n.26, 96, 102, 105, 106, 107,
   108, 117, 126, 132, 137, 144n.30, 159,
   162
'gentlemanly capitalism' 185
George, Eddie 137
Gerschenkron, Alexander 27, 29, 186, 209n.7
Ghilarducci, Teresa 197, 210n.21, 211n.24
Giddens, Anthony 34
Gillespie, R. 64
globalisation 11, 12, 20, 25, 28, 30, 31, 33, 36,
   38, 61–2, 75n.24, 106, 136, 140, 142n.18,
   145, 149, 156, 163, 164, 176, 178n.15,
   181, 183
globalisation thesis, 'business school' variant
   30
   see also globalisation
Glyn, Andrew 31, 64, 70, 149
Goldstein, Don 200
Gould, Bryan 126, 183, 203
Gould, Philip 96, 103n.8
Gourevitch, Peter 27, 165, 191, 209n.10
Gramsci, Antonio 10, 45, 71, 154
Grant, Wyn 39n.6, 209n.14
gross funds 200, 210n.20
growth dynamic, indigenous 160, 164, 169,
   175

Habermas, Jürgen 147
Hall, Peter A. 44, 178n.11
Hall, Stuart 10-11, 29, 43, 44, 45, 62, 72n.4
Halpern, David 179n.17
Hands, Gordon 98–9
Hantrais, Linda 142n.11
Haq, M. 37, 69
Harman, Harriet 120
Harrop, Martin 23, 134, 144n.30
Hart, Jeffrey A. 27
Haseler, S. 53
Hassam, Gary 4
Hausbanken 187
Heath, Anthony 23, 24, 35, 40n.17–18, 76, 97,
   140
Heath, Edward 165
Heffernan, Richard 15, 177n.8
Helleiner, Eric 37, 156
Her Majesty's Stationary Office (HMSO) 127
Hewitt, Patricia 96
Hills, John 70
Hinich, M. J. 76, 85
Hirschmann, Albert O. 165, 187, 209n.11
Hirst, Paul 28, 30, 136, 142n.18, 160, 163, 165,
   166, 177n.1, 178n.16, 206, 211n.28
Horioka, C. 178n.15
Hotelling, Harold 76, 83, 85–7, 89
House of Commons 137
House of Lords 38, 131–2
Howell, Chris 108, 179n.19
Howell, David 6, 39, 56
Howells, Kim 111
Howerd, Michael 139
Huber, Evelyn 27, 54, 64
Hughes, Colin 4, 16, 18, 20, 58, 96, 102
Hutton, Will 22, 27, 59, 64, 126, 165, 185, 188,
   195, 209n.6, 209n.7, 209n.9, 211n.24

'ideal collective capitalist' 153, 177n.4
ideational and material 34–6
industrial policy 38, 70
Industry Forum (Labour Party) 170, 203, 209n.13,
   211n.27
inflation, control of 124
Ingham, Geoffrey 165
insider-trading 191
Institute for Economic Affairs 168
Institute for Fiscal Studies 168
Institute for Public Policy Research 168
institutional investors 196–203
institutionalism 43, 193–6
intentionalism 32, 37, 38
   see also structure and agency
International Monetary Fund (IMF) 3
International Social Security Association 26
investment 73–4n.14, 74n.21, 124, 138, 144n.27,
   147, 149, 170, 178n.15, 187, 192, 194, 198
   foreign direct 127, 155, 178n.14
investment ethic, indigenous 181, 196–203,
   207–8
Italy 26

Jacques, Martin 29, 43, 62
Jeffery, Charlie 169
Jenkins, Patrick 18, 43, 75n.25
Jenkinson, T. 27, 189
Jessop, Bob 29–30, 34, 43, 44, 47, 65, 69, 70,
   72n.5, 121, 166, 211n.28
job seekers' allowance 121–2
Johnmann, Lewis 39n.6, 209n.14, 210n.15
Jones, Tudor 16, 17
Jowell, Roger 24, 76, 140

Kavanagh, Dennis 20, 21, 22, 40n.14, 59, 60, 140
Kay, J. 69
Kennedy, J. F. K. 6
Kenny, Michael 5, 9–10, 16, 17, 20, 22, 40n.11,
   41n.21, 76, 103n.1, 141n.1, 144n.31
Kerr, Peter 20, 21, 43, 47, 72n.5, 72n.7
Kester, W. C. 190, 209n.10
Keynesian welfare state 27, 71
Keynesianism 3–4, 8, 11, 28, 33, 61–2, 65,
   75n.24, 165
King, Anthony 23, 72n.11
King, Desmond S. 147
Kingdom, John 67–8
Kinnock, Neil 5, 16, 18, 96, 102, 134, 155
Kirscheimer, O. 103n.1
Kitschelt, Herbert 24, 27, 56
Kitson, Michael 22, 59, 178n.9, 192, 207
Klein, Naomi 110–11
Krieger, Joel 60
Krugman, Paul 74n.20
Kuhn, Thomas S. 44, 72n.6
Kurzer, Paulette 28

labour-market deregulation 11, 136
labourism 23, 28, 64
Larner, Wendy 39n.8
Layard, Richard 22, 144n.35
Lee, Simon 39n.6, 188–9, 208n.3, 209n.8, 209
   n.14
Leibfried, Stephan 142n.11, 142n.18
Lein, D-H. D. 149
Lent, Adam 72n.8
Letwin, Sophie 63, 72n.4
Levitt, Theodore 30

Leys, Colin 4, 6, 19, 20, 22, 44, 66, 67, 68, 96, 102, 111, 141n.1, 150, 158, 165, 173, 209n.6
liberalism, market 54–5
Liddle, Roger 3, 4, 5, 6, 9, 18, 20, 39n.10, 178n.10
Lindblom, Charles 60, 146, 147, 159
Local Government Act (1988, Section 28) 51
Longstreth, F. 39n.6, 209n.14
'loony left' 50
Lowe, A. 39n.6, 209n.14
Lowe, Rodney 21
Lukes, Steven 41n.25

Maastricht Treaty 142n.11
    Social Chapter 111–13, 142n.11
Maddison, Angus 187
Major, John 20, 33, 135
Major government 70, 160, 195
Maltby, Tony 26
Mandelson, Peter 3, 4, 5, 6, 9, 18, 20, 39n.2, 39n.10, 96, 178n.10, 179n.19
Manning, D. 69
Margetts, Helen 23
Marlow, J. D. 21
Marquesee, Mike 6, 16, 141n.1, 142n.13
Marsh, David 2, 20, 21, 30, 31, 38, 43, 44, 45, 47, 71n.2, 72n.5, 72n.7, 75n.24, 108, 142n.7, 142n.18
Marshall, Gordon 62, 74n.19
Martin, S. J. 211n.28
Marx, Karl 12
Marxism Today 10–11, 62
Mayer, C. 190
McAnulla, Stuart 20, 22, 47
McNamara, Kathleen 34
McSmith, Andy 144n.28
media, deregulation 129–30, 144n.28
median voter 76, 97, 99–100, 102, 134
Megarry, Sir Robert 199–200
Megarry judgement (1983) 199–200, 202
Mercer, Helen 39n.6, 209n.14, 210n.15
mergers 190–1
metropolitan development agencies (MDAs) 205, 211n.28
Michie, Jonathan 21, 27, 59, 69, 70, 178n.9, 179n.18, 192, 207, 208n.4
middle class 24
Miliband, Ralph 155
Milne, Seumas 122
miners' strike (1984–5) 4, 50, 141n.4
Ministry for Women 118, 120
mode of regulation 28
modernisation
    industrial 8, 22, 165, 166, 169, 203
    of Labour Party 2, 3, 4–5, 9, 10, 12, 14, 15, 19, 28, 31, 32, 33, 34, 38, 58, 60–6, 101, 105, 111, 123, 134, 145, 150, 157, 181
modernisation thesis 58–9, 60–6, 73n.12
Moene, O-K. 28
Mommen, André 14
monetarism 68, 184
Monopolies and Mergers Commission 127, 133
Moon, Jeremy 43, 44, 71n.2
Morgan, K. O. 155
Morris, Peter 21, 22
Morrison, Herbert 56, 72n.10
Moses, Jonathan W. 28, 155

Mulgan, Geoff 11
Munger, M. C. 76, 85
Murdoch, Rupert 143n.28

Nairn, Tom 23, 130, 185, 186, 188, 209n.6, 209n.7
National Association of Pension Funds 210n.22
National Coal Board (NCB) 199
National Executive Committee (NEC) 5, 96
National Health Service (NHS) 52, 119, 120–1, 122, 138
National Institute of Economic and Social Research 73n.13
national insurance 124, 127
national investment bank (NIB) 125, 126–7
National Lottery 133
National Union of Mineworkers (NUM) 199
neo-conservatism 44
neo-liberalism 10–11, 14, 27, 28, 29, 30, 44, 53, 60, 62, 63, 65, 68, 71, 74n.21, 75n.26, 105, 135, 136, 149, 161, 164, 167, 174, 178n.16, 184
New Jerusalem 7
new model party 6, 95–6
new realism 1, 140
new right 1, 9, 64, 141
'new times' 1, 8–11, 62, 145
new world order 1
New Zealand Labor Party 39n.8, 136
Newton, Kenneth 141n.2
Newton, Scott 22, 192
Norris, Pippa 23
North, Douglass 103n.3
Norton, Philip 72n.11
Notermans, Ton 28, 64
novelty
    concept of 12–14
    of New Labour 3–8, 11–38

O'Leary, Brendan 80
O'Shea, A. 72n.4
Obstfeld, Maurice 178n.15
Offe, Claus 146, 147, 177n.4
Office of Fair Trading 133
Ohmae, Kenichi 30
oil shock (1973) 3
Old Labour 3, 8, 12, 15, 17, 33
Oppenheim, Carey 70
Ordeshook, P. C. 76, 85
Organisation for Economic Cooperation and Development 26
Ormerod, Paul 74n.20
Orrù, M. 27, 209n.10

Padgett, Stephen 26
Panitch, Leo 4, 6, 19, 20, 22, 56, 67, 96, 111, 141n.1, 150, 173
Panorama (BBC) 138
paradigm shift 44–6, 66, 178n.11
Parker, D. 69
Parliamentary Labour Party (PLP) 5
parsimony 36, 41n.24, 78
partnership, public–private 114, 127
Pashukanis, E. V. 146
Paterson, W. E. 26, 64, 72n.10
Paulson, B. 76
Pearce, G. R. 211n.28
Peffley, Mark 74n.18
Peltzmann, S. 149

pension funds 197–203, 210n.20
  regional 203–4
pensions 25–6, 118, 120, 122, 139–40, 143
  n.20–1
Perryman, Mark 141n.1
Petty, R. E. 60
picketing, secondary 109, 110, 141n.6, 141n.7
Pierre, Jon 203
Pierson, Paul 28, 122–3, 142n.11
Pimlott, Ben 21
Piven, Frances Fox 24, 74n.21
Policy Review 9, 16–17, 18, 19, 20, 42, 48, 58,
  59, 60–1, 63, 66, 73n.12, 74n.17, 75n.21,
  96, 126, 150, 153, 183, 208n.4
political economy
  classical 1
  comparative 27, 29, 54, 185–7, 192–6, 209n.9
  global 8, 15, 28, 30, 31, 33, 61, 63, 65, 106,
   184
  new 1
political sociology 23, 24
politicism 37, 38
politics of catch-up 42, 59, 60, 66, 70, 76–7,
  101, 134, 158, 159
policy paradigm 45–6
poll tax 51
Pollard, Sidney 39n.6, 166, 209n.14
Pollin, Robert 27, 69, 165, 186, 188, 208n.4,
  209n.7, 209n.8, 209n.10, 211n.23
Pontusson, Jonas 54
Porter, Dilwyn 22, 192
Porter, Michael E. 27, 209n.10, 211n.24
portfolio investors *see* institutional investors
post-Fordism 20, 28–30, 62
post-revisionism 16
post-Thatcher settlement 53, 59, 65, 160
  see also consensus, post-Thatcher
post-Thatcherism 47
post-war settlement 71, 165
  see also consensus, post-war
prawn cocktail offensive' 149
preference, distribution of voter 89–92, 96–8,
  103n.7
preference-accommodation 60, 66–7, 68, 95,
  100, 135, 146, 151, 158–9, 173, 174, 176
preference fixity, of voters 83, 94, 95–6
preference-shaping 60, 68, 70–1, 75n.27, 83,
  135, 146, 158, 159, 161, 174
Prescott, John 139, 144n.36
privatisation 127–8
Przeworski, Adam 57, 136, 146–8, 150, 151–5,
  157, 173–5, 179n.21
psephology 23, 34–6, 40n.16
public choice theory 77
public sector borrowing requirement (PSBR) 49

Railtrack 127–8
Rapkin, D. P. 74n.20
rational choice theory 78
Reaganomics 65
recession
  manufacturing 74n.15
  responses to 191–2
  regime of accumulation 28
regional bonds 205
regional development 203
regional development agencies (RDAs) 125,
  204–6, 211n.27, 211n.28
regional economic fora 206–7

regional invesment banks (RIBs) 125, 126–7,
  206
Regional Policy Commission 203, 205, 211n.27
regional training agencies (RTAs) 206
regulation theory 29–30
Reich, Robert 30, 135
Reiger, Elmar 142n.18
revisionism 16–17, 39–40n.10, 53, 60–6
Reynolds, P. 160
Rhodes, R. A. W. 20, 43, 44, 45, 47, 71n.2,
  72n.5, 72n.7
Riddell, Peter 43, 46
risk aversion 189–90
Robins, Kevin 114
Ronge, Volker 146
Rosamond, Ben 110, 141–2n.7
Rose, Richard 36, 141n.1
Rothstein, Bo 54
Rowthorn, Bob 70
Rubery, Jill 65
Russell, Lord Conrad 22, 143n.23
Rustin, Michael 62

Sabel, Charles 114
Sachs, Jeffrey D. 30
Sanders, David 23, 24, 25, 35, 59, 66, 67, 70,
  72n.11, 76, 103n.2, 120, 141n.3, 177n.8–9
Särlvik, Bo 23, 34
Sassoon, Donald 26, 149
Savage, S. P. 43
Scharpf, Fritz 28
Scherman, K. G. 26
Schlessinger, T. 211n.23
Schmidt, Vivien A. 155
Schumpeter, Joseph 80
Schumpeterian workfare state 29
Scottish Parliament 131–2
Seldon, Anthony 21
Self, Paul 76
Seyd, Patrick 58, 66, 141n.1
Shanks, M. 39n.6, 209n.14
Shaw, Eric 4, 16, 18, 39n.10, 40n.13, 57, 58,
  60, 67, 73n.12, 73n.13, 74n.18, 74n.19,
  76, 95–6, 102, 141n.1, 156
Shonfield, Andrew 27
short-termism 165, 187, 188–9, 197, 201
Skocpol, Theda 153
Smith, Adam 76
Smith, John 5, 16, 134
Smith, John Grieve 27, 69, 70, 179n.18, 184,
  191, 208n.4
Smith, Martin 5, 9–10, 16, 17, 18, 20, 22,
  40n.11, 40n.14, 41n.21, 58, 63, 66, 76, 95,
  103n.1, 141n.1, 144n.31, 159
Smith, Paul 6, 39n.7
Smithies, Arthur 83, 87
Smyth, G. 23
Social Contract 142n.10, 166
Social Democratic Party (SDP) 41n.23, 97
social democracy 9, 10, 11, 15, 26, 27, 28, 30,
  33, 41n.20, 43, 53, 54–8, 64, 97, 105, 106,
  136, 148, 150–5, 157, 159, 163, 172, 173–
  4, 176, 178n.14
  definition 57–8
'social dumping' 70
social justice 4, 160
'social-ism' 8, 53
socialism 8
  market-research 66, 102, 158

socially responsible investment (SRI) 200, 202, 203, 210n.21
Soete, L. 207
Soskice, David 69, 193–4
Sowemimo, Matthew 72n.8
Spear, Joanna 16
Sprague, J. 147
stakeholding, regional 169
Stephens, John D. 26, 27, 54, 64
Stephenson, H. 43
sterling 75n.24, 192
Stoker, Gerry 211n.28
Stokes, Donald 76
Stones, Rob 69
Strand, J. R. 74n.20
Straw, Jack 139
structural dependence thesis 136, 146–62, 172, 177n.7
structuralism 32, 37, 38
structure and agency 31–4
Sugden, Roger 27, 70, 165, 208n.4
Sun 143n.28
supply-side economics 75n.28
supply-side intervention 8, 60, 70, 74n.21, 124, 140, 170, 203
supply-side rigidities 75n.28
supply-side socialism 8, 22, 75n.21
Swank, Duane 146, 147
Sweden 26

taxation 125–7, 146, 149
taxpayers' revolt 26
Taylor, Charles 147
Taylor, Gerald 16
Taylor-Gooby, Peter 29
Temple, P. 69
Terry, Les 10
Thatcher, Margaret 20, 21, 33, 44, 75n.25, 135, 142n.20, 195
Thatcherism 9, 43–54, 57, 58, 62–3, 65, 68–70, 166
    contraditions of 68–70
    employment policy 50
    implementation gap 47–8
    legacy 20, 43–8, 49–52, 53–4, 59, 72n.7, 122–3, 157, 158, 159–62, 167, 172
    privatisation policy 49
    reform of local government 51
    social policy 52
'Thatcherite instinct' 46, 167
Thatcherite revisionism 42–3, 48–54, 58, 59, 62–3, 70, 72n.8
'Thatcherite revolution' 43–4
think-tanks 168, 183, 208n.4
Thomas, A. H. 26
Thomas, Richard 122
Thompson, Grahame 28, 30, 136, 142n.18, 163, 177n.1, 178n.16
Thompson, J. 188, 190
Thompson, Noel 6, 67, 150
'three-day week' 141n.4, 165
Thrift, Nigel 114
Tiratsoo, Nicholas 8, 22, 155, 209n.14, 210n.15

Tomlinson, Jim 1, 8, 22, 39n.6, 155, 161, 209n.14, 210n.15
Toronto Star 111
Toulouse, Chris 141n.1
trade unions 5, 33, 49, 50, 55, 109
Treasury 123, 125, 126
Trustee Investments Act (1961) 199, 202
Tyson, Laura 186

unemployment benefit 121
University of Industry 132

Vickers, J. 69
Vittas, Dimitri 209n.12
von Weizsacker, C. C. 103n.5
voter leakage, problem of 87, 94, 98–9
voting, spacial theory of 76, 83–92

Wade, Robert 163
Walker, A. 26, 70
Walker, C. 70
Wall Street 149
Wallerstein, Michael 28, 136, 146–8, 151–5, 157, 173–5, 179n.21
'war of position' 45
Ward, Hugh 60, 103n.3
Warner, A. 30
Watson, Matthew 19, 22, 27, 28, 36, 37, 59, 69, 70, 73–4n.14, 74n.20, 75n.24, 126, 142n.18, 30, 177n.6, 178n.9, 181, 184, 188, 200, 208 n.5, 211n.26
Webb, S. 70
Weiss, Linda 37
welfare state 25, 28, 165
    retrenchment 120, 123, 136, 140
'welfare-to-work' 119, 121
Welsh Assembly 131–2
Whiteley, Paul 58
Wickham-Jones, Mark 4, 19, 20, 28, 40n.14, 57, 65, 72n.11, 73n.12, 95, 97, 141n.1, 144n.34, 145, 146, 147, 148, 149, 150–62, 172–6, 179–80n.20–3, 208n.3
Wighton, David 210n.22
Wilson, Harold 5–6, 7, 8, 39n.3, 39n.4
Wilson government 3, 5, 6, 7, 193–5, 209n.14
Wincott, Daniel 34, 210n.16
Winter of Discontent 4, 38–9n.1, 111, 141n.4, 166, 178n.10
Wintour, Patrick 4, 16, 18, 20, 58, 96, 102
Wolfe, J. 72n.4
Wood, Ellen Meiksins 147, 178n.13, 178n.16
Wood, Stephen 179n.17
Woolcock, Stephen 27, 165, 190, 191, 209n.10
Worcester, Kent 141n.1
workfare 121, 123, 143n.22
working class 24

Yarrow, G. 69
Young, Hugo 134
Young, S. 39n.6, 209n.14

Zysman, John 27, 29, 39n.6, 165, 186, 18 192, 209n.12, 209n.14